The Lived Experience of Improvisation

The Lived Experience of Improvisation
In music, learning and life

Simon Rose

intellect Bristol, UK / Chicago, USA

First published in the UK in 2017 by
Intellect, The Mill, Parnall Road, Fishponds, Bristol, BS16 3JG, UK

First published in the USA in 2017 by
Intellect, The University of Chicago Press, 1427 E. 60th Street,
Chicago, IL 60637, USA

A catalogue record for this book is available from the
British Library.

Copy-editor: MPS Technologies
Cover designer: Emily Dann
Production manager: Richard Kerr
Typesetting: Contentra Technologies

Print ISBN: 978-1-78320-673-5
ePDF ISBN: 978-1-78320-674-2
ePUB ISBN: 978-1-78320-675-9

Printed and bound by Bell and Bain Ltd, Glasgow

Contents

Preface

The book is intended for a non-academic as well as an academic audience. I hope the book will be of interest to musicians, teachers, those new to ideas of improvisation, those interested in inter-disciplinary improvisation, researchers and others. As the themes of educational inclusion are very much tied to improvisation in the book, I hope that those who plan and influence educational practice may also be interested.

Part 2's themes of improvisation were developed from a complicated and lengthy process of analysis of interview transcripts involving a huge number of documents that are not included. Instead, selective quotations are used that represent these themes. Sometimes quotations encapsulate multiple themes and these become motifs within different chapters. Central to Part 2 is my own interpretation (Interpretive Phenomenological Analysis) and Part 1 aims to make this perspective clear by explaining some of my own experiences. On grounds of avoiding repetition, I deliberated about the inclusion of Part 3, the edited interviews, but on balance decided that these should be there: each of these interviews provides an additional contextualized perspective, based as they are on very different histories, and together they represent a first-order body of knowledge of improvisation. The interviewees are Mick Beck, John Butcher, Tristan Honsinger, Sven-Ake Johansson, George Lewis, Roscoe Mitchell, Maggie Nicols, Pauline Oliveros, Bob Ostertag and Alan Tomlinson. Their concepts, ideas, views and beliefs about improvisation provided the material for analysis and I sincerely thank them for these contributions.

My improvisation research has been ongoing for around ten years now, and there are a great many people I wish to thank for having aided my thinking. Although too numerous to list, among them are Oleyumi Thomas, Andrea Lowe, John Tchicai, William Parker, Chris Chafe, Matthew Rose, Paul Stapleton, Peter Pilbeam, Steve Noble, Simon H. Fell, Adam Bohman, Mark Sanders, Raymond MacDonald, Fred Frith, Evan Parker, Andrew Wass, Julie Myers and Lydia Rose. I want to thank those at Banff Arts Centre; the Improvisation as Community and Social Practice project (ICASP); musicians in the Bay Area improvised music scene in California, the London Improvisers' Orchestra and the great many musicians as well as dancers in Berlin with whom I've collaborated; and students and staff at Daniel House School, Hackney, London.

Following work in theatre-in-education, I taught and found disaffected, bored students to be something of a norm, one that echoed my own experience at school. In drama and music

I also found that these same students were likely to be the ones who seized the chance to express themselves and excel. The energy and motivation were there but not directed, and students' potential was in effect being wasted. Education is often constructed in a way that will suit some, who will do well, while just as many, if not more, will not. Many don't or can't 'fit in' with the given construct on offer, drama and music in education can be particularly revealing of this dilemma. Within this picture, improvisation can play a central role.

Chapters 1, 2, 3 and 4 explain the context of improvisation, the reasons behind this book, the primary reference being experience. For Chapter 2, this comes in the form of a history of improvisation across different disciplines, chronicling the range of interest in improvisation. Chapter 3's context of improvisation is provided by personal experience in education, music and drama. The issue of improvisation's highly complex relation with understandings and constructs of knowledge is explored in Chapter 4 and is, by nature, academic – it includes a description of the method of study, phenomenology. The book can be read from beginning to end: its parts and chapters can equally be read independently. For some, the main interest may be in the themes of improvisation found in Part 2 within which teachers may choose to begin with Chapters 7 and 9 as well as Chapter 3. I hope that those with an inter-disciplinary or trans-disciplinary interest in improvisation will find Chapters 2, 5, 6 and 10 of particular interest. Musicians may well find Part 3 a good place to begin.

I use the term *enacted* improvisation in the book. *Enacted* grounds improvisation in the realm of experience. It refers to doing, involving action and actants (actors): those who perform through improvisation. Enacted improvisation implicates the theme of the body that ties all of the other themes. *Enacted* also helpfully links to many theories that support improvisation, for example: enacted cognition, situated cognition, activity theory, autopoiesis and others. The term *enacted* improvisation reiterates the importance of doing for discussion.

The study has focused on *free improvisation* in particular for which the initials FI are used. *Free improvisation,* or *open improvisation,* is used primarily as a way of delineating the term from the broader term *improvisation,* in order to signify an ongoing, developing activity rather than a style.

Part 1

Chapter 1

Human Improvisation

W e like to describe the world in terms of fixed structures while our being is a creative response within changing structures, a truer description of being is through creative improvisation. Improvisation is a pervasive aspect of being human, in every sphere of life, enabling existence; life without the improvisational response is difficult to imagine. From an evolutionary perspective the capacity for improvisation is there for good reason. There is a need to more fully understand the processes of engagement in improvisation. Improvisation is clearly evident in performing arts, performing makes processes apparent as things are seen and heard, in so doing, we become aware of how performance occurs. Understandably we identify improvisation with such performing arts but this has also led to an over-identification. Improvisation is within all areas of existence; the process of mutation in evolution is itself highly improvisatory. Unsurprisingly improvisation is found in every sphere of activity and can be better acknowledged as a human capability.

This book explores the established practice of improvisation in music and, in particular, free improvisation – the creation of not-predetermined music in the act of performance. Improvisation in music is interpreted as a social example of the human capability of improvisation. The book considers what the lived experience of improvisation in music, represented by themes, also tells us about improvisation as a phenomenon across experience. Within a range of activity and disciplines, there is growing interest in the potential of improvisation. The agency of improvisation, as a capability, is the focus and the exploration of the *lived experience* of improvisation in music forms a case study for the broader experience. The question of theory's relation to the practice of improvisation becomes central to the book's themes and the intention has been to write in a way that is of use to both non-academic and academic readers.

The book gathers a 'body of knowledge' of improvisation in music from an international community of practice in which improvisation is central. Ten practitioners from Europe and North America took part in interviews: Roscoe Mitchell, Maggie Nicols, John Butcher, Pauline Oliveros, George Lewis, Mick Beck, Tristan Honsinger, Alan Tomlinson, Sven-Ake Johansson and Bob Ostertag. The criteria for inclusion was that participants should be very experienced in the practice and I was interested in diverse perspectives. The method of inquiry, phenomenology, focuses upon and interprets the particular within the participants' experience (idiographic) rather than seeking an aggregate of opinion across a larger sample. The practitioners have spent their working lives with the advanced practice of improvisation in music and developed sophisticated understanding – recording and analysing this important body of knowledge is a way to better understand the phenomenon.

The research developed from work as a professional saxophonist and teacher of drama and music, which included work in special educational needs and with excluded students. The research is informed by an early training and career in drama and theatre-in-education in which improvisation processes are centrally important for devising and developing socially orientated, educational drama work. Three studies concerned with the practice of improvisation in music, drama and education contexts have helped develop the research perspective (Rose 2003, 2008, 2013).

The book describes improvisation's unique relationship with *learning* and how, at the same time, constructs within education can be resistant to the modes of creative, collaborative, embodied learning that improvisation presents. This has led to the need to grasp the at times thorny issue of improvisation's relation to education. The fault-line of this relationship illuminates important underlying issues regarding the phenomenon of improvisation and contemporary educational practice. In order to examine what occurs in the experience of improvisation, rather than how presuppositions within education may possibly relate to the phenomenon, a distinction is made between education and learning – in this way the potential of improvisation remains the primary focus. The question of improvisation's relation with education draws out fundamental themes concerning the nature of our learning, questioning suppositions about what happens during the significant portion of our lives we all commit to education. Competition that prioritizes individual over group learning; de-contextualized teaching; assessment; the significance of 'voice'; the role of the teacher and related themes are explored.

The way in which the concept of improvisation becomes constructed is centrally important as this defines its role in practice, in education and elsewhere. I have approached the study of improvisation aware from the outset of the importance of improvisation as enacted and how this can become too readily problematized and marginalized by academic structuring that values the written over that which is achieved through or represented by doing. There has been an institutionalized resistance to acknowledging, and therefore valuing, the potential of improvisation. It should be emphasized that formal understanding of composition and improvisation practice is simultaneously embedded in and largely constructed through education. At the same time, it has become clear in research that teaching itself benefits from the agency of skilled improvisatory interaction that can clearly enable and enhance teaching-learning relationships. Paradoxically, the formal space dedicated to the sharing of knowledge and its development, 'education', has had difficulty responding to the capability or understanding presented in the form of improvisation. Recognizing improvisation's lack of acknowledgement and its relative absence from formal education is important if we are to understand how potential may become realized.

Presenting a picture of improvisation that has value in and beyond academia inevitably leads to a repeated self-questioning about the kind of narrative that is being developed and what that signifies. Immediately there is a tension: improvisation is so pervasive and 'shape-shifting' that the adoption of too straightforward a correlation with theory is obviously questionable. Improvisation certainly presents itself in many guises within and across disciplines and these themselves interrelate with one another. In this way the themes of improvisation are co-present and overlapping in a necessarily complex manner. Reflecting this, theory from a multitude of disciplines is relevant and necessary in the discussion of improvisation. At the same time overly focusing on a particular area of theory and the associations that this brings with it can pull away from the truth of improvisation as practice. In 1997, Ornette Coleman and Jacques Derrida performed together in Paris, playing and reading, in the course of which Derrida was booed by the audience. Without wishing to negate Derrida's contribution, this seems to me to offer an illustration of the practice theory dichotomy – audiences understand how value is taken from improvisation through the experience of the activity, theorizing the activity is not the activity and a lack of awareness of this can pull in the opposite of the intended direction. Focusing on practitioners' experience has addressed the need for narrative that becomes developed from grounded experience.

The concept of *being* illuminates improvisation in a number of ways. In my 2008 study of improvisation and education, improvisation became represented in the findings by four features: *Awareness, Social, Play* and *Unknown*. Understood as working together, these were encapsulated by the term *being*. Describing the activity of improvisation did not benefit from overly categorizing and instead was more helpfully explained by not fragmenting. Interviewees consistently described improvisation in terms relating to *being* in the act of improvisation. The need for immediacy and spontaneity in order to compose in the process of performing requires a particular presence within engagement in improvisation. The demand of composing in real-time emphasizes this presence. Improvisation's interrelatedness with the theme of *being* subsequently influenced the design and choice of method for the research project that followed, 'Improvisation, music and learning: An Interpretive Phenomenological Analysis' (2013); this study provides much of the content of the book. The method was phenomenology, the study of *lived experience* through which the project explores the practice of highly experienced improvisers. Through this method, the researcher's subjectivity and perspective are overtly acknowledged (through the conceptualization of *interpretation*).

Exploring improvisation's relationship with *being*, Heidegger's (1962) examination of 'Being-in-the-world' became significant as it includes a re-examination of the 'background' or supposition upon which knowledge is based. Free improvisation's potential for the interrogation of the 'boundaries' of musical experience similarly re-examines this 'background' as a traditional or formalized construct that is not necessarily already fixed. The question of being becomes compounded as the most influential book on the subject was written by, to say the least, a highly controversial author. Heidegger's philosophy, and 'Being and Time' in particular, has had a major influence within philosophy and this has extended, unusually, to other diverse disciplines. At the same time, Heidegger also became an ambitious member of the Nazi party in the 1930s. Unsurprisingly, views on his work are easily polarized and have not been aided by an unwillingness to acknowledge either the significance of the influence of the work on the one hand, or the extent to which he envisioned his role as Nazi thinker on the other. Simon Critchley (2009) has put it in this way:

> There is no way of understanding what took place in continental philosophy after Heidegger without coming to terms with "Being and Time". Furthermore, unlike many Anglo-American philosophers, Heidegger has exerted a huge influence outside philosophy, in areas as diverse as architecture, contemporary art, social and political theory, psychotherapy, psychiatry and theology.

The theme of being and improvisation resonates through the book's other themes. In his interview, Lewis explains how in improvising: '[…] *you're part of an environment and also creating an environment* […]' – interpreted here as being-in-the-world. The opportunity presented by free improvisation in music of creative, collective, embodied, real-time experience provides an instance of '[…] the human world coming into being' (Bachelard 1958) through artistic practice. In John Butcher's interview he similarly describes the shared activity of free improvisation as *an unrepeatable moment*. Created through the act of improvisation, the human world is realized through playing: in the process of 'holistically' composing in real-time, we create the environment, or world, through our being/improvising.

Interrogating and being clear about the terms of reference of improvisation in order to better understand the phenomenon is fundamental. This book's central focus is with themes of free improvisation (FI) within musical practice, and to this end Chapter 2 describes the distinctive development of free improvisation in the United Kingdom. Key figures emerging in the 1960s and 1970s: Cornelius Cardew, John Stevens, Derek Bailey and Evan Parker and groups: AMM, Joseph Holbrooke (trio), Spontaneous Music Ensemble (SME) and the Improvisation Music Company are discussed with reference to the sociopolitical context of the period. The increased interest in inter-disciplinary arts activity and the democratization in musical practice are also discussed in relation to ideas of composition and improvisation. This includes the work of John Cage, the Fluxus movement, Morton Feldman, Karlheinz Stockhausen, Terry Riley and others. Improvisation's diversity is then described by means of the range of research in different areas of activity with examples from music, drama, dance; organizational theory, management and finance; sport; fire-fighting; reflexivity theory; sociology, anthropology, philosophy and others.

Chapter 3 provides a personal perspective by explaining why and how I began researching improvisation while working as a teacher and musician. The interviewees' experience is central in the book and so too is the way lived experience has led to and shaped the research approach. The chapter discusses how improvisation is as important for successful learning and teaching as it is for improvising musicians and drama practitioners and describes the relatedness of improvisation processes in drama, music, teaching and counselling in education.

Chapter 4, 'Improvisation and Knowledge', highlights the under-acknowledgement of improvisation by exploring conceptions of creativity, how practice and theory are situated and how perceptions of improvisation are influenced by the ways in which knowledge is constructed. The chapter also describes the phenomenological method of research that contributes to Part 2 and the book's central Chapters, 5 to 9, in which the themes of free improvisation are explored.

Within the globalized context of personal, social, organizational and political life improvisatory processes are apparent and need to become better understood. Contemporary questions in art, education and elsewhere become very much addressed by the scope of the social phenomenon of improvisation. Improvisation in music offers clarity of practice that other disciplines have looked to in order to better understand their own areas. The analysis of the practice of improvisation in music contributes to uncovering the nature of the broader phenomenon. One outcome of this is that improvisation can become more fully understood as a human capability (Chapter 10), and so too themes of improvisation found in the study of the phenomenon in music may become understood as transferrable to other areas of activity.

Chapter 2

The Development of Improvisation

In order to better understand improvisation within the contemporary social world this chapter explores the development of improvisation practice. There are three sections: 'The Emergence of Improvisation in Arts'; 'The Emergence of Improvisation in Music'; and 'The Range of Improvisation'. The background of improvisation in arts is explored and the development of improvisation in music is described in detail. The account of improvisation's 'freeing' during this period describes a body of practice in music that developed during the twentieth century. The chapter then discusses the range of improvisation and the increasing interest in improvisation in different areas of activity.

The Emergence of Improvisation in Arts

During the past half-century or so, improvisation has become clearly apparent across the arts. The artistic landscape can be thought of as simultaneous pockets of activity that may or may not be connected, and within these pockets the improvisational feature of practice can be identified. Musicians, dancers, theatre practitioners, performance artists and visual artists have increasingly developed practice in a manner in which they set their own agendas, seeking new forms, innovating while generating their own scripts and scores through practice. Also, improvisation becomes a common strategy within the more broadly termed sociopolitical arts. It's good to remember that much of this work, by its nature, was not well publicized and has remained 'unsung' as it eschewed the kind of attention sought by and associated with more commercially driven concerns, and within this picture, equally significant well-known and little known groups and individuals were practising. Within different arts, improvisation's role was centrally important in the development of practice and performance. The act of improvisation, self-creating, means that much of this work, across disciplines, has a distinct sociopolitical character as the individual and group 'voice' that improvisation lends itself to is foregrounded and asserted: 'voice' is an identifying feature of improvisation practice across disciplines. As the breadth of such activity is huge, and well beyond the scope of this chapter, three illustrations of practice are cited, as examples, in which improvisation's role is central: fringe or alternative theatre in London, England; the Fluxus movement; and the Situationist International. These examples are chosen as they are not the most obvious, but provide an indication of a broader tendency with arts. They reflect the 'performative turn' of the 1960s – as the focus on the *activity*, across arts, supersedes the art object – in music the score, in drama the play-script, in visual art the object. Frequently improvisation in arts is restricted in discussion to more narrow terms of reference, typically: jazz, theatre sports and, if extending to visual art, abstract expressionism; and the presumptions about improvisation leading from this narrow reference create a limitation that distorts the ensuing discourse. Improvisation has always been a great deal more pervasive. Whether historical movements have highlighted the process of improvisation themselves, and some have not, is a different question that, in part, also reflects the developing use of language, for example, 'performative' is a comparatively recent term. While many arts groups and movements are not necessarily identified with improvisation per se, nevertheless, improvisation – adaptable, responsive, creating 'in the moment' – is a consistent feature within different areas of practice. The third section of this chapter, *The Range of Improvisation*, provides numerous examples of the identification of improvisation within human activity beyond the arts.

The performance and rehearsal spaces of Oval House in South London, UK, became an important 'home' for fringe and political theatre in the 1970s for such seminal groups as People Show, Welfare State, Crystal Theatre, Hesitate and Demonstrate, Pip Simmons Theatre Group, Lumiere and Son and many others as well as groups from other countries. Devising theatre for 'community' was central within this activity and young people's theatre, and theatre-in-education were a significant part of the work. Improvisation enabled the creation of a more sociopolitical arts practice, concerned less with fixed outcomes or definitive performances and more with adaptable, changeable, collaborative, 'living' art with a focus on 'the now'.

Reflecting these same features in performances, events and installations employing multimedia, those associated with the Fluxus movement resituated art practice through an inter-disciplinary focus with emphasis on interaction and collaboration, spontaneity and improvisation, frequently away from art gallery. Examples are found in the work of Yoko Ono, Dan Graham, Alan Kaprow, George Maciunas and Vito Aconchi. Fluxus represented an intermedia, do it yourself attitude that blurred boundaries of practice and art/audience relations. With foundations in music, Zen, design and architecture – 'the essence of Fluxus has been transformation' (Friedman 1998). Although improvisation is not a directly stated aim, the very choice of the name, from the Latin *in flow* makes clear the practice's relation to what improvisers in music do – its features and outlook consistently align with those of improvisation. Fluxus used 'scores', often instruction pieces for activity to be performed and Friedman has described Fluxus activities in terms of musicality. While individuals may have made the score, anyone can create in an open manner. For example, in Philip Corner's 'Piano Activity' (1962), instructions for creating sounds from the piano for any number of players was famously performed by Maciunis and others whose interpretation led to publicly destroying the piano. Uncertainty and risk are present. In Ono's 'Cut Piece' (1964), the invitation for those present to cut the dress she is wearing, how this is carried out and with what effect, is not predetermined. This same open interpretation has been applied to the production of art objects initiated by instructions.

In France, formulating new art practice as political challenge became the raison d'être for the Situationist International (1957–1972). Guy Debord and the Situationist activity became centrally important in the Paris 1968 uprising; famously, the graffiti that appeared around the city that came to characterize this period is attributed to the Situationist manifesto, for example, 'Beneath the streets the beach'. Capitalism's increasing dominance of every area of life, termed 'the spectacle', was challenged by the attempt to rediscover lived experience by way of creating 'situations'. For example, through the improvisational strategy of psycho-geography, cityscapes were re-interpreted by personal mapping in the act of *derive* – walking following an intuitive, not-predetermined path. While psycho-geography is not labelled as improvisation, its whole purpose is to allow for the not-predetermined, by remaining open and responding to what is occurring in order to uncover meaning within the city and landscape. The Situationist influence is now broad and can be found in political thought, art, television production, music and in the work of writers such as Will Self (2007), Ian Sinclair (2003) and James Atlee (2009, 2015).

In the UK, and elsewhere, there was a backlash against sociopolitical arts during the 1980s. The political shift of Thatcherism's monetarism and its championing of boom influenced consumerism, together with a concerted campaign in the UK to quash the power and influence of the trade union movement, contributed towards an environment that was increasingly hostile to arts as sociopolitical practice. The majority of groups did not survive within this new economic climate – such arts practice represented the antithesis of the privatizing goals in the new political environment.

From the 1960s, drama became embedded in education in the UK as an educational tool, and the agency offered by improvisation was central to this. Drama is extensively, pedagogically employed to 'look at ourselves and the world around us', often by means of thematic exploration and portraying roles through improvisation. The use of drama methodology employed for educational potential provides an example of improvisation's inter-disciplinary nature (see Chapters 5 and 6), where a practice from one area, in this case theatre, becomes employed in another, education. The reasons why drama became embedded within UK education are numerous. By the 1950s and 1960s, the period in which drama began to become broadly established in education, beyond being solely identified in terms of texts and stagecraft, a canon of influential, experimental work was available, for example, Stanislavski (1936), Brecht (1964), Grotowski (1968), Artuard (1958), Littlewood (2006) and Brook (1968). Such work contributed to new thinking and developments in theatre and during the 1960s sociopolitical and experimental theatre flourished. The first UK theatre-in-education (TIE) company became established at the Belgrade Theatre in Coventry (1965) followed by the growth of such activity across the country. Within the emergence of drama in education, the agency of improvisation played a key role, providing a methodology capable of bridging theatre practice and educational aims. As well as providing a method within the subject area, improvisation provides a medium for the development of learning across subject areas. Children are frequently cited as 'natural improvisers' and it is for good reason that serious drama activity, at all levels, can be developed through immersion in play activity, for example, professional actors/directors may use simple games to develop insight of character and dramatic themes.

Beyond Fluxus and Situationist activity, the evolution of 'contemporary' art practice itself can be viewed as a kind of ongoing, collective improvisation with fine art. Characterized by experiment, innovation and radical expression that includes the personal and the political, contemporary art practice has successfully proliferated in the UK in particular. Multidisciplinary practices that can include sound, music, film, video, text, events, participation, performance, walks, installations, found objects, 'ready-mades', mixed media, emerging technology and social intervention are all now valued within the term 'art' and its curatorship. Contemporary art practice is now regarded as somewhat characteristic of UK culture and its relationship to education can be traced to developments within art schools in the 1960s and 1970s. Influential art schools, mainly in London, employed practising contemporary artists who, in turn, regarded the intake more as artists than students. The characteristic acculturated self-determination of art students since that time contributed to the diverse practices we are aware of today. Tangentially, the connection between art schools of the 1960s and the development of waves of music groups in the beat, pop and rock domain is also educationally informative. Members of The Beatles, The Rolling Stones, The Who and subsequently Roxy Music and Sex Pistols amongst a great many others spent time at art school – not music school. There are specific influences such as Gustav Metzger's auto-destructive art on Pete Townsend's guitar smashing and John Lennon's connection to performance artist Yoko Ono that further affirm the linking of experimental art and music practices. Moreover, these groups worked with awareness of how to be successfully creative within the total contemporary form that pop music presented – through sound, image and the range of media. The music of this period from the UK remains celebrated and influential throughout the world. While experimental practice in drama and fine art became embedded in education, with highly successful outcomes – enriching individuals, communities, institutions and national culture, music education, on the whole, was less able to embrace developments. The complex reasons why this curiously contrary dynamic has arisen between real-world contemporary practice in music and education are explored in Chapter 4.

Within this emerging picture of inter-disciplinarity with, for example, music as art, art as performance, drama as education and so on, the merging of creative, artistic practices and the crossing of boundaries is thematically important. Improvising saxophonist Peter Brotzmann (Rouy, 2014) continues to work in visual art and has described the influence and fondness of the Dutch art group CoBrA and Nam June Paik (Fluxus) (Brotzmann and Rouy 2014). When asked: '[...] so you make connections between music and painting?' He replies, 'I don't make them they are there. It's the same person [...]' While 'disciplines' encourage us to conceptualize phenomenon, and our individuality, within their own terms of reference, like an innocent and unruly child, improvisation happily crosses such boundaries – Chapter 6, *Process*, discusses numerous examples emerging from the interviews that reflect this.

Artists from different fields were influenced by one another's practice. With an inter-disciplinary methodology and political antecedence, Fluxus' different practices were greatly influenced by composer and theorist John Cage. Cage's relation to the idea of improvisation is complex and I will return to this. The question, 'but, is it improvisation or is it something else' is common. In conversation, a professor at Stanford University commented to me that for a friend of his, a Country session-guitarist, there was no such thing as improvisation, in playing he reproduced all he did and improvisation had no role. In that context, he may well be partially right – reproducing predictable elements in order to 'deliver' a commercial product within such a closely prescribed genre. Although, as music sessions can typically be unpredictable events, a reordering of known material will, by necessity, become improvisational. Jumping from country to twentieth century art music, John Cage's work is often assumed to be not improvisation. Cage's non-identification with jazz has led to a misleading impression, and in his early and late composing career, Cage dealt overtly with improvisation. In practice the use of 'indeterminacy' and 'chance' can be highly improvisatory – adaptability and fluidity are integral to their success at the point of performance. Cage's influence is clearly evident in Berlin's Echtzeitmusik (real-time music) scene. The inception of the Echtzeitmusik scene mirrored this ambivalent relation with improvisation. However, the current diverse set of practices found within Echtzeitmusik is certainly improvisational. Creating parameters for playing does not necessarily negate reliance on the improvisational in the process of realising music. Tuba player Robin Haywood (Blazanovic, 2012) describes how he was interested in sounding and not responding as a compositional strategy. While that is not a jazz kind of 'call and response' improvisation, playing 'in parallel' has been in common use, for example, in minimalism and with the group AMM's improvisation approach and elsewhere. Others within Echtzeitmusik have described the idea of depleting a sense of narrative in the music; although the presumption that playing less (reductionism) leads to less narrative is debatable, it may be that that the opposite effect is achieved. The continuing discussion of improvisation's presence is healthy. To reduce all to improvisation, or worse, a style of improvisation is absurd – as practices continue to develop and diversify improvisation is rightly a contested term.

The Emergence of Improvisation in Music

Improvisation's profile in music during the past century has been notably intercultural: African American music in particular, employing improvisational practices centrally, has greatly contributed to a reordering of the Western music agenda, squarely re-introducing improvisation as a robust creative practice that demands attention (Lewis, 2008; Berliner, 1994). While this section's focus is with the emergence of the practice of improvisation in music, there is also the broader emerging picture of improvisation, found simultaneously in different activity.

Improvisation's presence within music making is, and always has been, ubiquitous (Bailey, 1992). Contemporary terms that have been coined relating to such practice are wide: free jazz, experimental music, spontaneous music, conduction, sound painting, jazz, jamming, non-idiomatic, intuitive music, open-form improvisation, open, contemporary improvisation, creative music and others. Chance, aleatoric and indeterminacy are also, in practice, tied to processes of improvisation. Categorization in music is imprecise although there are also, increasingly, 'sub-genres' that relate to improvisation: noise, electronic, onkyo, lower case, Echtzeitmusik and so on. Most of the terms described are relatively recent, and while we can delineate between them, they all rely upon the centrality of creating new music through performance: improvisation. More importantly, improvisation is also, by nature, a continually evolving practice and, as the contemporary international scene reveals, practice is certainly not as fixed as these descriptors suggest. As new formations occur, these, by definition, do not adhere to neat categorization. While styles of improvisation and their products are clearly evident, improvisation is fundamentally an activity that is more fully understood in terms of processes.

In recent years, there has been an exponential growth of interest in improvisation activity in music, but it is equally important to recognize that improvisation is, as Anthony Braxton has suggested, an ancient musical practice, improvisatory music has always been around, it just hasn't been documented. As well as the all but forgotten forms of improvisation found in classical music, the practice of improvisation is evidenced in different cultures: within folk music, experimental music, rock music, jazz, old music, 'new' music and elsewhere. The growing area of music specifically delineated as *improvised music* or *free improvisation* in which musicians commit to a relatively open form of not-predetermined musical performance is of specific interest here. The term *free improvisation* can be blurred by its capacity to embrace styles and musical approaches found in other forms of improvisation. Again, it is helpfully thought of as an activity; and the activity of free improvisation has the capability to include genres. (There is a distinction here between the evolving process of inclusiveness of other forms and John Zorn's approach to the collaging, or hopping between musical styles.) Thinking of improvisation as solely 'jazz' is very misleading although it remains surprisingly common even in recent studies of improvisation. A 'stylized' form of jazz has become institutionally colonized providing an 'acceptable', sanitized face of improvisation that has been bent towards institutional aims – resultantly, improvisation's profile and potential have often been diminished within education (see Chapter 7). Moreover, the terms of reference for the study of improvisation are important for developing a robust conceptualization from which the human capability of improvisation can be better understood. In Berliner (1994) and Sawyer (2003), jazz is evoked as a descriptor and used synonymously for improvisation and Sawyer develops broad theories of collaboration from the model of jazz. Jazz is primarily based on 'tunes', for example, the interpretation of standards, written compositions and the principal improvisatory element being the solo with accompaniment, from a rhythm section that follows 'the changes' (harmonic structure), while meter is strictly adhered to. Free or open improvisation differs significantly; its premise is to negotiate the emergent, together, through which form is created. The scope is much broader than jazz. Many established writers rarely even mention free or open improvisation, except in passing, which is at odds with the international growth in practice and the potential offered by theorizing an open form rather than closed style of improvisation. Of course, jazz is very important in the field of study, most notably within the North American perspective. However, as the following chapter describes, the scope of improvisation's potential for implementation goes far beyond the limitation of jazz as a model and is better understood in terms of the broader interpretation of free or open improvisation that can extend across disciplines.

In music, the terms *improvisation* and *free improvisation* often lead to misunderstandings stemming from assumptions regarding different intended meanings and associations. Writers describing improvisation often highlight the development of musical ideas in the act of performance (Nettl and Russel 1998; MacDonald, Wilson and Miell 2012; Kenny and Gellrich 2002). For a musician whose knowledge of music is in a particular musical area (e.g., Gamelan, Sufi, Flamenco, Indian music, Blues, Baroque, Rock etc.), the term *improvisation* suggests a specific approach within those idioms. *Free improvisation* differs significantly. While it remains true that free improvisation is the creation of music in the act of performance, for free improvisation it is the act of improvisation that leads to form. Improvisation is commonly understood as an aspect of a form, for example in jazz. Free improvisation has no such already fixed rhythmic or harmonic framework for creating music in the act of performance; it employs a not-predetermined approach. This distinction is significant – the 'freeing' of improvisation from the notion of being defined idiomatically allows for the emergence of improvisation's agency as it is through the activity that individuals and groups can choose to shape the form. *Improvisation* is used here as an encapsulating term, while *free improvisation* also makes it clear that the creativity is open and not dependent upon a predetermined structure or form, the creative form is open. Landgraf's (2011, p. 70) comment is useful, '[…] art's ability not only to frame the necessary as contingent, but also to represent the contingent as necessary for art'. The negotiation of this contingency is grist that provides purchase for the experienced creative improviser; it can be described as a 'problem-seeking' approach through which the music's becoming is an outcome.

While it is not the intention of this book to present a history of free improvisation, some background is necessary and helpful for those new to the music of improvisation. Accounts of free improvisation are often problematic; confusion between the biographical and the breadth of development of the phenomenon typically leave important aspects to one side as they focus on particular individuals and places, whilst the complexity of concurrent international activity can lead to significant figures being left out of the picture. The aim of this section is to describe the development of *free improvised* music as a process and activity mainly from the 1960s and 1970s. Born in London, UK and having lived and worked there for most of my life, I have, unapologetically, a Londoner's perspective of free improvisation, and London represents a significant history of the music. However, in the course of improvisation research, it became clear that the phenomenon of improvisation is not only local, although local identities become formed through improvisation practice, it is more broadly represented by descriptions that are not bounded by statehood, as the diversity of practice found in the interviews makes clear.

The initial development of free or open improvisation was gradual, overlapping and simultaneously occurring in different countries around the world at this time. In Italy, the

Gruppo di Improvvisazione Nuova Consonanze: Bertoncini, Branchi, Evangelisti, Kayn, Macchi, Morricone, Vandor, were a group of composers (formed in 1964) who performed using free improvisation practice, exploring instruments for their sound producing possibilities. In Germany, the influential developments of Stockhausen in electronics extended, for a time, to an Intuitive Composition approach in the late 1960s, effectively indistinguishable from some free improvisation. Simultaneously in Germany, Peter Brotzmann, Peter Kowald and Sven-Aka Johansson were exploring the extreme sound possibilities of instruments associated with jazz: saxophones, double bass and drums in a high energy, free jazz, exploration of sound. Also in Germany, pianist Alex von Schlippenbach began to move from 'club jazz' music into concert settings, where extended structures incorporating improvisation could be performed with, for example, the Globe Unity Orchestra. In Holland the group, The Instant Composers Pool (ICP), begun by Han Bennink and Misha Mengelberg, conflated ideas of composition and improvisation through various strategies that were shared within the group whilst retaining a clear jazz character, often with the inclusion of musical and visual humour. In the former USSR, and in Russia in particular, the attraction of improvised music was celebrated as an opportunity for expression by the Ganelin Trio and others within the political restrictions of the time. In Japan, there was a clear influence of US free jazz on players such as Kaoru Abe and Masayuki Takayanagi as they developed their distinct form of improvisation improvisation-based music, often characterized by the intensity familiar in later 'noise' music from Japan and elsewhere. Obviously these references to developments other than in the UK do nothing to *explain* the emergence in different locations; they do, however, illustrate the range of more or less simultaneous developments, the diversity of practice and multiplicity within the emerging free improvisation practice.

Creative processes are evolutionary, shared, necessarily complex and influenced by other disciplines and while significant figures within a movement become rightfully acknowledged, it is within an essentially evolving environment. Balancing narratives of improvisation and free improvisation that typically fix upon a few albeit significant individuals, we can also acknowledge an 'unofficial' history of the music (Fred Frith mentioned this idea in a conversation in 2008). Music without pre-determined structure was being explored in different, if less clearly demarked, ways, for example: in undocumented amateur music sessions; through professional jazz performance and recording (Joe Harriet, 1961); by exploring new compositional approaches; through intercultural musical activity (South African group Blue Notes became exiled in the UK in 1964); through rock music experimentation (Amon Düül, 1969); in developing newer paradigms suggested by electronically produced music (BBC Radiophonic Workshop, created in 1958); through built instruments (Hugh Davies, 1965; Francois and Bernard Baschet, 1955); and through the combining of such activities, a practice that later becomes clearly demonstrated within contemporary improvisation. At the same time, composers increasingly considered aspects of improvisation and this is discussed in the following section.

Free improvisation is an imperfect term, and opinions on the 'free' part of it vary and can typically include, 'nothing is free' to 'if it's free why is it often the same'. The focus on *free* in this discussion is as signifying the not-predetermined, emerging aspect of the process. However, the incorporation of the term *free* also carries particular associations with the 1960s and 1970s during which time the music developed; there is the obvious connection to the term *free jazz* and *free* also reflects the spirit of popular, political activity of the time. The left-wing political convictions of founding, influential figures in the development of *free improvisation* in the UK, notably John Stevens, Paul Rutherford, members of AMM, Maggie Nicols and others, reflect this zeitgeist – similar attitudes were largely shared by other musicians across Europe (Brotzmann and Rouy, 2014). The music has a clearly identifiable political antecedence; this is expressed through the approach in performance as well as, for example, the setting up of independent, DIY record labels in order to publish music without abeyance to 'record business' interests. The musical agenda was self-realized in its inception, development and production. This radical, politically informed attitude to creating performance and art was also commonly shared across artistic disciplines during this period. Recordings of free improvisation of the period can often be 'challenging' for those unfamiliar, and awareness of this political context can provide a useful 'way in' to more fully understanding the musical choices and approaches being taken. Notable assertiveness, abrasion and unorthodox musical interaction presented in low budget recordings can also dupe an uninitiated listener into being distracted from what commonly involves extremely high levels of technical expertise.

The writing of practitioners Derek Bailey, John Stevens and Cornelius Cardew are important in revealing different aspects of these musical developments. Bailey's 'Improvisation: Its nature and practice in music' (1992) surveys the musical practice from a personal, musician's perspective. Bailey is often cited as helping re-define improvisation through the introduction of the terms *non-idiomatic improvisation, idiomatic improvisation* and *not-predetermined.* It can be argued that a kind of generic free improvisation has developed, leaving doubt about the validity of the idea of a *non-idiomatic* improvisation. Nevertheless, the parameters indicated by these imperfect terms have provided much needed signposts demarcating free improvisation from other forms. Much of Bailey's project can be interpreted as a questioning of conventions surrounding music, recognizing how his musical concerns did not necessarily rely upon assumed, musical constructs. For example, Bailey had a preference for the idea of *playing* rather than *performance*. This emphasis creates an unpretentious shift of focus towards the act of creating music in real-time and at the same time challenges the music/show business aesthetic of 'putting on a performance' on behalf of management and public. Bailey's choice to commit to free improvisation also lent his professional credibility to furthering the form. Prior to this move he was an active working guitarist in radio, television, theatre, jazz and elsewhere, playing with many well-known jazz musicians as well as backing 'show-business names' of the period (Watson, 2004). Pursuing this free improvisation approach, he played with a wide range of established performers from different musical disciplines, as well as dancers. In Bailey's 'Company' concerts, diverse international musicians, with and without experience in improvised music, met and performed for consecutive days – the event ran annually across two decades. Often held in London but also in other parts of the UK, as well as in New York, Marseille and Japan, 'Company' became an important focus for the development of emerging free improvisation. Performances would explore the possible configurations that may include unusual combinations: rock guitar, 'classical' violin, tap-dance, voice, electronics, Butoh (dance) and clowning, as well as the more expected saxophone, trombone, trumpet, double bass, drums and so on. 'Company' was celebrated for the adventurousness of its programming, with outstanding levels of musicianship, representing a range of musical backgrounds and using the not-predetermined, free improvisation approach. It also drew, at times, large audiences that included the uninitiated, and reviews in the mainstream media helped advance the recognition of free improvisation.

Drummer John Stevens emerged as centrally important in the development of free improvisation practice in the UK. His ideas, skill and drive influenced not only the development of groups he was a member of, but also those musicians' subsequent development (Maggie Nicols). Free improvised music coalesced during a period of about two years (1966–1968) in late night performances at The Little Theatre Club, St Martin's Lane in London's West End. Here The Spontaneous Music Ensemble (SME) began as a collective, becoming Stevens' ongoing project for the realization of concepts of improvisation in practice through to his death in 1994. Early collaborators included Trevor Watts, Paul Rutherford, Dave Holland, Kenny Wheeler, Evan Parker, Derek Bailey, Barry Guy, Bruce Cale, Jeff Clyne and others. From the recordings of SME can be traced the move from 'free jazz' (the initial influence of Ornette Coleman's approach is apparent on early recordings) to something new: free improvisation. Conventional instrumental roles become diminished; the collective sense of 'time' is more open to interpretation; and the idea of the 'solo' is surpassed by collective improvisation in which the music is generated through interactive playing rather than pre-composed frameworks. Stevens influenced and encouraged others, 'He opened the door for me when I wasn't ready,' (from a conversation with Evan Parker, 2010), and persuaded a reluctant Kenny Wheeler to participate not having played in 'free' settings previously. Stevens' group of that period included bassist Dave Holland, who shortly after joined Miles Davis' group in his *Bitches Brew* (1970) period. Descriptions of Davis' group of this time usually focus heavily on the 'electric' turn (featuring Holland on electric bass), but as far as the musical process is concerned, a significant portion of that group's live performance is collective free improvisation (Davis, 1970).

Stevens' influence and commitment to realizing ideas in music extended to passionately informed teaching, reflecting his belief in music as sociopolitical practice. An often-cited text for implementing improvisation activity is his 'Search and Reflect' (1985), a manual format, compiled with associate musicians Ollie Crook and Julia Doyle at Community Music. Here Stevens collated his exercises developed during his involvement with Community Music, London in the 1970s and 1980s. 'Search and Reflect' (1985) provides group exercises that identify elements of creative musical interaction as improvisation is focused by simple yet precise instructions. Views of 'Search and Reflect' vary widely. While it can provide a useful way into improvised musical activity, and is regarded well by some established improvisers, the manual style format may lead to a restricted impression of free improvisation practice, particularly for those unfamiliar with the context that gave rise to the development of free improvisation.

During this period in the UK, free improvisation emerged in different ways. AMM developed their distinct sound approach to music making, establishing a lasting, influential group identity through improvisation practice that continues to be highly influential. AMM's musical approach differed from SME's: while the groups shared a largely jazz background, SME's practice retained the play and response interaction associated with jazz contexts. The music of AMM developed to become more concerned with the possibilities of exploring the improvised juxtaposing of sound created through the musical/sonic interests of individual members. This approach included an investigation of objects' and instruments' sound producing possibilities, including, for example, the sounds found through tuning a radio. The influence of AMM and their working methods is apparent within current improvisation activity, noticeably in London and Berlin and elsewhere. This influence is also continued through the ongoing workshop activity of drummer Eddie Prevost, a founder member of the group.

The relation of improvisation in the UK and Europe to musical developments in the United States is complex. It is convenient but inaccurate simply to describe music from the US at this time as jazz and free improvisation as distinctly European. The multiplicity of practices within improvisation's emergence across disciplines has already been described, and 'European' influenced improvisation was, and is, evident in many locations in the US while free improvisation in the UK developed largely through musicians who had developed practice in jazz, and who were, by default, highly influenced by key players from the US of that period. At the same time, it is clear that the assertion of identity through music, 'playing our own music', was, and remains, centrally important to the development of free improvisation activity. Developments in the UK's free improvisation were influenced by and at the same time a response to the US jazz legacy: employing an improvisatory approach and developing a distinct musical identity through different approaches. Some of these approaches were distilled from aspects of US jazz playing and others drew from European musical developments: Schoenberg, Webern, Stockhausen, Berio, Boulez and others. Perhaps one of the clear distinctions in UK developments rather than in Holland or Germany was a more concerted development away from such a US-influenced jazz legacy (AMM, SME, Alterations, Feminist Improvisation Group and others). This is, however, a complex, intercultural picture, and improvisation practice is certainly unbounded by statehood; examples of improvisation unrelated to jazz are also, unsurprisingly, to be found in the US: for instance the important San Francisco Tape Music Centre (1964), Improvisation Chamber Ensemble (1957) and elements of the groups of Roscoe Mitchell during the 1960s. The history of improvisation in music from the US has become globally influential and at the same time its multiplicity challenges easy categorization, even the term *jazz* is so loaded with diverse associations that its utility becomes dubious. However, we can say that the largely African American movement of improvised music from the US in the 1950s and 1960s was undoubtedly influential upon the first wave of free improvisers in the UK, as it was in the rest of Europe. Examples of key influences include Charlie Parker, John Coltrane, Ornette Coleman, Cecil Taylor, Eric Dolphy, Max Roach, Ed Blackwell, Elvin Jones, Thelonius Monk, Sun Ra, Charlie Mingus, Lennie Tristano, Gunter Schuller and Albert Ayler amongst a large number of others. The influence of 'black music' is pervasive and significant. Additionally, The Jimmy Giuffre Trio's approach (Giuffre, Swallow and Bley [1962]: 'Free Fall') also influenced UK developments in free improvisation: much of the instrumental playing and realigning of the composition/improvisation relationship on this recording suggests the later developments in free improvisation.

Composition most often implies *written* composition, and the presumption that the experience of sound in music can be faithfully and best represented by dots and lines on paper is commonly unchallenged. It is the tradition of written composition that tends to be regarded as the bedrock of 'serious music'. Within the discourse of improvisation and composition, it is the cultural connotations suggested by the terms that often become strongly evoked. In the West, written composition is often aligned with 'high art' sensibilities and aspirations, and has had an associated distancing from improvisation. Paradoxically, classical music's estrangement from improvisation is relatively new, in terms of that music's history, and many of the most highly esteemed classical composers were celebrated for their skill in improvisation, these include J. S. Bach, Mozart, Beethoven and many others. While these composers are held in high regard through the legacy of their 'works', their extensive use of improvisation has become under-acknowledged, leading to an altered picture of the nature of their creativity. Reclamation of improvisation as a legitimate approach to creating music has not come from the 'classical' music but other forms of music making throughout the world and African American music in particular.

As developments in improvisation took place, so too were written compositional approaches being reconsidered. While improvisation is described as the generation of musical ideas in the act of playing or performance, 'composition' has most often inferred the written (to the extent that 'the music' is often used, erroneously, to mean notation). Some composers began to be interested in the wider possibilities offered through 'indeterminacy', the 'aleatoric', or 'chance' and other strategies. In this way, composing activity extended to include players in the compositional decision-making. However, decades prior to this, others, principally African American, had been engaged in compositional processes that featured the unique practice of players. For example, Duke Ellington built an orchestra of fluent improvisers, distinct voices, for whom pieces would provide playing vehicles. George Lewis has explored the significance of the dividing of 'white' and 'black' music in the important 'Improvised music after 1950: Afrological and Eurological perspectives' (1996). The separation of, and assumptions regarding, 'serious' (white) music and 'jazz' (black) creates a cultural legacy that is still very apparent today. By acknowledging the scope of improvisation, the prejudicial assumptions that support this separation become challenged (see Chapter 7).

There is an imbalance between the status and support afforded to 'the composer' and that of improvising musician who composes at the point of performance. Naming the composer of a piece of music defines legal ownership and affords cultural status. Notation is frequently taken to suggest a definitive representation of a piece of music, a practice that may service the desire for ownership and control and at the same time counters the true improvisational nature of much music making. Foregrounding improvisation within the structure of a piece of music destabilizes the status of 'the composer'. The emergence, principally in the 1950s, 1960s and 1970s of what is generically referred to as the 'graphic score', illustrates, to some extent, the developing improvisation/notation relationship in composition. The move towards such alternative 'graphic scores' is, in many cases, an acknowledgement of how the process of music making is not necessarily best served by the established writer/performer relationship in which the extent of the musician's role is to interpret the composer's wishes. As John Cage described: 'When you get right down to it, a composer is simply someone who tells other people what to do. I find this an unattractive way of getting things done. I'd like our activities to be more social – and anarchisticly so' (Cage, 1969). Composers of graphic scores include Morton Feldman, Micheal Nyman, Gordon Mumma, Christian Marclay, Karlheinz Stockhausen, Steve Roden, Terry Riley, Christian Wolf, Gavin Bryars, Barry Guy and Gyorgy Ligeti, amongst many others. While the term 'graphic score' is very broad, pieces often call for decision-making on the part of the player, and this may extend to the fundamental musical content, its instrumentation and number of participants. As a result, the player's 'palette', 'language', choices and identity become essentially important to the piece's performance. In this respect, graphic scores can be viewed as contributing to a broader move towards the increasing acknowledgement of improvisational practice, with the performer's unique voice becoming rightly recognized as legitimately compositional.

The idea of developing a system of codification in sound for visual art that would then dominate visual art practice is, of course, absurd. However, the equivalent, a visual system of 'reading' music (or pitch and meter), came to be accepted without question as defining of Western music. Braxton (Lock 2008): '[…] this concept of two-dimensional pitch in the Western music system is a form of reductionism compared to what is actually happening'. The broadening of the compositional focus to include the potential of sound making through improvisational processes opens the door to the consideration of sound in ways that 'dots' on the paper can never reflect.

Prior to his involvement with AMM, Cornelius Cardew's work in composition included collaboration with Stockhausen (Tilbury, 2008). His political and philosophical commitments became realized in such work as the graphic score, 'Treatise' (1963–1967). This piece provides a good example of how the composer/performer relationship can become realigned and the importance of improvisation within this. Performers of 'Treatise' are required to make decisions about every aspect of the music, through the openly subjective interpretation of the 193 pages of shapes and contours. The number of performers and instrumentation is also open and the piece was purposefully written and presented as free standing, without notes of guidance or instructions (Cardew published text reflecting upon the piece some years later). While we identify Cardew as the composer, 'Treatise's' realization is by means of the performers' ability and willingness to create with the shapes. Cardew's intention was precisely directed at drawing upon the responses of individuals and groups of musicians. Such a graphic score forms an important stage in development towards a fuller understanding of improvisation's potential in creating real-time composition. As the performer and composer roles became less rigid, the softening of boundaries led to a more aesthetically diverse, inter-disciplinary relationship making way for further fundamental questions regarding the nature of the relationship between the visual and the aural. The influence of Cage typifies the inter-disciplinary, cross-fertilization of the period; as well as in music, his writing, approach and attitude affected and continue to influence compositional approaches in visual art and dance.

Graphic scores can express mindfulness of the player's potential contribution in the process of composition; other ways of engaging the agency of improvisation have also been developed. Lawrence D 'Butch' Morris's 'Conduction', a method of working with hand signals/gestures, conducting musicians without a written score, has become adopted and adapted in numerous countries for its utility in facilitating large improvising ensembles in particular. Similarly 'Sound Painting' developed by Walter Thompson uses signals to the same end and has been employed in much the same way – notably in educational contexts in the US. Idiosyncratic hand signals have, unsurprisingly, been widely used by bandleaders in different fields, for example, by Count Basie and Frank Zappa. Zappa employed extensive, precise personalized ways of communicating the direction of the music through detailed visual signals with the band Mothers of Invention. And John Zorn developed his 'game pieces', for example, 'Cobra' (1984) in which rules cued through cards and hand signals guide players through unfolding sections of dynamic improvisations as they compete to play in different formations. Games that introduce chance for instant composing are also far from recent. In the eighteenth century, numerous composers designed dice games through which musical choices are made in performance (Berkowitz, 2010).

Despite improvisation's pervasiveness, support for such activity within arts funding and education in the UK (from primary through to higher education) has been lacking – in contrast to support for composition. In discussions of improvisation and composition, frequently one is set against the other, creating the false impression that they are separated activities and somehow in opposition. More accurately improvisation and composition are part of the same activity of creating music – improvisation can usefully be viewed as a compositional approach. The historical evidence of their mutual benefit abounds and the separating of practice has been acculturated rather than pragmatic – the reasons for this are explored in Chapter 4. As improvisation is ubiquitous, its inclusion is fundamental – those wishing to become professional musicians need to be skilled and experienced in all areas of practice if they are to not only to survive but flourish.

Berlin is currently one of the busiest centres of improvised music as musicians have gathered there from all over the world. Echtzeitmusik (2015) is commonly used in Berlin to describe this large music scene with an evolving diversity of musical practice. In the 1990s, the musical interests of a small group of musicians (Ignaz Schick, Burkhard Beins, Axel Dorner, Robin Haywood, Andrea Neumann, Michel Vorfeld and others) came to characterize the scene's music through the use of quiet playing and silence. For some, there was an attempt to create some 'blue water' between their activity and that of free improvisation, largely associated with older musicians. The funding of concerts, festivals and the publication of a book (Beins et al. 2011) and a thesis (Blazanovic, 2012) has positively projected the Echtzeitmusik ethos. As the discussion of 'reductionism's' importance has ebbed, the picture of diverse practices, clearly employing improvisation is more clearly revealed. Although those attracted to the scene have often cited reductionism as a defining characteristic, a closer look reveals questioning of 'the R word' (Beins, 2011) by many of those involved. The Echtzeitmusik (2015) online calendar shows how the scene consists of almost entirely improvised and related musical activity that can be more fruitfully described by its diversity. The Echtzeitmusik tag has served musicians closely identified with that scene by forming a response to the weakness of describing a life of practice in music as 'improvised music', or as being an improvising musician. To say 'I play improvised music' can be almost as vague as saying 'I play composed music' – although some musicians may well understand the intended cultural meaning, organizations and funding bodies may well not. The Echtzeitmusik term also serves a second purpose. 'Musical identities' are important and powerful (MacDonald et al, 2002) and for individuals musical choices are an important part of personal development. It is noteworthy how the more ardent defenders of the Echtzeitmusik 'ethos' tend to be younger musicians – for them 'Echtzeit' is their music, their scene.

The Range of Improvisation

The increasing research interest in improvisation across disciplines tells us more about its character within and throughout experience. As well as in drama, dance and music, improvisation research extends to psychology, pedagogy, philosophy, sociology, anthropology, law, literature, post-colonial studies, gender-studies, human-computer relations, emergency response, fire-fighting management, negotiation, sport, architecture, medical surgery, management, marketing, entrepreneurship and the military, and the extent of research continues to grow. Acknowledgement of the full range of improvisation allows us to better view its potential and implementation critically. The themes of improvisation, Part 2, describe the innately social, collaborative features – its interconnectedness with learning offering an ethical creative process. Only from awareness of all the implication of improvisation can a truly useful and ethical conceptualization of improvisation become developed. This section includes quotations from Ludovica Leone's (2010) survey describing a variety of disciplinary perspectives of improvisation. Improvisation beyond the arts has been described in the following ways:

> On the spot surfacing, criticizing, restructuring, testing of intuitive understandings of experienced phenomena [...] Knowing in action [...] Reflection in action.
>
> (Schön, 1983)

> Substantive rather than temporal convergence of planning and execution.
>
> (Miner, Bassoff and Moorman, 2001)

[…] discovering the future that [action] creates as it unfolds.

(Barrett, 1998)

Organizational improvisation is a type of short-term learning, where experience and related change occur at or near the same time.

(Bergh and Lim, 2006)

[…] robust models that do justice to particular difficulties in which people find themselves.

(Brown and Duguid, 1991)

[…] combining limited structure with extensive interaction and freedom to make changes […].

(Brown and Eisenhardt, 1997)

Making do with minimal commonalities and elaborating simple structures in complex ways.

(Eisenberg, 1990)

A just in time strategy.

(Weick, 1987)

As long ago as 1983, Schön used 'surfacing' to describe improvisation, a term that, to my knowledge, has not been used in improvisation in music. It is useful as it suggests the internal, individual processes that can become shared. The 'substantive' (Miner, Bassoff and Moorman) is also a helpful description of improvisation's responding to real events as they unfold. Not-predetermined improvisation in music occurring in the present, through the ability to play successfully in a substantive manner, within immediacy, is what leads to interesting music. For Barrett, the temporal nature of improvisation is imaginatively described as 'discovering the future': or allowing creativity in action to unfold in circumstances that change to reveal outcomes, rather than depending solely on past plans. Bergh and Lim link improvisation with learning – a centrally important connection that is fully explored in Chapter 7. Brown and Duguid's description of improvisation as a response to 'particular difficulties', and the 'freedom to make changes' further indicates the specific nature of improvisation's potential. Brown and Eisenhardt, and Eisenberg's complimentary descriptions of moving from the simple to the complex, is thematically echoed in descriptions of processes in the natural world and improvisation in Chapter 6. Weick's idea of improvisation as a 'just in time strategy' reminds us of the equally valid common use of the term: the way improvisation becomes employed in order to correct a situation or save us when things go wrong. The following descriptions of improvisation come from strategy and structure research.

Efficiency generate new combinations of resources, routines and structures which are able to match the present, turbulent circumstances.

(Ciborra, 1996)

Use structure in creative ways that enable the altering of the structural foundations of performance.

(Hatch, 1999)

Making decisions and adapting to changing needs and conditions [...] ideas emerge in new and creative ways not planned by the performer.

(Crossan, White, Lane and Klus, 1996)

Hatch's description of improvisation as altering structure through its process is a helpful clarification of the much misrepresented relation between improvisation and structure. Frequently improvisation and structure are described as separated (Sawyer, 2003) whereas the two work together – and can be part of the same process of creating – improvisation creates 'structure that supports'. In this way *free* improvisation provides us with a more helpful indication of improvisation's broader potential than forms in which structure is thought of as separated from the improvisational content.

Leone's survey of organizational improvisation has also included descriptions of improvisation from studies of music and theatre as well as sport and in Chapter 6, the collective, creative strategies used within basketball, arising from Lewis' interview, are compared to approaches within music.

Music and theatre:

Playing the game; setting to solve a problem with no preconception as to how you will do it; permitting everything in the environment to work for you in solving the problem.

(Spolin, 1963)

Sports:

Reading and reacting in parallel [...] Dual tasks [...] Perspective-in-action [...] Thinking-in-action.

(Bjurwill, 1993)

Improvisation's fluid quality contributes to its offer of agency. Fluidity or adaptability has been an important feature of both the inter-cultural history and inter-disciplinary activity described previously. For this reason, while *describing* the improvisation phenomenon contributes to the development of understanding, seeking to overly *define* may introduce a restricted view. George Lewis, in his interview, describes the '*agility in the term*' and elsewhere dancer Steve Paxton has called improvisation '*a word for something which cannot keep a name*' (1987). Outstanding exemplars of original improvising musicianship are commonly referred to when describing the music; however, resisting these as *defining* the *process* of improvisation allows for the ongoing development of creative practice. This point becomes highlighted in the discussion of inclusive educational practice in the following chapter in which improvisation's unique, creative potential is viewed primarily as an invitation for the inclusion of difference, one that is not furthered by overly prescribing the activity.

How helpful is it to think of improvisation in music as a model? Improvisation in music is frequently used as a metaphor and this is an important aid for understanding the scope of improvisation's potential. Improvisation in music is also widely used as a model that can illuminate other areas of activity. However, the intended meaning in 'real-world' contexts other than music, or drama, can often remain less than clear. Engaged in, for example, drama activity it would be unhelpful to limit our descriptions of improvisation to a musical model, so too in other areas of life, such as teaching and beyond, the metaphor's overuse can limit understanding of the capability. To this end, the terms of reference have increased importance if we are to develop an accurate picture of improvisation that is of use, for example, in education.

Peters (2009) aims to develop a concept of improvisation through a wide range of philosophy. In marked contrast to the descriptions of improvisation presented earlier, Peters' 'Philosophy of Improvisation' characterizes improvisation's advocacy as a kind of naïve utopianism, or 'love-in' as he puts it. The 'touchy-feely' factor is certainly present in some arts practice, but if we look at the activity of significant pioneers in the field of music, is that a true picture? The seminal recordings of free improvisation of, for example, Peter Brotzmann's *Machine Gun* (1968), or Evan Parker, Derek Bailey and Hans Bennink on *Topography of the Lungs* (1970) certainly do not reflect a 'love-in' attitude. These highly influential recordings, together with many others of the period are an abrasive protest, a breaking with the past, creating a new vision, clearly reflected in the aesthetic of the sound – (quite apart from the way the musicianship is breaking new conceptual ground). Peters also avoids the discussion of improvisation's important and theoretically potent historical connection with radical politics – Black Power, Feminism, counterculture and so on. As such there is a false footing created by the dubious terms of reference from which the, albeit, wide ranging philosophy unfolds. Peters also chooses to use the example of a television series to illustrate his perspective of improvisation. Superficially the *Scrapheap Challenge* (RDF Media 1998) series correlates with improvisation – the game show requires teams to build machines from junk with which they compete. However, while the television format of the game show example may have been chosen for its accessibility, it does nothing to aid understanding of the social processes of improvisation. In his conclusion, Peters returns to what he wanted to leave behind, putting a slightly different spin on what is commonly referred to as 'being in the moment': '[…] any concept of improvisation worth considering must acknowledge the primary importance of timing, the decisive now so rigorously promoted by improvisers […]' (p. 165). 'Timing' is certainly important, but a concept of improvisation also needs to be located in the true range of experience found in improvisation that exists across experience.

Berkowitz's (2010) disciplinary interest also determines the representation of the subject. Marrying hard science with high art, Berkowitz rediscovers the improvisation approaches associated with 'great' composers through 'how to' texts from the period. However, neither of his two living proponents of classical improvisation has made use of these texts in the development of practice. This is something Berkowitz doesn't pursue – it would detract from the aim to explain improvisation by way of such texts. Improvisation's uneasy relationship with text, as well as the dubious nature of 'how to' approaches in relation to improvisation is discussed later in Chapter 4. In spite of the title 'The improvising mind: cognition and creativity in the musical moment', there is very little mention of creativity. Surprisingly, there is no conceptual consideration of the significant sociocultural history of improvisation other than the study of 'classical' improvisation practice from two hundred years ago. The social, lived experience is always present in improvisation and, perhaps, it is the eliding of this within the formality of academia that has partially contributed to improvisation's death in classical music.

The extent of development of improvisation activity is also reflected by the growth of research. Currently, improvisation research is very apparent in some locations. The largest of these is the Improvisation, Community and Social Practice (ICASP) project based in Guelph University, Canada that continues to grow. It involves three universities and a number of inter-disciplinary initiatives. Its online journal, *Critical Studies in Improvisation/ Études critique en improvisation,* currently contains nine editions covering improvisation from broad disciplinary perspectives. As the project's leader Ajay Heble describes, 'This research project plays a leading role in defining a new field of inter-disciplinary inquiry' (ICASP, 2015). The International Society for Improvised Music (ISIM) based in Ann Arbor, Michigan, USA has held annual international conferences since 2006 at which practitioners and academics perform and present (ISIM, 2015). Mills College, Oakland, California, USA has a long history of teaching experimental practice and Fred Frith has been running the Mills Improvisation Ensemble since 1999. Currently, Mills music staff who also specialize in improvisation include Roscoe Mitchell and Chris Brown and visiting staff include Pauline Oliveros and Zeena Parkins. The University of San Diego (UCSD) also has a significant history in the development of experimental practice in its music teaching (UCSD, 2015).

Sonic Arts Research Centre (SARC) at Queens University, Belfast, UK currently hosts the Translating Improvisation research project (AHRC, 2014). This explores how practice in music may inform the development of theory and practice in law with a specific focus on child protection in Northern Ireland. There are a growing number of other locations where improvisation is researched and taught including University of Edinburgh, Newcastle University, Glasgow Caledonian University, Surrey University, University of Oxford (Perspectives on Musical Improvisation), Rensselaer Polytechnic Institute (USA) and Exploratorium, Berlin Improvisation Research Group. Elsewhere in Europe, Brazil and Australasia there is some dedicated work on improvisation in music. Of course, the picture is also blurred by the enormous number of universities and academies teaching jazz that obviously include consideration of improvisation, albeit within the idiomatic limitation. Similarly music education that includes electronic music composition may have a comparable consideration of improvisation. Some conservatoires, such as the Guildhall, London, are also developing improvisation activity.

Chapter 3

The Agency of Improvisation

I'm sitting in a room, in a small school in Hackney which is in East London. It's ten to nine on a Monday morning in 2003. I'm a teacher of music and drama in this Pupil Referral Unit – a school for teenagers who've been permanently excluded from mainstream education. The door is kicked open and bangs against the wall, adding to the marks that are already there. I deliberately don't look up from my planner as four fifteen year olds bound into the room engaged in a highly animated, high-volume exchange. I stand up, and indicate the chairs that are placed in a circle and as the four sit down, they become more attuned to their surroundings and a further half dozen students enter the room and take their places in the circle of chairs.

"OK, Daniel, let's get started."

"I'm Daniel and… I'm alright." [Pause.]

"Charlene?"

"I'm Charlene… and I hate school, init …. Well I do."

[Laughter, a lot of talking until…] "Charlene…"

"What?"

[There's a lot of talking over the top.]

"Charlene, have you finished what you want to say?"

[Angrily] "Yeeees!"

The group continues around the circle each 'checking-in'. The Year 10 students, some of whom have been at the school for two years or more, are used to the ritual of beginning the drama lesson in this way. Its purpose is to create a focus on *listening* to one another equally and, in the precarious circumstances of exclusion, it provides a safe beginning for all. This is an important theme for these students. Habitual disregarding of the teacher, in the form of talking over, is also a way of asserting position in the pecking order. It is demonstrably clear that a willingness to listen has the capacity to directly affect all of the issues that are presented in this challenging educational context. A story emerges in the course of the 'checking-in' – an incident on the bus where a phone had been stolen and a fight ensued in which a knife was used. We discuss the events. We then move the chairs to the wall and roles are assigned to members of the group – one student narrates the story in careful detail and as she does so other students portray the sequence of events – when violence is portrayed it is done so in 'slow motion'. When there is agreement about the representation of events, students record the piece using video and a spoken narrative accompanies the action.

Their story's themes connect to a set text for the English GCSE, Shakespeare's *Romeo and Juliet*. We talk about why Shakespeare decided to open the play with young men fighting with swords and then discuss the killings that follow in the play from the feuding between the families, or gangs. We talk about the feelings involved and the play's tragic ending. Then we discuss friendship, affiliation and loss. We also talk about love and relationships and why Shakespeare linked the idea of gangs and love together and the effect that this creates. The group refers to 'Murder Mile', a stretch of the Lower Clapton Road in Hackney, and how a cousin was killed there. They also exchange a lot in the discussion in a manner that I am not able to be involved – using oblique references and slang to discuss events that are part of local shared knowledge. The session is exciting and I'm encouraged that their experience relates so immediately to the central themes of an author that, for many, even in mainstream settings, may never 'get off the page'. I imagine the small school is full of Romeos, Juliets, Mercutios and Tybalts. They leave the lesson talking amicably about the stories that have become used in the lesson.

Activity on 'decks', twin turntables and vinyl records becomes significant in the school. 'Doing decks' is aspired to by the younger ones and those who can skilfully mix records are revered by their peers. But, it's the additional use of the microphone and spoken word that is a revelation for me in the teaching role. Many of the students are aspiring bards, creatively honing language, often on a daily basis, keen to perform and develop their performing skills, many have an urgent desire to 'get on the mic'. Lyrics are both written and improvised – made up, co-opted, developing over time, reflecting musical and personal interests and are a ritualistic display, banter, competitive and celebratory – those who become outstanding acquire high peer status. Embracing this creative activity at the heart of the music lessons positively impacts on teacher/student relations and resultantly students want to come to school, to actively take part in lessons and, in the process, become favourable to the idea of education that has meaning for them. Over time, I also developed a resource of instruments (guitars, bass, drums, saxophones, cello, percussion, sitar, computers and software) and students were entered for formal, public examinations. It is the reference to, and inclusion of, students' own music, its legitimization, that leads to the wave of enthusiasm and motivation that goes across the school, supporting successful learning, and, in turn, contributing to the possibility of further education and reintegration within mainstream education.

For a time, one-to-one music lessons were possible with a small number of students who, for one reason or another, could not be integrated within the group sessions. One such pupil, 'Bobby' aged twelve, presented as a boy and was frequently in violent conflict with others arising from their perceptions of gender. Bobby was keen to do music and sessions led to devising lyrics, performance and working towards making a series of self-directed music videos, with guidance. With a very unstable background (typical of many students in this setting), difficulties were far from resolved and Bobby continued to get into trouble, often with the police, and there was repeated violence. The music sessions provided a dedicated, non-judgemental time in which to create with the music, sounds, ideas and imagery exploring style in performance, producing recordings that were shared with family and friends. Bobby brought her own musical interests to bear in the lessons, through which formal educational requirements unfolded, and, additionally, the issue of educational inclusion became addressed.

The approaches described in these three examples foreground improvisation as an aspect that is employed throughout music and drama and, moreover, within the entirety of the teaching and learning relationship. Formal educational requirements become successfully addressed by planning and action that allows for and seeks the emergent – by means of improvisation. The material content of the lesson *is developed through the specific context created by those involved, as with free improvisation,* and this provides a vehicle with which educational aims are successfully achieved. The experiences here indicate that, firstly, improvisation is a capability that can be engaged to provide tangible educational goals. Within the specificity of these examples, improvisation leads to particular, concrete solutions to educational difficulties and inclusion within the highly complex and fraught social dynamic resulting from educational exclusion (in an area of disproportionate unemployment and high levels of poverty). Improvisation's potential in education is by no means limited to the setting of exclusion (Sawyer, 2004, 2007; Lewis, 2000; Thomson, 2008; Schlicht, 2008); however, in this setting, workable solutions to far-reaching educational questions, such as the nature and practice of social inclusion, are foregrounded in a dynamic manner. For this reason, the example of exclusion provides a useful lens with which to examine education and improvisation.

In this chapter, my intention is to transparently explain how this interest in improvisation has become developed. As I write I am reminded how these issues evoke strong feelings about the treatment of some individuals in education. No doubt a psychoanalyst would say this is linked to my formative experience. Aged ten, following my mother's death, I 'went off the rails', my education rapidly declined, culminating in what would have been my own permanent exclusion had it not been for the coincidence of my father's new job out of London and the family move. There were nine children and I had little emotional grasp of the world, which was making no sense to me. As an adult I can recognize an affinity with students who 'don't fit' and are discarded, and, as a result, I am not put off by outward displays of challenging behaviour, that transgress educational boundaries. At the same age, ten, I got my first guitar – and while I had no formal lessons, and the music at school was unappealing, music became extremely important in my development, perhaps reflecting the same way that music became so important for these excluded students in the example of the Pupil Referral Unit.

I taught in this educational setting for eight years and the examples described are from the later period, when I had developed further skills and knowledge that additionally supported the work in this environment. The student intake in the Pupil Referral Unit was largely characterized as having, what is termed, Emotional, Behavioural and Social Difficulties (EBSD). There are a highly disproportionate number of black excluded pupils in the UK – approximately 10:1. Teenage students, while reflecting the local community's ethnic diversity, were predominantly of Afro-Caribbean descent or mixed race. There is a problematic disparity between the way mainstream education is constructed in the UK and the actuality of the population. Education reflects and embodies society's dominant values, and the number of black young people excluded raises important questions that need to inform thinking and approaches to teaching and learning, across education. The Education Act, 2002 deemed it mandatory for all pupils, regardless of 'permanent exclusion' status, to attend full-time education. Nationally, at that time, approximately 60% of daytime crime was attributed to young people not in school (according to government statistics reported in the press) – the decision to enforce full-time education for permanently excluded students was not motivated by educational concerns but the political desire for a response to rising crime figures. This led to increased pressure on the educational provision, usually in the form of Pupil Referral Unit to meet the new legal obligation.

Developing Improvisation as Pedagogy

Improvisation becomes developed through specific, situated educational processes, not in an isolated manner, and the purpose of this section is to provide a contextualized example of this. The detailed description illustrates how improvisation becomes significant for successful learning. Broadly, the intake of the PRU was disaffected, alienated from central concerns of mainstream education, routinely hostile and there was frequently violent behaviour. No music was on offer although pupils were often curious to discover if music lessons were possible. Over the course of several years I developed music resources and music teaching in the Pupil Referral Unit that became a popular feature of the curriculum. Students took public music examinations, gave performances and Ofsted (UK government inspectorate of education, 2003) reported the music teaching as 'excellent' and highlighted its role in successfully contributing to whole school practice and aims. Students' progress was very good and music was taught to all students each week and for some twice per week.

Students' previously negative, and for some traumatic experience in education contributed to very low expectations and many routinely presented challenging behaviour that undermined educational aims – confrontations with teachers were a daily occurrence. Through prior work in special educational needs contexts, I had developed knowledge and skills in counselling (RSA, Counselling in Education Diploma, 1992). This provided a valuable additional dimension to the teaching. As anger and conflict were part of the daily routine of the PRU, and for many this had contributed to their exclusion, I employed reflective practice that enabled better understanding of 'what is going on' while engaging with the curriculum. Primarily through reflective writing, this practice informed the development of strategies, forming a response to the daily challenges that were presented. The process helped develop planning for teaching and learning that was informatively contextualized by the day-to-day teaching experience. While very challenging, the work became increasingly rewarding. Part of the dynamic of the challenge being that when students were successfully engaged in music and drama, they were highly motivated in experiential lessons, energetically creative and often fearlessly participating, providing a very rewarding learning environment for a teacher to work in. Students' challenging behaviour was twinned with a strong desire to express creatively in music and drama. Rather than create a 'top-down' lesson, repeating a negative dynamic, I encouraged students' motivation by acknowledging and foregrounding their practical ideas. Students' clear and informed musical choices influenced the planning of schemes of work, and creative immediacy and adaptability were important features of lesson design. Successful lessons occurred through active engagement. Experiential activity was built upon students' desire to express in music and drama; embodying the potential for successful learning. Video recordings, made by students, of lesson/performance activity became integral to this learning process. Listening and viewing performances provided opportunities for analysis of musical elements; peer and teacher assessment; record keeping; clear evidence of successful, ongoing engagement; and an indication of progress in learning that contributed to formal assessment. Pupils developed an owned, positive culture of learning that carried into other lessons and the popularity and success of music and drama contributed to an overall improvement in school attendance.

As students' alienation diminished, the motivation to be involved in educational activity was clear. For example, one student with particularly challenging behaviour returned well after the end of the school day to enquire if he could bring his 'mates' in, not members of the school, to have a music lesson. Over time, the PRU developed a local reputation as a place to develop strong music of your own making and through that experience gain educational legitimacy, for example, by achieving good public exam results. Music teaching contributed towards inclusive education and the culture of the school environment became, as the Ofsted inspection (2003) reflected, increasingly positive.

Performance is an important and valuable concept in this setting and intersects drama, music, personal development and educational achievement. The term carries multiple, overlapping meanings for educational practice, reflecting the broader significance of performativity (Austin, 1962; Butler, 1993; Goffman, 1990). Performance is used to describe students' overall educational achievement in formal contexts. Performance is obviously tied to educational drama, the value of which relates to enacted, thematic work rather than necessarily training for theatre performing (although that may also be the case) and musical improvisation also only occurs through its performance. Additionally, those who work with students with 'Emotional Behavioural and Social Difficulties' may identify performance as resonant: the desire to find an outlet and audience for the expression of such difficulties is often presented through challenging behaviour, referred to as 'acting out'. Performance is also celebratory and, for example, I organized an annual whole school event in which students would gather and 'pass the mic' – leading to a non-stop session in which spoken word, dance, instruments and decks would become used in a continuous, improvised performance that gathered momentum as it unfolded. These overlapping themes of performance through educational achievement, drama, music, channelling personal expression and shared celebration became embodied in the context of teaching and learning in the Pupil Referral Unit.

In order to seize on the creative possibilities and opportunities for learning presented by students, the pedagogical approach reprioritized that which was fit for purpose, the adaptable, over a fixed modality. In this way, the use of improvisation in music and drama, as an essential teaching tool, became mirrored in the approach to teaching which developed as an adaptable process that valued the emergent. This creativity was harnessed within very clear parameters of: time, the use of space and equipment, and, of over-arching importance in this setting, a shared understanding of behaviour that was safe. The teaching methodology employed formal systems of record keeping and assessment, led to successful examination results, and contributed towards students' reintegration in mainstream education. The rigorous approach that centred improvisation generated effective, measurable outcomes that were acknowledged by government inspectors who visited nine lessons. This formal acknowledgement of the process' success squarely counters the myth that the advocacy of improvisation, or 'creative approaches', should be characterized as 'ecstatic' and 'utopian' (Peters, 2009).

Recording performances of music and drama also supported the aim of inclusion in other more holistic ways as students shared their positive experiences in education with family members and others beyond the immediate experience of school. The recording in this setting also fulfilled an important secondary function, relieving the wearing effect created by the emphasis upon the teacher as the continuous focus of control within the classroom: a particularly useful addition in this teaching context. Students' were encouraged to take control of decision-making and the of recording of group work – a process that requires collective cooperation. By means of this process, the fundamental educational question of how to manage challenging behaviour was successfully addressed within the group activity.

The Need for Improvisation Research

Teaching in this setting led to an interest in investigating the processes at work more formally. I undertook a Best Practice Research Scholarship (BPRS, DfES, 2003) involving an Action Research project called 'The uses of digital video recording for teaching and learning music and drama in a pupil referral unit'. The project was developed reflexively in response to the circumstances of the PRU: the over-arching aim being to improve the experience for all involved through better understanding of the processes at work. Through the study, it became apparent that the adaptability provided by improvisation allowed for an appropriately flexible response to the day-to-day changes in relationships and personnel – in this way, students' emotional lives were acknowledged and accommodated within ongoing activity. The example at the beginning of the chapter illustrates how drama made use of students' immediate experiences. Encouraging students to explore aspects of their experience in words, and subsequently through role play and dramatic action transformed what could, as experience had shown, otherwise easily become a source of conflict within more conventional methods. As students experienced the potential expressive value of the improvisational drama form, and gained confidence in their ability, they became willing to explore more expansive, conceptual themes through which further learning took place. The experiential nature of 'doing' drama led to the development of communication skills; creatively expressing emotion; accurately reflecting events; developing ideas through role play; discussing narrative choices; exploring and learning about 'the self and the world around'. Working with communication and self-awareness in this way became highly relevant – as one headteacher put it: 'This is the most important work these students are doing in school'. Students responded well to this experiential approach through which their *life-world* (Husserl, 1982) was valued and integrated in the learning, rather than negated by the educational construct.

The need to more fully understand the potential agency provided by the processes of improvisation was clear and this informed the aims of further research. Work with permanently excluded pupils is under-researched and provides specific challenges for teachers, and Chapter 4's section on power and improvisation discusses why this is so. Teaching in this setting benefits from all available personal knowledge and skills; in this way, it is already improvisational. Explaining some personal background explains how inter-disciplinary connections were made that aided teaching and informed research. Work as a musician with a primary interest in improvisation influenced the teaching approach; this involves collaboratively performing music that is not-predetermined. With a background as an electric guitarist and songwriter, over the course of several decades (and moving to the saxophone) I became increasingly interested in the practice of improvisation in musical performance, and free improvisation in particular. With training in drama, I worked in theatre-in-education and toured schools, prisons and hospitals (Fish Theatre, Half Moon Theatre, Royal Court Young People's Theatre, Old Vick Young Peoples' Theatre, Thorndyke Theatre, Stirabout Theatre in London and elsewhere). I subsequently taught in colleges, schools and was a visiting lecturer. Improvisation has been a significant feature across all of my drama work. The later interest in free improvisation in music provided a wide variety of collaborative performance contexts, that has included various forms of electronic music, prepared pianos, objects, built instruments, field-recordings, work with dancers, playing with film, live animation, using graphic scores, work with artists, as well as with more traditional instruments such as double bass, drums, guitars and orchestral instruments and also solo work. *Free* improvisation has provided the methodology through which this variety of collaborative and solo practice has been developed.

Tacit understanding of improvisation practice in music influenced my thinking and approach to working in the challenging teaching setting of the Pupil Referral Unit. Improvisation in musical performance is developed by listening, responding sensitively and creatively to material that is presented by others: allowing for others' music as well as your own, negotiating, makes it possible to create something new together. The thinking that underpins free improvisation was being employed within the overall pedagogical approach. Students would introduce their own musical material and decisions in performance-based activity. In music and drama lessons, students' contributions became essential ingredients and in this way the learning activity was necessarily inclusive. Using the ethos derived from free improvisation in music, without a score or conductor, the individuals' choices within the group created the music or dramatic action. Openness to the possibilities presented by students provided direction for productive teaching and learning and led to progress in a cyclical manner. Over time, students began to adopt and 'own' this way of successfully working as a shared milieu. Free improvisation is participatory and autonomous in character: individuals contribute in the way in which they see fit and in the process the group music is created. The inherent social agency of the open, free improvisation approach was very valuable in this educational setting. Additionally, as lessons became more self-determined the teaching role adjusted (the role of the teacher is discussed in Chapter 7). Regardless of the subject, this way of thinking influenced the kind of interaction that was taking place in the room and during this period I also taught English and Citizenship.

Although Ofsted inspection assessed the teaching positively (advocating Advanced Skills Teacher status), there was no formal acknowledgement of the over-arching ways in which *improvisation* was influencing successful processes of teaching and learning in music and drama. The lack of overt acknowledgement of improvisation was reflected by the inspectors' choice of language; the term *improvisation* may have been interpreted as countering such intended formality, expressed by the concern for the maintenance of structure, assessment, monitoring, accountability, measurability and so on. Nevertheless, the recognition of the process' benefit in relation to such formalized criteria was clear. The need to more fully understand the relation between improvisation and educational practice led to the further study that is described in Chapter 7, 'Articulating Perspectives of Free Improvisation for Education' (Rose, 2008).

The aims of engaging active, autonomous learning (Bonwell and Elison, 1991) and educational, social inclusion (Ainscow and Booth, 2003) are furthered by knowledge and practice of improvisation. Employing improvisation processes through planning as well as implementation in teaching necessarily mirrored the openness to creative possibilities that is required in music and drama activity. The example of the Pupil Referral Unit illustrates how improvisation processes become significantly interrelated. There is an under-acknowledgement of improvisation's inter-disciplinary potential in arts and beyond. Furthermore, the agency of improvisation illustrated here suggests a phenomenon that is not necessarily best represented by bounded disciplines. In this way, the terms of reference of improvisation and its framing can be reassessed – improvisation is in need of redefinition. For example, drama training and experience shaped the organization of the teaching of music lessons and as such applied improvisation benefitted from inter-disciplinarity. In *Improvisation and Pedagogy: Background and Focus of Inquiry* Lewis (2008) asks three important questions, including, 'How can we extend the ways in which methods of improvisation developed in music can migrate to inform pedagogy in other fields?' We can also recognize how, for example, the pedagogy of drama and its use of improvisation can be a relevant social, artistic and educational tool elsewhere. With the aim of identifying and examining the social practice of improvisation, wherever it may occur, awareness of the benefits and limitations of advocating a solely musical model is also beneficial. It is exciting to speculate how, as improvisation research develops, knowledge of improvisation from the range of different areas will further cross-fertilize between multiple disciplines.

The work in this example of teaching is very much about negotiating educational difficulties productively and the case study draws out significant themes regarding the nature of improvisation and the way education is constructed. The heightened emotional intensity that typifies this setting generates a vivid illustration that foregrounds these themes. However, the themes of how learning takes place, the relations between teacher and learner, how social difference is contextualized within planning and implementation and the role of the teacher are equally relevant for mainstream and other educational contexts. The example also illustrates improvisation's relation with inclusion – a theme that is relevant to all disciplines, curriculum areas and places of education.

The Context of Improvisation

Lucy Green's *How Popular Musicians Learn: A Way Ahead for Music Education* (2002) describes an approach for teaching derived from an analysis of 'popular musicians' practice. The framing created by 'popular music' and the terms of reference that unfold from there contrast with the approach I've described in a number of ways. The sociopolitical context of all music requires that we acknowledge it in its own terms, ways of operating, function and so on, however it may differ from our own background and knowledge base. While 'popular music' has become a common category for examination boards and education, in terms of reflecting culture, it is limited. The institutional framing offered by 'popular music' comes from the background in which 'serious' or 'classically' related music dominates thinking and funding together with the maintenance of educational status quo – the label 'pop' assigns the other, while giving it some acknowledgement it remains not 'serious music'. When we come to the example of excluded pupils, it is clear how unhelpful framing can contribute to alienation – not just of these individual learners but to a broad base of culture. Green refers to 'popular music' as played on guitar, bass, drums and vocals broadly referencing the successful groups from the 1960s and the tradition of music that has followed from there. The book's pedagogical emphasis is on listening and copying and a session musician becomes a strong reference point for this concept – exemplifying the method. However, is it the purpose of music education to primarily focus on the reproduction of styles or is music more than that? While imitation and copying are a central part of enculturation in music, the example of the Pupil Referral Unit and the emphasis upon individual creativity on its own terms, regardless of style or genre, differs considerably. From an educational perspective, taking the activity rather than a style as the starting point situates all individuals and communities at the centre of the music curriculum. This in no way negates desired formal requirements, for example, developing understanding of musical elements, composition, instrumental technique and so on, as these features are available throughout music.

Can education be inclusive without expressly acknowledging different identities through its structures? The expressiveness of arts provides education with a particularly poignant reference with which to engage the full range of cultural possibilities. Music is inextricably tied to identity (MacDonald, Hargreaves and Miell, 2002) and, for example, the history of 'popular music' in the UK is tied to the cultural identity of groups such as The Who, The Beatles, The Rolling Stones, The Kinks and so on. But comparably powerful identifications are formed across music, in all cultures. Creativity can become acknowledged in the terms in which it is found. Both drama and music can be effectively developed by pedagogical design that makes overt acknowledgement of the identity of those present. Describing improvisation's implementation in a higher education context, Ursel Schlicht's article, "'I Feel My True Colors Began to Show": Designing and Teaching a Course on Improvisation' (2008) describes how allowing for the inclusion of different cultures is central to the design. Reflecting the characteristic potential for openness found in improvisation, this inclusive aspect is developed as part of the pedagogical approach. It is noteworthy that the approach is developed within an inter-disciplinary arts structure (The School of Contemporary Arts, Ramapo College, New Jersey) in which Schlicht draws upon the experience of her 'extensive history of intercultural collaborations'. In the examples described at the beginning of this chapter where drama and music experience and related pedagogies are employed in an inter-disciplinary manner, the lowering of disciplinary boundaries, in terms of thinking, planning and implementation, contributes to the inclusion of difference. Thematic similarities can be found in Stephen H. Lehman's (2008) account of alto saxophonist Jackie Mclean, who began to teach following involvement with the Living Theatre, where he was employed as a musician and actor. As Lehman describes:

After leaving the Living Theatre in 1961, McLean began to work with young people in African American communities throughout New York City. He worked with incarcerated youth as a bandmaster in a penitentiary and also contributed to programmes like Harlem Youth Opportunities Unlimited-Associated Community Teams (HARYOU-ACT) and Robert Kennedy's 'Mobilization for Youth' initiative, where he remained for almost five years [...] McLean's decision to work with troubled young people was, in part, a response to his need to find alternative sources of income after the loss of his cabaret card in 1957. However, it must also be understood as another instance of McLean's ability to respond, constructively and resourcefully, to personal and professional challenges. In this respect, McLean's ingenuity can be viewed as akin to his improvisational gifts as a musician: a positive response to change, opportunistic/creative solutions to problems that presented themselves, an orientation to social cooperation, and a careful attention to process.

McLean becomes a highly effective and influential teacher. Advocated for a university post by the students in response to the lack of 'black' music on offer and drawing from his professional, life experience as a musician, his teaching presents jazz as an American classical music (Lehman, 2012).

A lot of the time the very character of 'popular music' has problematized ideas of formal music education – as Green describes: 'none of the professional musicians [the cohort of interviewees] had a music qualification' (p. 145) and yet they have become successful in their own terms, in their own way through autodidactic practice. Pop music itself has developed through non-formal means. The way pop music from the UK in the 1960s and 1970s did outstandingly well without formal music education suggests the need for a more fundamental reappraisal of music education's role. The success of the groups mentioned previously owed little or nothing to formal music education (although, as the previous chapter describes, art school was a point of reference). The cultural context of the music, which includes how it came to be developed, is highly relevant and needs to be acknowledged within pedagogy. 'Popular music' emerged as very much an antidote to the kind of music on offer in formal education. In many ways, it also represented an opposition to the way in which ideas were being represented through formal education. Forty years on, things have changed but there remains a need to understand the cultural context of music, its power, influence and potential in its relation to individual and cultural identity. So, in referencing 'popular music', there is a need to critically conceptualize what that music means to the individuals involved. Session musicians have extraordinary skill and, for some, represent the apex of playing and working as a professional musician. However, overly focusing on that particular virtuosic specialism as an educational model relegates the much larger sociopolitical issue of music and creativity in education and what that means for individuals and groups. While it is possible to selectively choose aspects of non-formal practice that can be readily transposed to the formal setting, via the value system already in place, there are bigger questions raised by formal education's relation to non-formal practice and these are explored in Chapters 4, 7 and 9.

In marketing and selling, the music industry uses categorization for its own ends. In respect to education, there is something more humanly interesting about music's potential than defining musical boundaries in this way. The industry construct of 'World Music' is a case in point. For those seriously interested in different music, it is, at best, an absurdly vague term and at worst a way of collectively assigning music other than that which is considered culturally mainstream. Terminology tells us about the thinking behind the decisions that are being made in forming curriculum and left unchallenged the 'normativity' in much discussion of music education sustains a highly dubious status quo. For example, although classical music represents a tiny percentage of music sales (Small, 1998), it remains culturally dominant in policy and public spending and the legacy of its thinking influences how other music is situated in education. The vagueness of the term 'World Music', while gesturing towards other cultures, does nothing to reflect the diversity, scale or significance of musical activity. Returning to the example of the disproportionate number of black excluded students, we can make real connections between unhelpful terminology and conceptualization in educational practice and the constructs of 'educational exclusion' – alienation has consequences. For education we can more helpfully situate music as *lived experience*, an *activity* reflecting lives, rather than by such categories.

These complex educational issues that are social, cultural and political can become addressed through thinking that is strongly related to the practice of *free* improvisation. Rather than taking categorization as the starting point, the approach draws from those present in the classroom. Of course, genres and styles of music are significant but openness to what is present is necessary, and difference is always present. Education contributes hugely in forming identities: the students described previously are labelled as 'excluded'. This badge's negative association inevitably leaves a mark, affecting outlook, regardless of subsequent experience. In this way, the manner in which education is able to interrelate with different experience, for example in music, can determine education's success or failure, influencing the development of productive or alienated identities.

Maude Hickey (2009) rightly asks, 'Can improvisation be "taught"?' Hickey describes the openness and fluidity of free improvisation and suggests that 'authentic improvisation' cannot. Improvisation, and free improvisation in particular, can be better understood as a *pedagogical methodology*, and Chapter 7 explores the themes arising from improvisation's relationship with learning – improvisation is better conceived of as a process of learning rather than something that is taught. The aim in making use of a free improvisation approach differs from the teaching of, for example, harmony in music, or a set text in English, or algebra in Mathematics. Free improvisation requires decision-making that leads to content in a fluid manner and offers the potential for ongoing autonomous activity within the group setting, and, musically, it can be described as 'non-idiomatic' (Bailey) – it doesn't rely upon the learning of a single style. Within the contemporary educational culture with the heavy emphasis on continuous quantifiable results the more long-term social benefits that can derive from free improvisation as pedagogy are easily overlooked. Hickey describes how:

> Free improvisation begins with deep listening and reacting to the environment or players involved. Texts by Pauline Oliveros (2005), R. Murray Schafer (1986) and John Paynter (Paynter, 1992; Paynter and Aston, 1970) offer techniques and exercises for facilitating free and creative improvisation in the classroom with children of all ages. What is needed more than these, however, are materials specifically written for school practitioners [...].
> (2009, p. 294)

While specific materials can always have potential, and those cited are all significant authors, the gap in teachers' knowledge is due to the lack of exposure to practice. The knowledge deficit will become bridged by a combination of experience and theorizing. John Stevens' *Search and Reflect* (2007) has been available for over thirty 30 years (although it was out of print for some time), and while it offers specific material for development, there is not a theoretical contextualization that explains why these particular exercises have become developed – for this reason its principal advocates tend to be experienced improvisers.

Chapter 4

Improvisation and Knowledge

There is a tension between *practice*, the improvising musician's activity and *theory* within academia. It is not uncommon for professional musicians to be disdainful of the intellectualization of their practice; the different fields have different priorities. A particular cause of discontent can be the imbalance of remuneration for such theorizing of practice as, in general, there remains a dearth of funding for professional musicians engaged in improvisation practice. While some creative musicians do have academic work and have been involved in extensive research activity, such economic ironies indicate the continuing broad imbalance between *doing* and *theorizing*. While, historically, academia has had difficulty recognizing improvisation, there is currently an increasing growth of research interest in improvisation, for example, ICASP, Canada; POMI, SARC, University of Edinburgh, UK; ISIM, Mills College, UCSD, USA; Agosto Foundation, Czech Republic; Exploratorium; BIRG, Berlin, Germany; and elsewhere. Theorizing by musicians contributes to redressing the picture and texts by Derek Bailey, Anthony Braxton, Pauline Oliveros, George E. Lewis, Bertram Turetsky, Cornelius Cardew, Ursel Schlicht, Dana Reason amongst others are important. Related to the *theory* and *practice* dichotomy are the themes of ex-nomination (not-naming) and subjugated knowledge that are explored later in this chapter. The importance of improvisation as *doing,* understood through practice, is further explored in Chapters 7 and 8.

Improvisation activity carries with it different kinds of knowledge, that can be musical, social, cultural and political, and yet, 'Improvisation enjoys the curious distinction of being the most widely practised of all musical activities and the least acknowledged and understood' (Bailey 1992: ix). Bailey's quotation carries a double signification: it is not only a comment upon the range of improvisation in music but also reflects the ways in which we construct and acquire knowledge. If, as Bailey suggests, improvisation is ubiquitous, why is it so little acknowledged or understood? In music and beyond, there is a disjunction between what we do in the world, improvisation, and constructs found within education. While there are an increasing number of texts concerning improvisation and education (Lewis, 2000; Hickey, 2009; Borgo, 2007; Sawyer, 2008; Ford, 1995; Allen, 2002; Bailey, 1992; Oliveros, 2005; Schlicht, 2008; Stevens, 1985 and others), the underlying issue of improvisation's absence in formal contexts is under-explored. Much of education's construction has been resistant to improvisation's meanings, as improvisation doesn't necessarily play by the familiar 'rules' of reproduction, text and hierarchy. However, as improvisation research increasingly includes a critical reading of its social importance, and is occurring in different fields, knowledge of improvisation practice is becoming more broadly understood. Kevin Korsyn describes how:

'[…] music is always already post-disciplinary, it forms its objects with the aid of other disciplines which themselves are in flux'; for this reason, Bailey's 'curious distinction' between improvisation and education can be addressed by multidisciplinary and inter-disciplinary research in improvisation that works with the grain of this 'flux'.

(2003, p. 42)

Creativity and Education

Improvisation in music is a creative practice, and creativity is frequently referred to as fundamentally important for education (Robinson, 2001; Cropley, 2001; Craft, Jeffrey and Leibling, 2001, and others). The questions this raises relate to discourses of epistemology, structures in education and pedagogy. Influential double bassist and professor Bertram Turetsky (2010) with over three hundred compositions written for him has described creativity in music as 'Not accepting the status quo'. Participation in free improvisation is not dependent upon 'the status quo' – instead its practice allows for creating something new.

The inclusion of creative activity contributes to broad educational aims of development in learning (Swanwick, 1979). Describing how industries experience a deficit in aptitude for creative thinking in human resources, and the ways in which this impacts negatively at the broader level of the economy, Ken Robinson (2011) advocates the urgent need for creativity in education. Robinson points to inherited, outmoded structures within education as inappropriate and ineffective in meeting contemporary educational needs. One particular example of creativity embodies many of the themes that become relevant for the improvisation/education discussion. He describes the experience of a student who was regarded by her school as having behavioural difficulties, and before an educational board whose job was to find a suitable alternative educational placement. By chance, one of the board's members noticed how the girl was dancing outside the room while she waited. She was successfully placed in a dance school and went on to become one of the world's best known and financially successful choreographers: 'She wasn't bad: she needed to dance'. Evoking the 'Cinderella'-like narrative, the account successfully draws attention to the way mainstream educational structuring can fail to recognize and celebrate creativity and, as in Chapter 3, fail individuals through labelling that positions them as problematic. The point is well made and, by chance, the story has a happy ending.

There can be a tendency in discussions of creativity to overly focus on the extremely successful, for example, the child prodigy, the inordinately 'talented' and so on, contributing to the damaging myth that creativity is only for a 'chosen few' rather than importantly acknowledging everyone's creative potential. This view of creativity as the exception rather than ubiquitous has been highly detrimental in the development of education for all. The myth also reinforces the ways in which education values the achievement of the individual over that of the group, although why this should be the case typically remains unquestioned. There can be an overly narrow perception of the nature of creativity – for example, as Anthony Braxton puts it, '[t]here has long been an inability on the part of Western culture to deal with the realness of "form" in non-western creativity and the actualness of what that form celebrates' (Lock, 1999). Acknowledging creative improvisation within education, developed through group activity, contributes towards redressing this. This lack of acknowledgement of the benefits of collaborative, creative improvisation reflects practice in education that needs to be challenged.

> If you have a road map that tells you how to get somewhere then fine, when you get there leave the map and go and do your business – why I'm going there is for some kind of relationship whether with nature or with some people, now that's the heart business. Leave the map we're going to do the heart to heart. That's the difference between African and European culture – see we work from the heart, European culture works from the theory, so you take theory and you apply it to everything and you clamp it down – if it don't fit then they say it ain't valid.
>
> (Oleyumi Thomas in Rose, 2008)

Improvisation develops through experiencing activity, but, as Robinson describes, education has firmly established an academic hierarchy within the curriculum: textually orientated study at the top and that which involves doing or making at the bottom. Oleyumi Thomas creates a clear distinction between theorizing and direct engagement: 'Leave the map we're going to do the heart to heart [...]'. As Thomas poetically suggests, the 'heart business', the relationship with 'nature or with some people', is of a different order from theory. Education often assumes a neat relation of theory and practice, although embodied understanding of that which is practised occurs through lived experience. As such, understanding of improvisation is developed through practice, and research is developed from this lived experience.

If, as Bailey suggests, improvisation is '[...] the most widely practised of all musical activities [...]', its absence from discussion in formal contexts is at odds with its pervasiveness. Improvisation is often not named and therefore under-acknowledged within musical practice – the reasons for this are complex. This not naming, or exnomination, is often linked to the retention of hegemonic power (control by the dominant order). In other words, a strategy for negating something that may be troubling can be the denial of its presence. Examples of exnomination have been described in relation to class structure and racial subjugation. Barthes (1972) links the middle-class' use of 'common sense' to the imposition of a particular set of unchallenged values. Lipsitz (1998) has described how 'whiteness is everywhere, but very hard to see', – suggesting how this lack of self-acknowledgement contributes to a retention of dominance, as Fiske describes: 'the means by which whiteness avoids being named and thus keeps itself out of the field of interrogation and therefore off the agenda for change [...]'. Lewis (1996) discusses the unwillingness to acknowledge the place of improvisation within 'white' developments in the field of experimental music as a feature of the 'investment in racism'. He challenges the dividing of 'black' and 'white' experimental music practice, indicating the way improvisation has become distanced over the last hundred years or more within ideas of 'serious' musical development. This lack of acknowledgement of improvisation practice is reflected in different ways, for example, *Musicology: The Key Concepts* (Beard and Gloag, 2005), while rightly reflecting a range of theory understood as important for the contemporary study of music, contains no entry for *improvisation*. Undoubtedly, the lack of acknowledgement of improvisation in formal contexts is self-perpetuating: it is common for trained musicians to be wary of improvisation due to their lack of exposure to the practice within formative education and of course these are likely to be the very people who go on to teach.

The sociopolitical themes of creativity are well represented in Anthony Braxton's *Tri-Axium Writings* (1985). In Locke (1999), Braxton the African American composer, musician and writer vividly recounts how, at the age of thirty, all of his contemporaries from school were either in prison or dead. Braxton's work in music can be interpreted as a hyper-creative response to his environment: he has led groundbreaking groups with highly esteemed musicians in the United States and Europe; he released the world's first entirely solo saxophone album, *For Alto* (1970); his compositional output is numbered in the hundreds and includes operas. Braxton's immense, three volume *Tri-Axium Writings* is an exploration of creativity that becomes emblematic of the dividing of musical practice: its scope is wide and yet it is only published in a limited manner and remains very difficult to access. The work shows the influence of the political momentum associated with the 1970s 'Black Consciousness' in particular. Braxton's aim is to reveal the significance of what he terms the 'reality of creativity' and the implications of this for humanity: '[...] what I hope will be a massive body of alternative literature on creative music'. With the aim of not misrepresenting the multiplicity of creativity, Braxton develops terminology to critique the phenomenon leading to the infamous use of idiosyncratic phrases found throughout the three volumes, for example, 'physical and vibrational universe', 'affinity postulation', 'multiple develification', 'progressional transfer cycles' and so on (the glossary of which is thirty pages in length).

Braxton describes the way creative practice in music has provided communities with an expressive voice, while at the same time the advancement of Western classical tradition has become stifling. He advocates discourse about creativity that moves away from addressing superficial aspects – principally marketability. Seeking to reassert the potential of creative music, he views the music's history, future, forms, functions and qualities as 'dangerously neglected'. The challenge for the reader is to, for example, go from the cosmic, to the detail of bebop, to the history of the Western canon and meantime relate all of this to 'different time zones' within the non-linear format of the three volumes' cross-referenced layout. Describing the potential of creativity in music that Western cultural developments have marginalized, eroded, undervalued, becoming bereft in the process, Braxton's themes connect to Jacque Attali's (1985) analysis of the development of aural culture, the economy and society. Braxton's notion of 'The Spectacle Diversion Syndrome' clearly forms connections to Guy Debord's

Society of the Spectacle (1995). For Debord, this was an over-arching concept: 'the Spectacle' as an omnipresent, controlling denial of truth, resulting from the later stages of capitalism's evolution rather than what Braxton describes more simply as 'America's bizarre understanding of entertainment without spiritual or functional (living) intent […]'. While *Tri-Axium Writings* reflects the politics of the period, the questions it raises regarding the nature and practice of creativity remain equally valid for today.

Power and Improvisation

The gap between improvisation and formal education, that is the failure to acknowledge 'all the form it [creativity] can represent', can also be understood in terms of the 'field' (Bourdieu, 1977) of education. Those who practice improvisation will not necessarily share the same priorities as those propagating education: 'If it's going to be a musicology thing, or a thing that includes the AACM and talks about all this other stuff, I'm not going to participate' (Muhal Richard Abrams on the documentation of the AACM, in Lewis 2008: xxiv). Hegemonic power determines institutional structuring and education and this may represent that which is being opposed by the act of improvisation. African American history has famously shown improvisation as a vehicle of self-assertion and resistance (Fischlin, Heble and Lipsitz, 2013; Berliner, 1994; Lewis, 2008; Heble and Wallace 2013 and others). It cannot be assumed that demonstrating academic understanding will lead to the inclusion of improvisation practices – sociopolitical improvisation is not necessarily amenable to constructs and traditions found within educational practice. Education is unequivocally empowered by legislation; for example, the law states that all under the age of sixteen in the UK attend full-time education, and this inescapably informs teacher/learner relations. But power can also be asserted in response: improvisation offers a *creative* forum for such assertion. *Free* improvisation is an open form through which participants may engage on their own terms; it is a means by which other, subjugated knowledge (Foucault, 1970) may become included and thereby legitimized in the process.

> Power is not simply repressive; it is also productive […] Power subjects bodies not to render them passive, but to render them active. The forces of the body are trained and developed with a view to making them productive. The power of the body corresponds to the exercise of power over it. Hence the possibility of a reversal of that power.
>
> (Sheridan, on Foucault, 1980, p. 218)

Improvisation, creating music through doing, is not dependent upon a written score, and while we are encouraged towards the idea that music is synonymous with the written, knowledge in musical improvisation is expressed through action. Dominant textually orientated traditions and processes for teaching and learning are questioned by *improvisation as doing*. The marginalization of improvisation is often inaccurately explained by way of some innate difficulty with its nature rather than, more truthfully, a problem arising from education's inherited, unquestioned paradigms. For example, the hierarchical privileging of text, 'core curriculum' subjects (English, Maths, Science) take a large percentage of the curriculum time; the arts, crafts and sports are considered flexibly. An overemphasis on text in the culture of education, 'textocentrism' (Conquergood, 2002), can compound the lack of acknowledgement of improvisation in music as a form of embodied, or enacted learning (Chapter 8).

Researching Improvisation

A common thread in the discussion of improvisation, pedagogy and research is the abiding need to resituate music as an activity (Small, 1998). In contrast, traditions of musicology and music funding have heavily supported the construct of the 'work' (Goehr, 2004). Green (2002) describes how, with musicology's failure to address improvisation, in the 1970s some shifted to the study of performance (Blacking, 1973). In UK schools, there were some extraordinary developments in the late 1960s and early 1970s using child-centred learning methods that focused on the group working together (Paynter and Aston, 1970; Shafer, 1967; Self, 1970; Dennis, 1969, 1970), albeit largely in reference to developments in 'serious music'. Keith Swanwick (1979) continued this re-thinking with the introduction in the curriculum of ideas of composition, audition, performance, with literature and skills (CLASP). This repositioning of music as an activity leads to questions about how it is effectively researched.

Richard Scott discusses some of the dichotomies created by improvisation research. He emphasizes the importance of recognizing how improvisation's problematizing of approaches to research forms part of its essentially difficult character; he also recognizes the importance of experience.

> [...] it seems to me that Bailey is in many ways correct to emphasise the 'personal' aspect of improvisation over the concept of improvisation as general and somehow agreed upon activity [...] Bailey's warnings about the 'coherent partial view' notwithstanding, the *primary* secondary sources in this investigation are the perceptions and experiences of the musicians and listeners themselves, and it is difficult to imagine where else we could begin.
>
> (Scott, 2014)

Scott also calls for the investigation of improvisation as 'not so much multidisciplinary as antidisciplinary', questioning the limitations of 'disciplinary' thinking for meaning making in improvisation. Disciplinary dependency, lacking self-reflection, will contribute little to improvisation research. The 'hard to pin down' quality, common in discussions of improvisation, is reflected by Scott's comments on the disciplinary difficulties presented by improvisation research. This ineffable feature has also contributed to a position, taken by some, in which improvisation in music is viewed as somewhat beyond understanding (anti- intellectual attitudes, as well as those attributing mystical qualities to improvisation, may reflect this). However, as Chapter 3's description of the experience of education indicates, we can say that improvisation is an artistic, social, communicative activity in music and elsewhere that lends itself to understanding in the same way as other important activities in life. An appropriate research approach can itself helpfully contribute to positioning the subject within the breadth of its social, communicative and artistic context.

Although Aaron Berkowitz (2010) examines numerous historical accounts of 'classical' musicians' instructions for improvisation, his two 'classical' improviser interviewees, Robert Levin and Malcolm Bolson, make no use of these accounts and reflect how 'my experience is my teacher'. Levin is himself a passionate and articulate advocate of improvisation (Levin, 1992). While Berkowitz clearly supports the lineage of 'classical' music, the 'improvising mind' (2012) of the title suggests the need for a much broader appraisal of practice in improvisation and research that includes the centrality of the sociocultural and pedagogical contexts.

In contrast, the importance of experience for research is the starting point of Sudnow's *Ways of the Hand* (1993). This first person phenomenological study of learning to play jazz piano is a detailed account of his personalized processes, reflections and actions in the course of developing capability as a jazz pianist. In general 'how to play' texts are presented by experts, by reversing this Sudnow cleverly provides a significant perspective of learning by a learner. The learner becomes the teacher. Sudnow's 'production account' (influenced by the sociology of Irving Goffman, Harvey Sacks and Harold Garfinkel) also appropriately reflects musicians' autodidactic or self-directed approach to learning (see Chapter 9). In this way, the account also addresses the imbalance between formal education and its structures and the more lived experience of learning through engagement with practice, beyond academia. *Ways of the Hand* has been influential beyond music and its primary significance is for the development of understanding embodied learning, this is discussed in Chapter 8 *Body*.

Improvisation research benefits from inter-disciplinarity. Pianist Sudnow trained as an ethnographer and social scientist, this background is reflected by his choice and delineation of method. So too, Berkowitz's study employs neuroscience and musicology. The first study of improvisation, Ferrand (1961), drew from music history, music education and dance. This study of improvisation draws from the multiple disciplines of music, drama and education. Sudnow's study of learning also brings with it some ideas that differ from free improvising, or creative music making: there is a tension between the emphasis with copying and being creative. Sudnow describes in detail absorbing as much of jazz pianist Jimmy Rawles' performance as he can. This emphasis on copying is an accepted feature of jazz. For example, for the saxophonist in jazz, the canon of Charlie Parker and John Coltrane is widely positioned as a standard against which playing may be measured – 'absorbing' or getting as close to the original as possible is encouraged and rewarded. While this is a complicated issue, in improvisation the personalized voice is emphasized and self-determining is a significant, unique feature of improvisation in music and beyond (see Chapter 7).

The Research Approach

The findings of the study 'Improvisation, Music and Learning: An Interpretive Phenomenological Analysis' (Rose, 2013) form the basis of the discussion in Part 2 of this book and the remainder of this chapter explains the methodological approach that necessarily includes discussion of relevant theory. This aims to explain why and how the examples from the interviews have become used in the discussion. This section's inclusion may be of particular interest to those with an interest in research in music, drama and education.

Improvisation is 'enacted' experience coming into being through doing – and in no other way – in practice, knowledge in improvisation is expressed through action and so research can begin by acknowledging this. Phenomenology is the study of experience and as Merleau-Ponty (1962) describes there is a difference between first-order knowledge of experience and second-order knowledge of science. Recording and analysing personal experience found in the ten interviews uses an idiographic approach (it focuses on understanding the particular and the individual); in this way, it values and reflects experience. This leads to the question of interpretation in analysis. The study of interpretation, hermeneutics, and phenomenology are joined in Heidegger's work; Schleiermacher (1977) and Gadamer (1990) are also key figures in the development of hermeneutics. Heidegger's interpretation of phenomenology leads to the need to address meaning that readily presents itself, 'appearance', as well as additional meaning that may be hidden. Gadamer describes the process of interpreting as one in which we are constantly projecting meaning in our attempt to understand and this becomes revised as textual meaning is understood – a process in which we introduce 'fore-meanings and prejudices' at the same time:

> [...] a person engaging with a text is prepared for it to tell him something [...] the important thing is to be aware of one's own bias, so that the text can present itself in all its otherness and thus assert its truth against one's own fore-meanings.
>
> (Gadamer, 1990, p. 269)

Through this reflexive process, we can better understand how we are conceiving of an object. The method of the study: *Interpretive Phenomenological Analysis* (Smith, Flowers and Larkin, 2009) makes use of a *hermeneutic circle*. This is explained as interpretively moving back and forth between the part of a text and the developing understanding of the whole (Schön, 1983; Smith, Flowers and Larkin 2009). The iterative (repeating, back and forth) process allows, for example, the meaning taken from an interview extract to be reflected upon the entire set of transcripts and vice versa. Within a continuum of cross-referencing in the development of meaning, the hermeneutic circle and reflexivity are synergetic, as it becomes possible to monitor ways in which interpretation is developed in the course of analysis. The hermeneutic circle functions at a number of levels, lending itself to the formation of different relationships between understandings in the process of analysis. The process also forms a 'double hermeneutic', as the researcher is making sense of the participant's sense making (Giddens, 1987).

The aim is to explore the creative process of improvisation in music with a specific emphasis on investigating its potential for learning. Interpreting ideas, views and beliefs derived from the experience of practice contributes to lessening the problematic distance between academia and improvisation practice. A body of knowledge of improvisation in music has developed within an international community of musicians, and this research project records and interprets this knowledge in order to further understanding of the practice of improvisation in music. 'I am not so much interested in constructing a building, as in having a perspicuous view of the foundations of possible buildings' (Wittgenstein, 1981, p. 458). The research project seeks to create a 'view of the foundations of possible buildings' through the interpretation of experienced improviser's accounts of practice. Interviews with those from within this community of practice were chosen as the best means of recording such a body of knowledge. The criteria for participation were a high level of experience of professional practice in improvisation and that improvisation should form a central part of practice. Diversity among the cohort was sought in order to benefit from a range of perspectives. The study encompasses interviews in the US, Canada, the UK and Germany and includes female and male, European, African American and other North American participants.

With the findings of the earlier study (Rose, 2008) citing *being* as an encapsulation of the characteristics of free improvisation, thematic connections were made with phenomenology. For this reason the works of Martin Heidegger (1962), Maurice Merleau-Ponty (1962), Edmund Husserl (2001) and Franz Brentano (1995) and others are thematically important for the study. With the interest in improvisation and education, Michel Foucault's (1970, 1980) work on the relationship between power and knowledge also influenced the research approach. 'How have my objects of knowledge and the questions I seek to address to them been produced' (Foucault, 1980, p. 134). Asking the question, '*What is the place of improvisation in your practice?*' provides for the semi-structured interviews, the vehicle through which interviewees' experiences become described in the ways in which they see fit. By this means, experience becomes framed by the interviewee and optional prompts are used (rather than directing the interview via pre-determined questions). The focus of the study is with *free* improvisation – the act of creative music making, or composing in the course of performing, with a specific interest in the broad relation between improvisation and processes of learning. Jurgen Habermas' (1975) perspective of participatory social justice and education (leading to action research) also influenced the research approach for improvisation and learning. So too, Henry Giroux's (1983) radical pedagogy reflecting the human agency to affect resistance, contest, express cultural struggle, and challenge hegemony also contributed to shaping the research perspective. Kevin Korsyn's *De-centering Music* (2003) has been influential: modes of research have been critiqued in light of the academic legacy and tropes they may seek to uphold and reflect. Bourdieu's work on 'reflexive sociology' and the concept of social strategies as conscious as well as unconscious also contributes to thinking: '[…] it is because agents never know completely what they're doing that what they do has more sense than they know' (Bourdieu, 1993, p. 69).

In order to understand and communicate experience, phenomenology aims to 'go back to the things themselves' (Husserl, 2001). Through the phenomenological approach, the lived experience of improvisation is recorded, interpreted and contextualized, and the method's flexibility lends commitment to the subject of research. Idiographic IPA is concerned with specific, subjective phenomenon and the focus of analysis is with participants' interpretations of their *life-world* experience. It seeks to 'go deep' in establishing meaning in research by means of detailed, thorough analysis of a relatively small sample – understanding of the particular leads to reflections upon the universal (Warnock, 1987). The idiographic approach is suited for understanding experiential phenomena of particular individuals. The 'particular' may lie with an individual's experience but may equally be found in experience's relational quality, reflecting Dasien (Heidegger, 1962) as embedded in the world of things and others. (This contrasts with a nomothetic approach in which aggregation and inferential statistics lead to generalization based upon averages rather than individual experience.)

The human capability of improvisation forms activity we are all engaged in. While research is characterized as 'academic', improvisation is not 'academic'. An approach that can embrace life as it occurs is a 'good fit' for the subject. Elsewhere IPA has been used in studies of the psychology of health care (Smith and Osborn, 2007; Brocki and Weardeon, 2006; Arrol and Senior, 2008; Thompson, Kent and Smith, 2002 etc.); and in studies of sexuality (Lavie and Willig, 2005; Flowers, Duncan and Knussen, 2003; Ruben, 2004). IPA has been used in studies of music (Holmes, 2005; Faulkener and Davidson, 2004, 2006; Bailey and Davidson, 2002, 2005; Davidson and Borthwick, 2002; Burland and Davidson, 2002). Samson (2007) in particular has focused on the construction of identity and free improvising duos. IPA has also been used to examine 'major events', for example, that which may involve psychological distress associated with a medical procedure (Brocki and Wearden, 2006) or the effects of events upon the self, for example, Oakland's (2010) study of redundancy among choristers.

As the complex phenomenon of improvisation in music is culturally located, the cohort of interviews was set at ten, a large number for the in-depth nature of an IPA study. However, in this way it has been possible to reflect on difference within practice and analysis has established meaning that is confidently interpreted beyond the local. The large cohort has not detracted from the idiographic commitment of the method. The individuals' experience of improvisation means that the cohort represents a homogenous group within an international community of musicians identified through the shared practice of improvisation. Interpreting diverse voices from both Europe and North America has contributed to the breadth of the study. Seeking the universal through the particular remains important while developing group themes. It has been possible, however, to identify 'the particular' as significant across cases as well as within single cases.

The aim of Part 2's design is to avoid fragmentation as the chapter's themes of *Process, Learning, Body* and *Approaches* are not only related, but also embedded within one another. To develop understanding of the whole, it has been necessary to identify components, although ultimately these parts are recognized as not existing in isolation but within the whole picture of improvisation practice. The five chapters have been structured in a manner that reflects the phenomenological aim to identify the *particular* of experience. Much of these chapters forms a dialogue between the themes expressed by participants and researcher's interpretation; the discussion also broadens through further contextualization. For the purpose of clarity, themes are illustrated in some sections by quoting single interviewees and at other times quotations from across interviews are employed. And while documentation from the process of analysis is far too great to include, superordinate themes: *Process, Learning, Body* and *Approaches* are understood as shared. The phenomenological aim is to not presuppose the nature of improvisation in music, to this end the *lived experience* is prioritized. In this way, the inherent practice/theory dichotomy in the study of improvisation is addressed.

Part 2

Chapter 5

Recognizing Improvisation

Improvisation as Composition

Improvisers share responsibility for the creation of music in performance; participants *compose* the music through improvisation activity. Musicians know this, but at the level of institutionalized funding and education, the point needs to be asserted. This is a major shift in generally accepted, formal understanding of how music is created and benefits from reorientation. In a variety of ways, interviewees made reference to the practice of improvisation as composing and themselves as composers. '*They're effectively three mutual composers going out and creating their music, which is a continually evolving body of music through the practice of improvisation.*'[1] (Butcher, p. 4, l. 1, on the The Schlippenbach Trio [Alexander von Schlippenbach piano, Paul Lovens drums, Evan Parker saxophones]). The idea of 'mutual composers' is important. Improvisation actively negates the divide between the performer and composer roles – resulting in 'mutual composers': composition in an embodied form in the act of improvisation. Characteristic of such real-time composition is a continually 'evolving' music, evidenced by this trio's forty-year plus history of activity. Improvisation also forms composition in ways that are not necessarily about a long-term group evolving. Derek Bailey expressed interest in not seeking to maintain long-term groups, for him this moved away from the productive immediacy of the improvisation encounter (although this is also countered by the recurring musical relations that were inevitably developed). Temporary groups with a shifting membership are as common as fixed groups in free improvisation and, regardless, the music that results is in effect composed by the group. The development of individual's musical material and the ability to make creative use of it in the group context lead to the composition of the music, by the group.

The flux in perceptions of improvisation and composition was well illustrated at a presentation in 2013 in Berlin: a performance given by members of a large group ensemble was followed by discussion. A composer-in-residence was spending time with small groups from the orchestra and developing a commissioned piece for performance. The musicians, all very advanced players, improvised together – the performance was satisfying and complete, although in the 'work-in-progress' circumstances with a slightly 'staged' air. The visiting composer, who I didn't know, looked on and discussion followed. Although the event was structured around the composer's presence, what remained unclear throughout the discussion was their role. For me, this illustrates a misunderstanding, or miscommunication of improvisation's potential. The event also shows the dichotomy arising from perceptions and expectations of 'the composer' and the activity of improvisation. With a group who are working well together, making excellent music, composition is already occurring and yet the inclusion of 'the composer' enables cultural status and the possibility of funding. The presence of the sponsor, unusual at events featuring improvisation, indicates the significance attributed to the event by the composer's presence. This example illustrates the underlying theme of improvisation's status. The role of 'the composer' can become clarified by acknowledging the capability for improvisation. Improvisation and composition are part of the same process and the redundant binary of improvisation versus composition in a misrepresentation. Of course, composers certainly can have a valuable role within and beyond traditional notation. On that occasion, I left without a sense of what contribution the composer would make to the development of a piece; the musicians, while supportive of the process, also seemed largely unclear, and some were openly dissatisfied. By acknowledging improvisation, a more truthful picture of what is happening in the world emerges.

For some the argument for improvisation as composition is countered by the view that it is a semantic discussion having no impact on practice, for example, that composers need to study theory for years and so on. However, improvisers typically develop a lifetime of practice in which knowledge and skills of creating music in real-time are developed and, importantly, experience of creating becomes developed through performance. And so, while strong arguments are made for preserving the institutional status of the composer, it is simply inaccurate to conceive of improvisation as any less significant; not affording improvisation equal status in terms of funding and educational opportunities is counter-productive.

'There's often the claim with composers that we, and I include myself in that [...]' (Lewis, p. 15, l. 30). Interviewees' descriptions of themselves as composers were nuanced. Some referred to the act of improvisation as composition (Butcher, Nicols, Lewis) and at other times as improvising forming real-time composition. And for some, musical practice encompassed careers in which they are known for commissioned written scores (Mitchell, Oliveros, Lewis, Ostertag) while equally, they pursued careers through the practice of improvisation (this reflects interviewees' direct reference to composing – other interviewees are also similarly involved in various composing activities). Between the open form of free improvisation and the written score that uses traditional notation, there is a growing multiplicity of approaches involving strategies of improvisation and composition as individuals and groups develop their own particular ways of developing music. Some established examples of this being 'Conduction' (Morris, 2014); instruction pieces (Stockhausen); game pieces (Zorn); and the range of graphic scores described in Chapter 3. In relation to the notion of improvisation as real-time composition, the Instant Composers Pool (ICP, Holland) and the Spontaneous Music Ensemble (SME, UK) can be acknowledged as highlighting improvisation as a compositional strategy. And, of course, within the ill-defined area of jazz from the US, composers such as John Coltrane, Charlie Parker and Thelonious Monk's compositions are improvisation vehicles that are characterized by difference at each performance.

Butcher describes a section of younger contemporary improvising musicians' practice: '[...] they're actually making music in a way which is more akin to a composed *process … and they're aiming for a particular kind of music and they're filling in the details through improvisation [...]'* (p. 2, l. 15). At a distance from the distinct history of free improvisation in the UK, the Echtzeitmusik (real-time music) scene in Berlin is in many ways at the forefront of improvisation practice; currently there are a plethora of venues and great diversity of practices becoming developed by musicians from many parts the world. Although, paradoxically, its initiation has also been an attempt to create some distance from free improvisation, or a style of free improvisation, and in the process define a cultural space (Williams, 2011) through which, for example, some funding has been possible. It is certainly true that some re-interpretation of reductionism from an earlier time contributed to the antecedence of this scene in the late 1990s. However, in terms of current activity within the scene 'reductionism' is no more present than, for example, 'noise' and 'electronics' – in practise these categories have a limited usefulness. Some influence from John Cage's thinking and AMM's performance practice has been consistently apparent. So what, if anything, distinguishes the Echtzeitmusik scene? It is currently characterized by a diverse, pervasive use of improvisation and often novel compositional strategies that themselves typically employ improvisation.

'[...] it's a very important thread throughout and I've always improvised. When I was composing music with conventional notation, if I got stuck I could improvise. So my composition teacher, Robert Erickson encouraged me to improvise and we were all encouraged by Robert Erickson to improvise [...] it's a very important thread throughout and I've always improvised' (Oliveros, p. 1, l. 7). The circularity between ideas of composition and improvisation supports the creative music process. Musicians refer to 'finding things' while improvising, these musical ideas may then contribute to personal musical 'vocabulary' also described as 'ingredients' (Butcher) and a 'grab-bag of ideas' (Ostertag). These 'ingredients' become options within the compositional choices made during future improvisations, reiterating the evolving character of real-time composition.

Mitchell emphasized a unified approach to composition and improvisation: *'I think that I study composition and improvisation as a parallel because what I'm striving for is to be able to create spontaneous composition. And I think that this helps me know how composition works and then you can apply these principles during an improvisation … if you look around at the great composers, I mean they all improvised. So I just feel it's important, for me, to study music as a whole'* (Mitchell, p. 1, l. 6). For Mitchell, improvisation and composition studied 'in parallel' suggest equality as well as some conceptual distance. The idea of 'spontaneous composition' also echoes the groups Instant Composers Pool and Spontaneous Music Ensemble. A drawback to these terms is that 'instant' and 'spontaneous' may convey an unintended superficiality that belies the integrity of the work of improvisation. The use of 'spontaneity' is explored at length in Chapter 9.

'I'm interested in being the performer as well as, if you like, the composer. And I do consider myself to be a composer it's just that most of my compositions are realised through comparatively spontaneous performance' (Butcher, p. 6, l. 37). Elsewhere, improvisation and composition are frequently discussed in ways that suggest they are opposed, thus obscuring their clear

creative interrelatedness that remains true across different kinds of music. When I first played guitar with friends, aged twelve or thirteen, we'd make music by inventing our own parts, whether through jamming on a riff, or as a response to an idea someone had. The onus was on the individual musicians to do what they could, regardless of whether it was a version of a song, a jam or building upon a chord structure and lyrics introduced by one of the group. The activity depended upon improvisation, although we didn't call it that, and it was essential to the process. This collective or ensemble composing practice is common across rock and pop and other music and is both accessible and productive at all levels of ability. It is a process through which individual and group knowledge and skills become developed and shared, and through which groups develop a 'sound' and identity.

The terms we use to conceptualize practice are important as they lead to how we perceive, support, teach, situate and fund musical activity. In her history of the musical 'work', Lydia Goehr (1994) describes: 'how and with what effect a concept shapes practice'. So too, developing a grounded concept of improvisation contributes to the shaping of practice. For education, the legacy of concepts such as 'the work', 'serious music' and so on not only influence the construction of curriculum, but also create a kind of cultural subtext that informs the reading of other music. Goehr describes how a narrow and dominant view of composing has led to 'cultural imperialism': '[…] many persons, convinced nowadays by the greatness of classical music, have found reason to describe all types of music in the world, of whatever sort, by means of a work-based interpretation' (1994). The shortcomings of this way of conceptualizing music are glaringly obvious when it comes to music of different cultures that share no commonality with the European concept of the 'work'. At worst, such a way of reading different music can also entirely negate the broad practice of improvisation.

Social Improvisation

'[…] what you're hearing is the flow of intelligence and thinking […] in these improvised music things, you're always hearing the intelligence and the intention regardless of what they're doing, you're always hearing it, but I sort of wanted to hear a lot of different variations for that' (Lewis, p. 12, l. 20). Recently there has been a surge of activity in large group improvisation and improvising orchestras are now fairly common in a number of countries. For some, large group improvisation is celebrated as contributing to the 'cutting edge' of the improvised music form. The emergence of these large ensembles reflects the extent of growing interest in improvisation activity. The nature of improvisation also means that performances involving large numbers of musicians can be organized relatively easily. It is a form that lends itself to educational contexts and Fred Frith (2007), Susan Allen (2002), Ursel Schlicht (2008) and Charlie Ford (1995) have all described working with large group improvisation in higher education. While jazz and improvising orchestras may be regarded as within different genres, there are noteworthy similarities in practice. Referencing the jazz orchestras of Duke Ellington, Count Basie and Stan Kenton, Mitchell describes how 'those groups learnt how to *play together* [...] *finding their sound together'* – as essential to their success, regardless of the individual virtuosity on hand. Lawrence D. 'Butch' Morris' (1947–2013) work significantly influenced the development of large group improvisation. His project initiated 'improvising orchestras' in a number of countries and their establishment has, in turn, influenced the development of others. Morris' 'Conduction', a system of using hand signals with which to guide improvisers, has held appeal for organizing large group improvisation. Some large groups have developed their own systems, reflecting the nature of the autonomous improvising activity. There is a tension between this and the open approach to improvising. Being directed alters the individual participants' autonomous decision-making, shifting the nature of the individual onus and group activity – improvisation's autonomous aspect is a key feature for learning (see Chapter 7). The recording 'Improvisations for George Rusque', London Improvisers Orchestra (PSI, 2009) is of interest in this respect as it represents large group free improvisation without such a guide, predetermined plan or conduction. Large group music making is a powerful phenomenon evidenced by football supporters, religious groups, school ensembles, marching bands, choirs and so on throughout the world. The potential social dynamic offered by improvisation within the large group context is both challenging and potent and this is explored in the later section *Ethics, Improvisation and Education.*

The question of how sound becomes organized in improvisation is highlighted by large group activity. Ornette Coleman (Litweiler, 1992) describes how in music, 'You only have so much space'. While I was participating in an improvising orchestra of over twenty players, a saxophonist sat in with the ensemble for two long sets, declaring at the end how much they'd enjoyed it – although they'd hardly taken the saxophone from their mouth for the entirety of the performance. Playing together at once, continuously, is one strategy among a great many, but one that will limit the options for musical development, as Mitchell describes in his interview: *'what kills improvisation is when there are no choices'*. Mindfulness of others' voices is an effective strategy for participation in the large group (as it is in small groups) and provides a way for establishing clear musical events, and this comes about by listening and a preparedness to 'sit-out'. *'[...] nobody felt the need to chime in or add a little bit, or adornment, and all those things you know, people didn't do that and so as a result you could hear that, it opened up the space, you could hear people play. Everybody likes the idea that they were being listened to and some people felt they were being listened to for the first time since they'd been in the group, that people were listening to them in a new way'* (Lewis, p. 11, l. 24).

The social aspect of improvising activity is recurrent across the interviews and has been reflected by diverse research (Sawyer, 2007; Small, 1998; Leone, 2010). For some this was directly stated while others reflected the social through descriptions of interaction giving rise to the music. Rather than focusing on a style, genre or particular history, describing FI as a *'socio-musical location'* (Lewis, p. 19, l. 32) reorders the act of making music, signalling improvisation's potential for diverse settings. For Lewis, this social setting reflects fundamental human questions about the nature of collective experience, the quality of communication and personal development: *'[...] there are bigger fish to fry in improvisation than aesthetics'* (Lewis, p. 8, l. 40). The social aspect of free improvisation is distinctive – the 'chemistry' developed by participants forms the content of the music, or score – change the people and the musical content changes. For education and community contexts, this social dimension provides a corner stone of theorizing improvisation practice and Chapter 7 explores this in detail.

The social context of improvisation in music is also complex, and, of course, reflects the range of musician's experience. Within working musicians' lived experience, knowing where the next gig is coming from in a highly competitive working environment is a priority and the aesthetics of those involved certainly contributes to their employability. We can acknowledge how within the field of professional music, there are inescapably less than ideal influencing factors, such as competition for livelihood, that also shape the social aspect. Following a passionate conference presentation advocating the potential socio-ethical feature of improvisation in music, a seasoned improviser dryly commented: 'That's not a picture I recognise'. The human capability of improvisation is available within the full range of human experience through which ethical choices become made. This does not detract from the ethical potential of the 'socio-musical location' but, if improvisation in music is used as a model, it can also be contextualized by the 'real-world' experience of musicians' lives. In his interview, Roscoe Mitchell describes the significance of working together, having learnt from the tragic histories of figures who suffered though lack of community. And Lewis' (2008) extensive history of the AACM similarly describes the assertion of community through music and improvisation practice. So too, in recent reflections Peter Brotzmann, the maestro of the 'terror sax' (whose sound and popularity also attracted punks and anarchists towards free improvisation), somewhat surprisingly also describes improvisation as a social practice: 'As I get older I see it more and more as a kind of social movement of what is possible' (Brotzmann and Rouy 2014). This is of note coming from this die-hard 'Soldier of the Road' (Josse, 2012) whose 1968 recording 'Machine Gun' was one of the most uncompromisingly abrasive discs of the past century. Brotzmann goes on to describe 'solidarity' as a necessary way of surviving in 'the music'. Once in common use, 'solidarity' now reads, sadly, as from another era and yet in Brotzmann's current view this represents 'what is possible' in the musical activity – a model of sociality.

Improvisation's complex socio-ethical dimension can also be understood through the broader sociopolitical context. John Coltrane's large group recording 'Ascension' was released in 1966 – the title clearly references spiritual transcendence; featuring a host of well-known musicians, this is considered widely as a landmark recording of large ensemble improvisation in the free-jazz vein. Employing a similarly large group, Peter Brotzmann's 'Machine Gun' (1968) is an equally noteworthy recording. The contrasting titles, and music, reflect the musicians' sociopolitical orientation. Coltrane's spiritualism was within a wave of new Black Consciousness in the US – a movement that encompassed artistic, political and social aims. Brotzmann's abrasive musical activity was within the emerging counterculture and the specific context of Germany's post–World War II renewal. At this time, positions of authority were still commonly retained by those who had been associated with the Nazi regime; the phrase: 'Don't trust anyone over the age of fifty' was common (from a conversation with drummer Willi Kellers). Slightly later, in 1973, the Red Army Faction (RAF) was founded with the symbol of the automatic weapon against a star and the Revolutionary Cells (RZ) developed at the same time. In the US, African American activism was encompassing: there was an outpouring of creative musical activity; the Black Panthers and Malcolm X; the adoption of Islam by many; and a broad exploration of spirituality. 'Ascension' and 'Machine Gun' both use minimal pre-composed motifs as a unifying starting point, while the collective energy of the improvising, or 'fire music,' is the modus operandi of their momentum. For some, these two examples of early, entirely male free jazz are dissimilar, for others they belong next to each other, regardless, the socio-political context of these recordings describes the environment within which they emerged.

Ethics, Improvisation and Education

The themes of improvisation, education and ethics are intertwined and this section explores how the activity of social improvisation in music carries with it an ethical dimension that offers a potent educational process. Improvisation's ethical potential has led to ongoing discussion (Cardew, 1971; Benson, 2003; Midgelow, 2012; MacDonald, 2013; Peek, 2011; Laver, Heble and Piper, 2013; Lange, 2011 and others). Ethics in improvisation is tied to communities and identities and the history of free improvisation in the UK provides numerous examples of distinctive voices emerging within the broader 'scene' of the time. Similarly the AACM nurtured individual musical voices within its organization (Mitchell). 'Authentic' and 'egalitarian' practices have been grounded by the strong identities of those involved. Ethical questions come into sharp focus when looking at specific examples. Acknowledging individual and group voice in free improvisation provides a starting point for educational activity (see Chapter 3).

For pedagogy, the ethics of improvisation is complicated by 'teaching' – teaching itself needs reassessing in order to more fully understand its relation to improvisation (see Chapter 7). Uncritical assumptions about teaching couple the activity with imparting knowledge – in improvisation's case, this easily becomes the teaching of a genre. It is principally for this reason that 'learning' is reprioritized over teaching in this book's title. Given the autonomous nature of the activity and *'the agility in the term'* (Lewis), describing free improvisation in terms of a genre that can be taught (in much the same way as a version of 'jazz' has become employed in curriculum) is a limitation. The potential agency of free improvisation and its ethical dimension are precisely derived from the 'socio-musical location' and that ethics can be 'taught' without very specific reference to the cultural context is the wrong way round. Teaching or aiming to reproduce a style of European contemporary improvisation is one thing, but the greater potential of improvisation's ethical content is revealed through nurturing learning in the sociocultural context in which 'voices' are found, and, as Chapter 3 has illustrated, this may have little or nothing to do with the *style* of European free improvisation. In other words, free improvisation's benefit is more as a process that is directed towards the concerns of those present than stylistic. In this way, it can contribute to an emancipating pedagogy (Giroux 1997; Freire 1970) and avoid, at worst, contributing to another kind of 'cultural imperialism' (Goehr) in which a set of external values become imposed. With education's insistence upon standardization and fondness for reproduction, differentiating improvisation's broad potential for learning from the teaching of a genre is important.

The ethical approach is grounded through a process of exchange that reflects personal musical histories: '*I come from jazz – but also soul, blues and also cabaret, theatre and you know we have both learnt the new language of the more abstract free improvisation but also can integrate the different roots and histories, our own personal musical histories as well, so I do feel it is a beautiful contradiction, you embrace what's gone before and replace it*' (Nicols, p. 5, l. 8). Aligning different personal and collective musical experience forms a source of creativity in free improvisation and Nicols' makes it clear that this can apply regardless of previous musical orientation: '*Everyone's creative – no negotiation*' (Nicols, p. 10, l. 3). With a willingness to engage and the shared development of trust in the process, acknowledgement of difference occurs at a musical and social level. The improvisation form's openness to difference brings with it the potential for social inclusion. Nicols celebrates the ethical potential of improvisation, tying the social with the musical – reimagining 'virtuosity' as social intelligence. '*[...] you become virtuosic in different ways but there is such a thing that I really love which I call social virtuosity, it's a collective virtuosity which is multi ... you know, not streamed. And again John* [John Stevens] *was a master of that – mixed ability virtuosity, that has its own particular power. There is something phenomenal about a group of different experiences, making really strong performance in music*' (Nicols, p. 10, l. 14). A professional jazz drummer, well known internationally, Stevens is widely regarded as central to the development of free improvisation in the UK, and beyond. But he was also known locally for his work with those without experience or expertise – for Stevens music making was sociopolitical. His conviction led him to become a facilitator and teacher in Community Music, London. '*John gave up a lot to become involved in Community Music, consequently a lot of Europeans don't know about John and just how crucial he was to the history of improvised music. Because he put his heart and soul into sharing that in community [...] John created excellence; he believed that everybody could achieve that kind of excellence*' (Nicols, p. 10, l. 36). Numerous musicians with very different backgrounds attended Steven's workshops and participated in freely improvised performances. (I attended a workshop series in London in which all the other participants were members of a Nigerian gospel choir.)

The early development of free improvisation in music commonly involved small group activity: duos, trios, quartets and so on. For some it is the small group that offers greater possibilities and freedom. Smaller units readily offer the space and opportunity for experimentation and expression for which free improvisation is celebrated. Large group activity magnifies the question of its organization and, for example, how individuality is balanced within the need to work together. The following extract explores this difficult key point and forms a case study that helps illuminate the interaction of social improvisation.

> *I remember this saxophone player who used to come, he's a crane driver, he used to drive these cranes, and he'd come into the London one* ['open-door', free improvised music session] *at about half past ten at night. And we had an L shaped room and he'd creep into the back of the L shape – and suddenly there'd be this absolute blast!! Absolutely deafening sound. And then of course what would happen is everyone would have a knee jerk reaction, so the drummers if they were there they would start hammering away – and then there was no space. And I remember we were talking about this and I thought, well how would it be if we didn't change what we were doing, when he started, what would happen and we tried that, and do you know something, the actual way he was playing was that he would do this blast and then he would leave this enormous space. So in actual fact he wasn't the problem, it was everybody else thinking, Oh, right, we'll all pile in now, even though they didn't want to. So it's that thing of being authentic, if you're truly authentic, I do believe that sooner or later it creates a space for everybody, so even somebody … he needed, he needed to play like that but he was also incredibly sensitive because he would play like that and we'd all, we wouldn't change what we were doing if we didn't feel like that – there'd be these huge spaces, where there were lots of little gentle things happening and then he would steam in again. So that was a real lesson for me [...] Being strong in your own centre, being really totally committed energetically to what you're doing. And then whatever anyone else is doing won't throw you off balance. And that's a lifetimes practice [...].*
>
> (Nicols, p. 13, l. 25)

There is a particular skill in identifying how the need of the individual may be reconciled or aligned within overall group activity – that may be potentially quite different in character. This account is not intended to be prescriptive of interaction as the infinite possibilities within improvisation and its interactions have endless scope for different ways of doing things; however, the clarity of this description of an extreme example illustrates a successful approach to creating the conditions for *heterogeneity* as a valued ingredient of FI. For Nicols, the social possibilities are prioritized and the unsaid understanding that nobody should simply ask '*this saxophone player*' to modify his approach is striking – instead, musical ways are sought that not only alter the effect upon the whole group, but also, in the process, unveil another unexpected aspect of this player's contribution: '*he was also incredibly sensitive*'. This echoes Lewis' point: '*You know, you are much more alive to possibilities for growth or change or interventions of different kinds*'. There is a challenge in finding ways to incorporate and value others who need to play differently and this requires commitment to the social context and imagination in influencing the group. Moreover, this process of inclusion, that sustains heterogeneity, is a necessary part of development in large group FI interaction. '*[...] you'd get a period where it would be the same people and it would get incredibly coherent, almost insular, almost to the point where it was stagnating. It was so perfect, it was so beautiful everybody knew each other so well. And then somebody would come that would just completely disrupt everything [...]'* (Nicols, p. 17, l. 3). Disruption may appear counter to the group's aim; however, this becomes a source of new creative response, as the group dynamic shifts. Commitment to the process of improvisation includes the need to respond and with that comes the incorporation of difference. In this way, difference provides a source of creativity that contributes to the group's identity. Here, FI effectively becomes a social practice focused upon: *'Mixed ability virtuosity. That has its own particular power'*. The heterogeneous character of FI reflects the diversity of its participants – too closely prescribing free improvisation imposes limitations.

This chapter is concerned with improvisation's potential and, of course, to a large extent education determines how practices are recognized and acknowledged, or otherwise. In jazz education, there has been a normalizing of content through the standardization of approach (Mantie, 2008) – largely, there's a 'right way' of doing things and within that degrees of expertise. If we think of the earlier music of Ellington, Monk, Parker and Coltrane and others, while the language they created has contributed to the subsequent 'standard' way to learn jazz, if introduced today their innovations would be, paradoxically, at odds with today's conservative jazz practice. All the significant figures in jazz history contributed something new. In order to remain vital, free improvisation, or creating at the point of performance, cannot be overly prescribed and this necessarily involves resisting a merely consensual approach. In this respect, improvisation can be understood as a kind of *paralogy*, with the acknowledgement of different simultaneous narratives, as illustrated in Nicols' previous description – logic may suggest that the group does well without the disruption of an outsider, but the process of improvisation develops and benefits through not being too tied to one way of doing things. This not fixed, potential instability gives rise to creativity and new opportunities within the continuum of the activity. As Lyotard (1984) describes: 'consensus is only a particular state of discussion, not its end. Its end, on the contrary, is paralogy'. Through the form's capacity for openness, difference provides a source of dynamic creativity. Not-predetermined improvisational performance occurs in radically differing circumstances as this extract from Bob Ostertag's interview illustrates:

The way we started the concerts were sort of composed because the Pope had just put out a record: Pope John Paul, I don't know if you know that? The Pope made a record it was on Sony. It was him reading Psalms and giving homilies over this sort of ambient, world beat grooves [...]. I immediately thought OK, so we need to sample the Pope. I mean we're PantyChrist. I wanted to put out another CD entitled: 'The Pope Remix' (laughs). The way the concert started was that Otomo (Yoshihida) and I went on stage first and made this big noise, blaaaa, and it gradually sort of settled down into a drone, it became quieter and quieter and the lights would go down until the stage was dark and there was just this drone and then we'd have this white down spot come on, with nobody in and then you'd hear the Pope's voice say, it was from the record: 'The man who does bad things avoids the light, for fear that his bad deeds will be exposed. But the man who does good things walks into the light'. And Justin (Justin Case) walks into the light where he just sort of has a grouchy

schoolteacher outfit on looking very angry with a cocktail. Walks up to the mike and says:
'Welcome to Bitter Mummy's Club Arioloa' (laughs) and that's how the concert began and
from there on it was improvised, no idea what was going to happen.

(Ostertag, p. 10, l. 3)

Within this, albeit, contentious performance the different cultural and artistic histories form the dynamic of the trio: Bob Ostertag, Otomo Yoshihida and Justin Case. In this way mutual regard is a way of working. As J. David Velleman (2009, p. 1) suggests, '[…] the grounding of morality lies closer to the social surface than philosophers like to think, neither in the structure of practical reason nor the telos of human nature but rather in our mundane ways of muddling along'. In this way, committing to the process of improvisation, creating through negotiating difference, is necessarily ethical.

Crossing Boundaries

The phenomenological approach of 'going back to the things themselves' shows improvisation as not necessarily bounded by disciplinary constructs. Improvisation's potential for inter-disciplinary activity is also distinctive. '*Music is just one domain of the improvisative experience, you know, and as you start to find out how vast that experience is, how many levels it has, you don't want to privilege music over all the others, which ends up making a limitation on it*' (Lewis, p. 15, l. 22). Improvisation not only raises questions to do with disciplinary boundaries, but also poses fundamental questions within the individually constructed disciplines, for example, What is the role of the teacher for free improvisation in music? (Chapter 7). How do we acknowledge this inter-disciplinary character through practice? How appropriate are disciplinary paradigms for improvisation research? Ostertag's previous description of improvisation in music involving electronics, drag-performance, theatre and an audience of rock fans crosses several cultural boundaries. Developments across the arts, beyond the gallery, concert hall and proscenium arch have resulted in practices that form different kinds of artistic interaction, and improvisation in music and elsewhere provides an effective motor within this broader cultural shift. The interviewees describe how improvisation practice in music readily forms connections to other practices. '*When I discovered improvisation* [in music] *I also saw a retrospect of Buster Keaton. I was living in Montreal at the time. I went to see all of his films. I saw many short films – and I'm absolutely sure that he influenced me completely in the fact that I'm in front of people. It's kind of like a fake thing, it's pretentious, and fake. SR: What is, the situation? Yes the situation is very unnatural, people are here and you are here […] from the beginning I was influenced by the theatre. And also reading Becket for the first time*' (Honsinger, p. 5, l. 12).

    The '*agility in the term*' improvisation (Lewis), its openness and lack of prescription, means that personal development of practice can be self-defining. While copying others is emphasized in theorizing jazz (Sudnow, 1993) and 'popular' music (Green, 2008), the interviewees' accounts are characterized by the development of distinctive individual practice, and to this end, improvisation becomes a form of investigation, of discovery. In developing personal practice in improvisation, awareness of other disciplinary practices is beneficial and in this process norms of musical presentation may become questioned. Johansson's distinctive, enigmatic approach to musical performance with percussion can be more fully understood in the knowledge of it having developed alongside an equally successful 'contemporary' art practice involving various media and performance – his engagement in music and art practice can be interchangeable. An early associate, saxophonist Peter Brotzmann (2013), also a productive visual artist, cites how during the 1960s cross-fertilization contributed to the development of arts practices – people from different areas spent time together and became influenced by each other's ideas and concepts; he contrasts this with the way practice is currently pursued in a more separated manner. SR: *'You mentioned an 'art sound'. I don't think Brotzmann or Kowald had come from music training background [...]* Johansson: *[...] Peter Kowald was a languages man. He studied linguistics and he worked as a translator in the court. And Peter Brotzmann was graphics, art.* SR: *There were some Fluxus ideas?* Johansson: *Yes [...] he was impressed by some of the people who were with the Fluxus [...]'* (Johansson, p. 3, l. 14). Elsewhere in the interview Johansson describes this trio's playing in the late 1960s as *'not music'* but a *'way to explore the instruments together. It was to find out what the instrument can do.'* (p. 2, l. 15). Such experimentation and interrogation of form and materials is a commonplace creative strategy within fine art education although underdeveloped in music education.

Although 'inter-disciplinary' can be used quite freely in academia, in practice the transfer of ideas from one area to another is not necessarily straightforward and work involves negotiation. For example, the fields of *art* and *music* carry nuanced sociocultural ramifications that need to be reconciled within professional aims. Johansson: *'I work as a visual artist and my scores and papers, it goes in the directions of scores and drawings, is integrated in the visual art scene. I am in the Biennale here* [Berlin] *I am invited as a visual artist, in the biggest house in Orienplatz but I also have a concert 21 July at the Kunst* [Akademie der Kunst] *a solo presentation. So I am also an artist special-musician. And also qualities from the visual art scene come into my work as a musician. So it's not from the academic school.* SR: *I've read that you use theatricality in relation to your work. Would you agree with this?* Johansson: *No. People see me moving from one to another they might see [...] but it's just music stuff, playing this and the other. A piano player has to stick to his instrument but my instrument is here, there and everywhere, more or less, so I have to move a bit, and they say it is theatre but it is, I have nothing against it but [...] I do visual acts but for me it is also music. I have a rubber cymbal. And people hear a big cymbal in their heads, sometimes and they see the cymbal. Not hearing, but they see the sound. I play with this seeing and hearing and turn it sometimes backwards round.* SR: *You play with the visual side which inevitably accompanies musical performance?* Johansson: *Yes. Expectations or the visualization of musical sound, in some parts'* (Johansson, p. 8, l. 1).

While improvisation's inter-disciplinary and trans-disciplinary potential is suggested throughout the interviews, it should also be acknowledged that a 'workmanlike' attitude is common among professional musicians (certainly in the UK); in seeking to maintain professional credibility, some musicians may also be wary of such inter-disciplinary association. The presentation of the personal and professional self also colours interpretations of FI (Goffman, 1990). For example, while sitting in with a directed ensemble in a performance in which instructions were unclear, a fellow musician whispered, 'Look like you know what you're doing'. The performative presentation of self and activity also contributes to shaping the improvisation.

'*I normally bring a theatrical element to my playing, something a bit visual. I mean I don't overdo it but, I mean, I don't stand* there *like a statue and play and twenty minutes later step from the spot when I've finished. I don't play like that. I try to use the space*' (Tomlinson, p. 6, l. 1). Tomlinson's professional 'no-nonsense' attitude is balanced with the use of some humour. It can be interpreted as an ironic reflection upon the dominant 'seriousness' presented in much musical improvising. What is elsewhere described in Tomlinson's interview as '*a bit of drama*' is also reminiscent of the comedic feature often associated with the Dutch improvised music scene. Typically, improvisers develop practice through an extensive, evolving process of playing and performing. A weakness of describing such multifaceted activity in 'inter-disciplinary' terms is that it may, for some, suggest a superficial mixing of practices. While it is possible to identify these other aspects, performance is integrated. Overly emphasizing the separate elements is to distract from the unity of improvisation in the course of performance. Nevertheless, the inclusion of different practices and the reference to their influence is strongly evident, reflecting the nature of open creativity. Mitchell: '*This was '61 I guess, so I was 21. I was 21 years old then, but we explored all kinds of things – all kinds of things. We'd go to art museums and maybe spend the whole day looking at different art, all these different things. It was kind of like a total world of learning […] what I've seen of people that are particularly talented, they usually can do almost anything in art, they have to decide which way they're going to want to go. Because out of that group of people we had Lester Lashley who is a very talented artist although he still plays, you know, art became his real focus. So, like I said it was a whole pool of learning, I mean you could learn things from all these different people and certainly the compositional process was very interesting. Each person has their own take on it,; the concerts were all different because each person would have their own take on that, I mean you were inspired*' (Roscoe Mitchell, p. 4, l. 32).

Openness to the influence of other disciplines is poorly served by compartmentalized thinking. Ursel Schlicht's (2008) lucid description of developing improvisation ensemble practice takes place within a department that has a history of cross-disciplinary curriculum design; the example's openness to other musics and practices is a feature of its clear success. In similar manner, the renowned Black Mountain College (Goldberg, 1998) in the US that featured Cage, Cunningham, Kaprow, Buckminster Fuller, de Kooning, Creely and many others was founded upon an ethos that nurtured inquiry regardless of the disciplinary orientation; in cross-disciplinary fashion, activity included a highly improvisational approach to programming artistic events.

Improvisation and Language

In order to acknowledge improvisation, it is necessary to reflect upon the way it is represented. In describing improvisation in music, it is easy to overlook what for some musicians is an intransigent difficulty: the phenomena of music and language are of a different order and language can never reproduce the experience of music. The experience of improvisation in music is often regarded as occurring without the need for its articulation in words and it is not uncommon for musicians to be sceptical about the benefits of discussing improvisation. It may be for this reason that the group AMM agreed in a 'manifesto' not to have pre- or post-concert discussion of the music with one another. For some the purpose of music, or art, is to express that which cannot be articulated in words. Primarily, enacting improvisation leads to the acquisition of knowledge of practice in a way that words cannot; describing music is never the experience of music. The examples of walking, swimming or riding a bicycle are comparable – we understand how to do such things through experience; similarly, in the creative process of improvisation doing leads to understanding. However, as this embodied action forms knowledge, it is possible to gain insight of improvisation through discussion of its experience and processes. Within the breadth of knowledge found in these interviews, there is a need to examine more precisely the relationship between discussion and the act of improvisation. Chapter 8, *Body*, explores this in detail. For some interviewees, their choice of language not only described the *lived experience* of improvisation, but is also suggestive of improvisation's relationship with language itself. Tristan Honsinger's descriptions, in particular, draw out underlying tensions between meaning created through the use of language and the act of improvisation. For Honsinger, descriptions were multifaceted and rich in metaphor, and free improvisation itself was described as 'this language'. The interview response is interpreted as a play between what we presume to understand by means of language and do not understand in relation to music and free improvisation. The limitations are shown up, suggesting that for Honsinger language is insufficient to describe what is taking place. He cites Buster Keaton and Samuel Becket as influential at the formative stages of becoming a professional improvising musician, and themes found throughout Becket's work (for example, *Waiting for Godot* [1956]) are reflected in the following extracts in which the choice of language also suggests inadequacies in attempting to achieve fundamental understandings. Additionally, Keaton (1889–1966) was clearly a specialist in communication without words.

It's... it's... like the theory of gravity, the gravita... that we are here... so, improvisation is up or down – in direction [...] This is an example of improvisation – the moment surprises you, but at the point of deciding to go down or up can be very important in the whole spectrum of the thing – it's kind of like catching something that is in movement – for me this is what improvisation is, the moment of change can be totally important to what comes (Honsinger, p. 2, l. 21). And: *We're talking about [...] well, I'll bring water into the discussion, because water is undividable, you can't divide water, water is one of the elements that you can't divide, alright air as well, these very important things that benefit us but are totally, these words, what is the word, water is of a consistency but it doesn't care about our practice of dividing. And I think something happens in music where the connection becomes one, then we're in the way of water and this would also be another way of saying its anti-gravitational in a certain way [...] When we become one, we are flying together and I think, yes I think music has this, we have made this language I think for some of these reasons – reasons to become one and to float I would say* (Honsinger, p. 3, l. 18).

Although the multiple metaphors may at first be confusing, their use draws attention to an additional, over-arching idea. Grappling with articulating the phenomenon of free improvisation, Honsinger's frequent switching between suggestive metaphors effectively emphasizes the way in which meaning here cannot, and should not be readily pinned down to a single idea, definition, model or analogy. The last sentence is thematically strong as ideas converge through mixed metaphors: *'flying together'* as *'one'* is reminiscent of the phenomenon explored by Csikszentmihalyi (1991), described as 'Flow', that of being in a fully immersed, concentrated, challenging, creative state. And improvisation is also described as a *made language*, developed so that we *'become one and to float'* for this unique, collective experience. Although we are examining free improvisation through the medium of words (employing a double hermeneutic in analysis), it is also essential to acknowledge that perceptual engagement in the process of free improvisation is not linguistic. Steve Paxton, known particularly for his work in the development of Contact Improvisation dance, has referred to improvisation as 'a word for something that can't keep a name' (1997), which echoes Lewis' *'[...] the agility in the term [...]'*. As improvisation exists in different ways, simultaneously, conceptualizing in terms of the co-presence of themes relieves the tendency to 'pin down', thereby foreshortening understanding of the phenomenon. Chapter 10 explores this necessary ambiguity in improvisation.

The comparison between improvisation in music and our use of language is common: improvising in sound is communicative and improvisers acquire 'vocabulary' – good 'conversations' emerge through the exchange with attentive listening (this has been discussed by Sudnow, 1993; Bailey, 1993; Berliner, 1994; Berkowitz, 2010; Frith, 2008; Benson, 2003). For Sudnow, his study is of a specific jazz piano style, and the precise content becomes defined, as he describes, through copying – within these terms of reference, the language comparison is used consistently. In free improvisation, the comparison to language is less secure. The diversity of creative practices means that playing can become continuously re-contextualized in different group settings and so the comparison needs to acknowledge fluidity, instability and the re-contextualization of material. Additionally, while the influential group SME retained the kind of dialogical playing found in jazz, call and response that could be said to correspond with language, the approach is certainly not defining of improvisation, which includes other strategies, for example, not responding, playing against, collective textural playing, drones and so on. In this way too direct comparison with language in free improvisation can be misleading – the extent of sound possibilities in free improvisation goes far beyond the limitation of the one-to-one relation that the analogy to language can suggest.

Improvisation and Being-in-the-world

'[...] you're creating an environment, you're also interacting with one – so you have to pay attention' (Lewis, p. 1, l. 6). Lewis' remark is encompassing; it situates us as part of environment rather than simply commentating upon it, implicitly at a distance. Of course, environment is an over-arching contemporary theme and this is a ripe idea for pedagogical reflection about initiating free improvisation activity. It also connects directly with the idea of improvisation as *being-in-the-world*. Our being is interpreting and constructing, a grasping of 'the world' by interacting with things and others – improvisation is through '*paying attention*', directing our perceptual and conceptual awareness within this environment of things, others and our selves at the point of performance. Linking improvisation with being also reflects the activity's essential pervasiveness. As Lewis puts it, '*Music is just one domain of the improvisative experience [...]*' (p. 15, l. 22). The question of improvisation's true range is highly relevant for understanding the improvisation phenomenon – this quotation is from the 2008 study: 'Articulating perspectives of free improvisation for education':

> The features that arise from engagement with free improvisation all point in the direction, to a greater or lesser extent, to what can most usefully be described as being. It has been possible to divide this concept further, but this continued analysis and further fragmentation has not been of use as it ignores the central unifying capability of the subject [...].
>
> (Rose)

In 'Imaginative listening and the reverberations of the world', Jeffrey Ediger (1993) explores the ways in which Merleau-Ponty (1962) and Bachelard (1958) describe the process of realizing being-in-the-world through two kinds of artistic activity: Merleau-Ponty through the act of the painter and for Bachelard the poet: 'Through the activity of the artist, drawing on powers of the imagination, the natural world undergoes a transformation by means of which the human world comes into being'. While poetry is privileged by means of its special relationship to language 'the house of being' (Heidegger, 1968, p. 64), improvisation in music's relationship to embodied, *real-time*, creative and collective experience provides a vivid example of '[...] the human world coming into being' through artistic practice'. In Heidegger's conception of 'being-in-the-world' (1962), *being* is described through our integrated experience of the world of one another and things, rather than divided subject and object; it is a holistic, temporal picture. The real-time composing dimension of improvisation highlights a particular connection to being-in-the-world: as individuals commit to creating music in real-time, the experience is not repeatable, engaging in making something new within that given time. In the process of composing in real-time we create the environment, or world, through our being/improvisation. In creative improvisation, our *being* becomes highlighted, as Oliveros describes when discussing listening: '*If you talk about being it's right in there, having awareness up-front*' (Oliveros, p. 6, l. 10). Improvisation's particular connection to authentic being-in-the-world is through playing. In the face of music as pervasive mass-media reproduction, improvisation provides a contemporary resonance, through what Butcher describes as '*this unrepeatable experience*'.

Lewis' discussion of music and the nature of the improvisation phenomenon extends across experience: '*Increasingly I find the same structures are active all the time. And so I can learn just as much from that process of walking down the street as I can playing with some certified person or even a not so certified person or group of people. And that's what comes from paying attention* (pause, laugh). *You know you are much more alive to possibilities for growth or change or interventions of different kinds – you're engaged in a continual kind of analysis of what's going on, what other people are doing, what the environment is doing*' (p. 2, l. 8). The description of a '*continual analysis of what's going on*' contributes to the major theme of *Learning* in Chapter 7; potentially, engagement with FI is a process of continuous learning, regardless of experience. The not-predetermined character of FI leads to continuing engagement with something not fixed – it therefore becomes inadequate to rely on a stock set of responses, if we do we foreshorten the possibilities offered by the particular group situation, at each given time. Rather, we '*pay attention*' to emerging opportunities and how we contribute towards and affect the collective musical continuum. Beyond music, improvisation in different areas of activity also reflects these features and in this way improvisation can also be understood as a human capability.

Note

1   Italicized quotations are taken from interviews included in the author's Ph.D thesis (2013). These interviews are also included in Part 3 of this book.

Chapter 6

Process

Evolution and Improvisation

I'm sitting on a train, returning from a conference at the Institute of Cultural Inquiry in Berlin and talking to a scientist, James T. Costa who has a new book about Darwin and Wallace – he's an evolution expert. I ask him if he thinks evolution is a kind of improvisation. He pauses for a long time, as the train moves along. 'Yes I do, particularly the mutation aspect'. He subsequently reflects upon how it is more the process of 'natural selection' improvising with the raw material initiated by mutation (which is random) that gives the evolutionary process its 'improvisational appearance'. Lewis' '[...] you're creating an environment, you're also interacting with one' can also be interpreted, broadly, as a description of evolution, or *development as an environmental response* and Butcher similarly describes improvisation as '*evolving*'. Newer understanding of processes in the natural world can also contribute to further understanding processes in improvisation. Nicols' description of permaculture (later in this chapter) has been influential in developing thinking, as has David Borgo's 'Sync or Swarm' (2005), in which his research interest in 'new science' has led to the exploration of improvisation and fractals in studies of Evan Parker's solo saxophone improvisations as well as the groups of Sam Rivers and Peter Brotzmann. In addition, Evan Parker (2014) has described his personal approach to playing through reference to bio-feedback systems. This section discusses self-organization, feedback, evolution and the process of improvisation. The related theory of autopoiesis (self-creating) is discussed within the thematic context of Chapter 8.

Our conception of the ways structures are produced is fundamental to the day-to-day understanding of our being-in-the-world. The choice of language is profoundly important in shaping our understanding of experience, and metaphors contribute to the embodiment of conceptualization (Lakoff and Johnson, 1980). In music, descriptions are often represented in a largely metaphorical manner, and the use of metaphors contributes greatly to conceptualizing and extending our grasp of music. Using language that *accurately reflects the process of improvisation* furthers comprehension. Over the last one hundred and fifty years, fundamental developments in the understanding of the way life develops have revolutionized our knowledge of the world (Darwin, 1859; Turing 1952; Belousov, 1985, Mandelbrot 1975). The process of adapting to environmental circumstances (adaptation), through which life has arisen, evolution, is improvisatory. The Newtonian metaphor of the universe was of a mechanical, mathematically reliable system and random behaviour was seen as an outside influence impacting upon it; the idea that patterns could exist without an external designer was inconceivable – this view has now been surpassed. Unsurprisingly, features of this former way of understanding the world are mirrored in the development of 'classical' music's presentation – the insistence on the fixed, written 'work' and an emphasis with hierarchy and status through the constructs of orchestra, conductor, composer and institutional prestige – such a way of thinking left little room for adaptive, emergent improvisation.

Self-organizing systems are found everywhere in the natural world and improvisation in music has the potential for self-organization – creating through indeterminacy, without an external designer, composer or conductor. We can describe this as a system of feedback. The output from one player becomes the input for another and so on, creating a musical continuum of real-time composition. This becomes highly complex as feedback occurs at multiple, simultaneous levels: within the individual's own playing, within the group, between pairs, between an individual and the entirety of the group sound, the group in its environmental setting and so on. While part of the improvising musicians' job includes awareness of the implications of developing complexity while playing, engaging in such a process that includes the element of instability, or uncertainty (mutation), is essential for the developing process. This involves acceptance of contingency and emergence within the process. Experience leads to valuing, and trusting in the uncertain element for its contribution within the feedback process. In these ways, participation in enacted improvisation is self-organizing. Evolution in the natural world builds on self-organizing patterns, and adapts systems to the environment; it is creative and based on simple rules and feedback, from which complexity spontaneously emerges; for evolution the feedback comes from the environment, favouring the mutations that are best suited to it, resulting in increasing complexity. These features of evolution can be used as descriptors, or metaphors for improvisation in music. Leaving the Newtonian vision of a world functioning like clockwork and instead looking at self-organizing systems describes the potential of the process of improvisation in music, valuing the possibilities of not-predetermined events, within developing, socially based structures.

Process and Product

Thinking of improvisation in music as a process opens the way to the activity's potential, allowing for the phenomenon's complexity. The focus on process in improvisation reveals its creative and social potential. The activity of improvising in music represents, in many ways, the antithesis of the concept of the musical 'work'. And while it is possible to argue for a canon of recorded improvised music, which could be regarded as works, this does little to advance understanding of the process of improvisation's potential. Conceptualizing the *process* of experiential improvisation aids understanding of the broader theme of music as activity.

In discussion, the process in improvisation is often contrasted with product. Sawyer (2003) describes the process of improvisation as the product, also citing Collingwood (1938) for whom the process *is* the work of art. Benson (2003) situates the musical product as belonging to the *activity* of music: 'From an *energeia* [activity] grows an *ergon* [product] – but an *ergon* that still remains *within* the play of musical *energeia*, and from which it cannot be disconnected'. The process/product relation in improvisation has been thematically emphasized in organization theory (Baker, Miner and Eesley, 2003; Barrett, 1998; Crossan, Cuhna, Vera and Cuhna, 2005). Durant (1989) describes how 'improvised music foregrounds – in its practice as well as in its name – the relationship between the *product* of performance (the musical "text") and the *process* through which that product comes into being'. While improvisation's process is undoubtedly of primary theoretical interest, it is also important not to contribute to an artificial process/product binary, thereby disassociating from aspects of lived experience. Firstly, recordings can be highly valued representations or documentation of practice, as such significant products of the music. Secondly, professional musicians, improvisers or otherwise earn a living at what they do, something that improvisation theorizing tends to overlook, and it would be inaccurate and a disservice to musicians to give the impression that the products of professional improvisers are unimportant. Commonly operating in highly precarious economic fashion, they are freelance and often need to accept work where and whenever it is offered. This can often lead musicians into situations in which they are badly paid. Musicians' recorded output, product, has contributed to ameliorating this situation – both through sales and increasing awareness of a musicians' activity (although the current economic viability of recording and sales is itself in question with the increased ease of free reproduction). In spite of the lamentable economic predicament facing most professional improvisers, true understanding of the creative and social potential of improvisation is revealed through examination of its processes. For Lewis, awareness of deeper potential in the process informs his aims. The process of improvisation shapes human interaction in making music. '*So you felt good and you got a good outcome for your piece and everyone liked it, so what, you know. I mean did you learn anything about the nature of [...] the things that you can learn from improvised music – the nature of consciousness or the nature of communication, things that really matter, things that you can really learn from improvisation, that you can learn all the time. And I thought that's why they were on stage but I guess what they really, what some of them were really on stage for was to create a nice commodity, that they could package in some way and that they could get a repeatable outcome from. That's a different problem, that's not my issue – not now, maybe it was a long time ago*' (Lewis, p. 12, l. 30).

Trust

Lewis interprets the potential of improvisation as much more than simply an aesthetic alternative to more traditionally composed music. The process of improvisation offers '*infinite possibilities*' for exploration through the relationships that are formed – potential that is applicable in different areas of activity. In the process of improvising control is shared – creating together in a not-predetermined fashion. Because of this, trust is functional in improvisation – enabling music, but trust is also an indicator of ethical social qualities relating to understanding of the self and the group: empathy, supportiveness, fairness, care and so on (Luhmann, 1979; Misztal, 1996). Through the experiential nature of educational improvisation in drama and music, trust becomes an integrated component that facilitates the activity's potential and development. At the same time, the educational potential of exploring trust through the forum of music and drama activities provides a means of engaging much more over-arching social, ethical themes, by means of experiential learning. Trust provides for work concerned with the nature of social structure and relationships however that may become thematically framed. Additionally, as the nature of trust itself remains not wholly understood, the immediacy of social improvisation also offers a means by which trust can be explored.

The following extract provides a perspective on the significance of trust in the process of improvisation. Nicols' description refers to the long-standing (over twenty-five years) regular, 'open-door' sessions where all are welcome to participate in undirected, collective free improvisation; previous experience is not a requirement and all levels of ability are welcome. '*There's an organisation called permaculture [...]. It's all about learning from nature, observing nature, which is what people did before, you know, before capitalism broke. Anyway, it's about minimum input and maximum output. You're learning about how nature functions and they have these different zones, and zone one is maybe your herb garden, it's close to the kitchen, zone two might be your vegetables and so on, bee keeping might be a certain [...] and then right to zone six which you leave alone, you don't actually interfere with, you just let nature do its thing. And so I often feel the Gathering* [open-door improvisation group/ sessions] *is probably, it's not exactly a six because we are in there energetically influencing things but it's probably zone five. Just let it be self-regulating, however chaotic that might be and trust that out of that chaos will come the clearings, will come the new growth, will come the coherence. And it does, when you trust it and if enough people trust it then of course that affects the whole thing*' (Nicols, p. 15, l. 1).

This idea echoes Lewis' description of *allowing* group development through the process of improvisation. Elsewhere Nicols emphasizes her '*love*' and faith in the potential of '*mixed ability*' creativity and at the centre of the environmental comparison is the importance of trust. Nicols' personal commitment to her vision of improvisation's potential has sustained the longevity of this group activity, attesting to the viability of the approach. Free improvisation's potential autonomous agency is foregrounded – reiterating Lewis': '*let them work it out*'. Oliveros also refers to the importance of trust in the process of improvisation: '*You have to trust the situation, you have to make it safe*' (Oliveros, p. 2, l. 26). Ways 'to make it safe' can be seen in different practices. Prior to performing, improvising dancers are commonly tactile with one another – the ability to perform freely is dependent upon mutual support, demonstrating that this is forthcoming furthers their process. The tactile behaviour contributes, along the way, to engendering trust. Similarly in drama, trust exercises often involve tactile, sensory interaction: touch, falling and being caught, demonstrating support of the other within the group context. In this way, trust supports and enables the process of social improvisation.

Risk

'[...] if new communication, a new experience doesn't happen then there is no reason to go on stage' (Johansson, p. 9, l. 46). Openness to participate in making something new reveals the importance of trust in the process, so too, the related feature of risk emerges from the interviews as important in the process of improvisation. The development of trust encourages the willingness to explore, to take risks in order to discover – these are two sides of the same coin – trust engenders the circumstances for risk, or the willingness to engage with uncertainty. In the interviews, the element of risk is manifested in a variety of ways. '[...] then that person is maybe trying to learn too – again it hinges on the personal transformation thing, how open are you? How vulnerable can you make yourself, how open to change, how malleable – mutable as I think Evan [Evan Parker] used to say [...]'. Discovery in the process, by definition, seeks the unfamiliar and in this way improvisation offers a process of learning (Chapter 7). This openness to develop necessarily includes a willingness to risk something new. Classical pianist Robert Levin, a strong advocate for reinstating the lost importance of improvisation in his field, describes how 'The most important thing is the willingness to take risks and the acknowledgement of doing so invests the artistic statement with a level of integrity, with a level of personality, a level of uniqueness that nothing else can do' (Bailey, 1992). And, 'There is nothing more risky than improvisation, but there is nothing more devastating to music's dramatic and emotional message than avoidance of risk' (Levin in Landgraf, 2011): (although Landgraf limits risk to the association with 'mistakes', or the deviation from the script). Saxophonist Peter Brotzmann (Brotzmann and Rouy, 2014) describes how risk is only possible with trust: '[...] between everybody [...] You have to take that risk that the whole thing could break down [...] risk can develop into something if you have the right combination' and [...] some great recordings that came out of such a process' (Brotzmann, Bennink and Van Hove, 1975).

In common usage, the term 'risk' is often referred to in relation to its avoidance; however, the risk of interacting within indeterminacy enables creative development – through improvisation. Within free improvisation's challenge to create music in real-time the possibility of failure is always present in the process – this can form part of the attraction, the excitement. There is a necessary mutual openness, a willingness to be challenged. To allow for that which is not previously well known, through the process of improvisation, is not 'playing it safe'. Ostertag identified the 'discovering new things' or willingness to seek the unknown as an important aspect in improvising: 'When I think of improvisers that really come to mind, who are really inspiring improvisers in that sense, the first one would be Monk, who every time he sat down somehow conveyed the sense that he was taking a really fresh look at the piano – look here's an E over here – how can I use that, and when you compare his various recordings he never plays the *same tune the same way twice. And he always conveys the sense that he is discovering, genuinely discovering new things, every time he sits down to play'* (Ostertag, p. 12, l. 32). While improvisers have their known materials, it is the real-time choices that lead to the possibility of newness in the process of improvising. Partly due to his use of space and unhurried timing, in Monk's performances the musical choices appear to be transparent. This *'discovering'* or searching quality is an integral part of the music's success and continued appeal, drawing the listener in as the music unfolds.

The element of risk also emerges in other ways. Taken to an extreme, risk can become more overtly displayed, relished while contributing to the structure of performance. *'[…] and they had no idea that Mike Patton wasn't going to be in the second set so (laughs) when Mike wouldn't appear and this guy in a women's bathing suit appeared in his place and started getting a tan with her tanning* lotion. *I think people were absolutely dumbfounded. People were like, what the fuck. I half expected that chairs were going to start flying* [laughs]' (Ostertag, p. 9, l. 30). The performance plays with uncertainty in a number of ways and it challenges audience expectations in the process. It is reminiscent of the risk associated with some 'rock and roll' bravura (for example, Iggy Pop) or the way some 'contemporary' art has employed risky 'shock' strategies. Aside from the theatrical, rock, noise, electronics orientation of the performers, within this performance, the approach is essentially one of open improvisation. Risk is present in a number of ways. There is the challenge to audience expectations when the 'star' they have come to see engages with distinctly other material during the first set, vocal sounds rather than lyrics. There is the tension created as, unannounced, he does not appear in the second set. There is also the challenge created by the unannounced drag performance before an unprepared, largely rock music audience. A challenge of a different order is present through the group's not sharing a common spoken language. As Ostertag finally puts it, *'this was not an easy band to book'.* Notwithstanding the group's difficulties in reception, it is the process of improvisation that gives rise to this intercultural cross-disciplinary performance.

Self-assertion

Across the interviews, the feature of risk was present: within the intricacy of how the music develops in the process of improvisation, within the dynamic of the group interaction, and also more widely in the sociopolitical setting. In Nicols' description of the Feminist Improvisation Group (FIG), risk in the process of improvisation is implicit through the challenge to male hegemony. Here, risk in the process of improvisation is inseparable from the groups' self-assertion. *'[…] you had musicians of phenomenal technique like Lindsey [Lindsey Cooper] and Irene [Irene Schweizer] and others who didn't have such a strong technique but were amazing performers and again that was really open and I loved the openness of that. What happened to FIG which was very interesting was, different male groups, there was* [names removed] *and they'd say: Well, we like you two, Lindsey and Georgie*

[Georgina Born] *but we think they're too theatrical. And then there'd be the jazzers like [name removed] going – Oh, we like you and Irene, you know, and there was a bit of divide and rule went on, because I think we were quite threatening and other musicians loved us like Lol – Lol Coxhill, Eugene Chadborn, Martin Altina there were lots of male musicians who were big fans but there were other men who really, really were threatened in fact* [name removed] *we did the Berlin Total Music Meeting and he actually complained about us. He said why did they book us, because we couldn't play our instruments. Well this is insane – you've got women like Irene and, you know, I could use my voice. And it was a huge hit as well the audience loved us but we were accused of being a novelty – you have no idea of the vitriol we got'* (Nicols, p. 21, l. 13). FIG's identity is tied by name with the feminist theme of struggle and this is played-out when met by the male questioning of the groups' validity. The group's inclusion of theatrical, visual and comedic elements also contributes to 'making waves' within the distinctly male musical hegemony of the period. FIG's willingness to risk characterizes their determined political assertion as the group becomes criticized on a number of fundamental levels.

Within the process of improvisation in music, themes of trust and risk are embedded within the broader social theme of *self-assertion*. This reflects Lewis' description of improvisation's potential for *'drawing larger lessons from improvisation'*. Nicols' experience, at times stark and painful, clearly informs personal development and a life's work in which the processes of improvisation are central. *'[…] it just became more and more of who I was, or who I am, and just felt more and more convinced that that's what improvising for me was, it was just a totality of whatever, of the history, the now, the other musicians, the environment, what's going on in the world, politically, all those things and … it varies all the time as well* (p. 7, l. 8). *'[…] thanks to people like Dennis Rose and John* [John Stevens] *who didn't take advantage of me, and who genuinely mentored me – because I mean there were men there who used me like an unpaid prostitute in many ways, you know. Because it wasn't like the casting couch, where you give me a favour […] no, it was literally you just service me, so that's um, quite a, quite a wound really in a way, and probably why, that's another reason why I worked, again not thinking about it consciously – why I, for me I was so driven to develop my voice as an equal instrument, with any male instrumentalist. That wasn't conscious, it really wasn't, but I know that I felt I had to prove that I deserved to exist, on that scene […]'* (Nicols, p. 22, l. 19). In Nicols' candid description, there is no shying away from harsh, formative experience – rather a learning from it. The determined expression of the personal as political is also a celebratory *life-world* account: improvisation provides Nicols with the means of expressing resistant, self-determination. She identifies the capability of improvisation as providing for her human need. Nicols is also adamant that, for her, the ongoing process of improvisation is an encompassing means of being and expression.

Jazz, *free* jazz and *free* improvisation have historical associations with emancipation – in North America, in particular, improvisation is theorized via its association with the expression of resistance (Heble, Fschlin and Lipsitz, 2013). The African experience of slavery and post-slavery is notably representative of self-determination that has been linked with improvisation and has been well documented within jazz, post-colonial and

African American studies. Examples found in the work of Amiri Baraka, (as LeRoy Jones, 1963), Billy Holiday's 'Strange Fruit' (1939), John Coltrane's 'Alabama' (1963), as well as Sun Ra, Anthony Braxton, Duke Ellington and the wide range of other artistic and academic work contribute to understanding improvisation's broader capability for self-assertion and political expression. The continuity of this theme in music can be seen in the form of hip hop and rap where the spoken word and pervasive media provide a very direct means of self-assertion. In music, the adaptability, mutability and contingency of the process of improvisation, regardless of its stylistic manifestation, have also given rise to self-assertion in the form of instrumental virtuosity – moreover, such activity has led to new musical developments. For example, saxophonist Charlie Parker developed his saxophone voice through the assertion of 'owning' the music; assertively re-defining its harmonic, melodic and rhythmic parameters in performance. Parker's radical musical developments and legacy are of such an order that no serious musician in the field, then or since, would remain unaffected. Similarly, within the Duke Ellington Orchestra, Ellington's innovative practice included composing designed to give voice to virtuosic musicians who were outstanding, distinctive improvisers – Johnny Hodges, Harry Carney, Cat Anderson, Paul Gonsalves, Ben Webster and many others.

Unlimited Process of Improvisation

The increasing research interest in improvisation in arts and beyond is, of course, largely guided by disciplinary concerns. But the broad range of improvisation also suggests improvisation's commonality across as well as within disciplines. The process of improvisation can be read as disciplinary but also in a broader manner, throughout activity, as a pervasive mode of human interaction – independent of disciplinary distinction. In this way, we can understand improvisation in music as a concern for music, but we can simultaneously interpret the example's relevance beyond the music discipline. Lewis's following interview extract concerns improvisation in basketball. *'[…] this guy Phil Jackson […] he's the coach of the Lakers, and he had this book right, and the book is all about improvisation, in basketball […] it's based on this theoretical book written by his assistant coach in the 50s […] he would say this funny thing like, the team would be loosing, and usually the thing is, you got somebody saying "the team is loosing take out person X and put in person Y". But his thing was "well the team is losing, we'll let them work it out" [laughs] […] that's why it's so entertaining to watch, even though I'm not a big basketball fan, you can see them working it out improvisationally, how to do things – it was an expression of trust in their ability to work it out for themselves. And I learnt a lot from that for improvised music'* (Lewis, p. 6, l. 21). With features of real-time development, performance and the importance of the group working well together, sport contributes clarity for understanding improvisation. Ross (2011), Buarque de Hollanda (2011) and Vaz (2011) have all explored improvisation in football, and Landgraf (2014) points to sports' 'presence', with its focus on the here and now. The influential basketball coach Phil Jackson, described in the extract, provides a noteworthy perspective:

> In the heat of the game, I simply tried to stay in the moment and make decisions based on what was actually happening [...]. Afterward, rather than trying to fix things myself, I let the players solve the problem [...]. Winning is about moving into the unknown and creating something new. Remember that scene in the first Indiana Jones movie when someone asks Indy what he's going to do next, and he replies, 'I don't know. I'm making it up as we go along.' That's how I view leadership. It's an act of controlled improvisation, a Thelonious Monk finger exercise, from one moment to the next.
>
> (Jackson, 2014)

As Lewis suggests, the example of basketball is informative for musical aims, and more broadly as a description of improvisation within human interactions.

The *process* of improvisation's mutability, its not-fixed character, contributes to the cross-disciplinary potential. Chapter 5 describes how the personal development of practice in improvisation has connections to other disciplines. The interviewees describe the *process* of improvisation in music in ways that relate to other activity. The relevance of conventional disciplinary boundaries may become less important through the process of improvisation and, as such, stylistic musical boundaries and separations between artistic disciplines are less rigid. While musicians engaging in improvisation may not necessarily be concerned, or even aware of the cross-disciplinary aspect, the process of improvisation in music is indeed open to other practices – a point that is also particularly relevant for understanding improvisation's true potential in education. Nicols describes an aspect of her performance: '*[...] my favourite, definitely, is when I trust and when I trust and just let things, you know whatever happens – if there's a baby, or if there's a bird, just be open to whatever's there is in that moment, in those unfolding moments, yes*' (Nicols, p. 7, l. 41). The possibilities on offer '*in that moment*' of improvisation are unrestricted and reflect the environmental context. Through the improvisational performance process, Nicols incorporates and responds to sound as it occurs and once more, trust is referred to directly, enabling the process. The following interview extracts further illustrate how other disciplines have been referenced within descriptions of the process of improvisation in music and suggest ways in which improvisation relates to other forms. The extracts also illustrate the breadth of activity and thinking within individual's practice.

> *And Terry Riley got a commission to write a piece for a film, a five minute film ... he didn't have the time to write the music so Lauren Rush and I went into the studio and we recorded five minute tracks for Terry, we improvised the music. That was my first improvisation in that way.*
>
> (Oliveros, p. 1, l. 21)

[...] we did written stuff, we did improvised stuff, it was lovely in a way and lots of different women came through that: Sylvia Hallet and all different women, women who were experienced, women who weren't. Wonderful, wonderful stuff we did and Annalisa Colombara, who's a visual artist, who did the most amazing slides as well and wrote a story that we did.

(Nicols, p. 24, l. 6)

[...] So I am also an artist, special musician. And also qualities from the visual art scene come into my work as a musician.

(Johansson, p. 8, l. 9)

[...] there's a change going on there. A lot of classical trained musicians are becoming more interested in improvising. People from all different fields of music are stepping out of the category, I mean. Charlie Parker wanted to study with Varese and someone else too, but who knows what Charlie Parker would be doing today if he was alive.

(Mitchell, p. 10, l. 14)

I normally bring a theatrical element to my playing, something a bit visual.

(Tomlinson, p. 6, l. 1)

So from the beginning I was influenced by the theatre. And also reading Becket for the first time.

(Honsinger, p. 5, l. 28)

The first set was hard enough for them because they had no idea it was going to be this noise thing and that Mike wasn't going to sing any words and they had no idea that Mike wasn't going to be in the second set so [laughs], when Mike wouldn't appear and this guy in a women's bathing suit appeared [drag artist] *in his place and started getting a tan with her tanning lotion [laughs].*

(Ostertag, p. 9, l. 30)

In the process of improvisation in music, there is a productive openness to other disciplines. For example, The San Francisco Tape Music Centre's early 1960s music performances combined with equally experimental work with light (Bernstein and Goebel, 2008). And Keith Rowe (2001) has described how in AMM, 'we were visual artists who also played musical instruments' and how this informed his early experimenting with other ways of playing. As Peter Brotzmann puts it, 'I don't make them [the connections between practices], they are there' (Brotzmann and Rouy, 2014). The association with other practices in the process of FI may be viewed as surprising in one way, given that its demands have also been described as a self-punishing form, a kind of 'hair shirt' (Watson, 2004), suggesting that nothing is required outside of the essential interactions of a paired down music, existing in the moment. However Watson's subject, improvising guitarist Derek Bailey's broader interest in improvisation (Bailey, 1992) also encompassed performing across disciplines with, for example, dancers Min Tanaka (Butoh) and Will Gaines (tap); a clown; and musicians from the variety of backgrounds and genres: classical, rock, funk, bebop, electronic, modern jazz and so on. The variety of activity and emerging relations arising from improvisation in music is a thematic undercurrent, an outcome of the music form's 'not-predetermined' character – it also indicates the breadth of the improvisation phenomenon.

Within music performance, the process of improvisation comes sharply into focus: as the performance is experienced, so too are the processes that enable performance. While we celebrate improvisation within music and other arts practices, particularly those involving performance, improvisation is also present as a capability within the range of human activity. *'Increasingly I find the same structures are active all the time […] you're engaged in a continual kind of analysis of what's going on, what other people are doing, what the environment is doing'* (Lewis, p. 2, l. 8). *'Music is just one domain of the improvisative experience, you know, and as you start to find out how vast that experience is, how many levels it has, you don't want to privilege music over all the others, which ends up making a limitation on it'* (Lewis, p. 15, l. 22). As well as looking at musical activity to describe the nature of improvisation, we can look across human activity to further understanding. The following is from an interview conducted in 2008: *'To me free improvisation is a paradigm for your life because your life is freely improvised and nothing else but free improvised. You think of it as having routine and so on but in fact it's freely improvised from the beginning to the end, your life is one long free improvisation […] you are actually freely improvising without being aware of it. When you're in some critical situation you sometimes become aware of it … I think it's good […] you can either go down and sink or rise up […]'* (Roger Parry in Rose). Rather than focusing on routine, Parry describes life as the human creative capability to respond to circumstances, and the opportunities offered by each day's difference. Similarly, while improvising musicians may have known materials, or 'routines', it is the choices they make in each new setting that lead to creative interaction as opposed to the repetition of the same. As improvisation is present within the range of human activity, in arts, communication, travel, domestic activity, work, sports, play, education and so on, confining the activity within one or more areas, or disciplines, *'ends up making a limitation'* on our understanding.

The human capability for improvisation is very apparent within the newness of the emerging technological revolution. Individuals and groups are acting with technology's potential in new and unforeseen ways, for example, through impromptu gatherings and events (Todd and Scordelis, 2009), hacking (Levy, 2010) and whistle blowing (Poitras, 2014). New technology's relationship with improvisation has significant implications. At a political level such improvisatory action, employing the Internet, has already contributed to major changes. During the events of what was termed the 'Arab Spring' (2011) (or as Robert Fiske puts it the 'Arab awakening' from the colonialist legacy of the Sykes-Picot Agreement), the world's media showed surprise at developments that took place in a highly improvisatory manner as, with the aid of social media, large numbers of people responded spontaneously, adapting to changing circumstances and organizing accordingly (for example, Tahrir Square, Cairo; Noujaim, 2013). Ongoing action of this type has contributed to the fall of five governments. Within this emerging picture, the potential agency of improvisatory organization remains highly socially and politically significant. The extent and potential of this activity have been signalled elsewhere by government reactions. Attempts have been made to directly prevent such difficult to control, spontaneous responses, facilitated through new media. There has been the shutting down of the Internet and blocking of mobile phone networks in Egypt, 2011; Myanmar, 2007; China, 2009; and the UK government has also explored ways to control social media following the England Riots, 2011 (during which, in response to a police killing, the usually highly territorial gangs of young people united and fought the police in London and elsewhere, and also caused widespread damage to property [Prasad, 2011]). Within the broader picture the lived experience of improvisation is revealed as cross-disciplinary and broader social and political themes become apparent. This in itself indicates the extent of improvisation's importance for learning and education.

Chapter 7

Learning

Improvisation-as-learning

The process of improvisation forms a continuum for learning. Within free improvisation's 'open-form' stylistic boundaries and musical language are not static; therefore, adaptability and developing knowledge are integral to successful individual and group activity. In this way the development of socio-musical relations and individual practice in free improvisation forms an ongoing learning opportunity – the not-predetermined activity leads to discovery and the emergence of something new. Reflecting this, a super-objective for the improviser can be to play effectively in a wide variety of contexts: '[…] what I've done, and continue to do, is try to improve, all the time, so that I'm able to speak in any kind of situation […] because it's also a thinker's game. So you want to be able to have the long-range thinking' (Mitchell, p. 6, l. 27). For Roscoe Mitchell improvisation remains a process that is tied to learning. What is expressed as 'long range thinking' is interpreted as developing ability to not only listen and contribute 'in the moment' but also to retain an overview of unfolding compositional structure; how momentary decision-making contributes to the whole. Progressing in successful practice forms a lifetime's activity that is tied to learning: '[…] I realised that if I didn't make it in music, I wasn't going to make it […] What I found is the only things that help you with music are the things that you really learn, the things that you don't really learn they're already out there haunting you, until you decide to really learn them' (Mitchell, p. 7, l. 18).

Real-time composing in music through free improvisation is characterized by immediacy in processing information; a deep conceptual knowledge of music; informed response; adaptability; compositional decision-making in inter-subjective interaction; understanding of collaborative processes; and the ongoing development of musical skill and knowledge. This very particular coalescing of skills and knowledge through group improvisation is significant for education. Margaret Donaldson describes how: '[…] some of the skills which we most value in our education system are thoroughly alien to the spontaneous modes of functioning of the human mind' (Donaldson, 1978, p. 15). Intelligence in improvisation is expressed through the activity's immediacy: '[…] what you're hearing is the flow of intelligence and thinking […] in these improvised music things, you're always hearing the intelligence and the intention regardless of what they're doing, you're always hearing it […]' (Lewis, p. 12, l. 20). '[…] you're communicating with one another directly' (Oliveros, p. 1, l. 43). Group improvisation provides an educational approach that seeks intelligence through the collaborative, not-predetermined activity.

During the last hundred years or so, the intellectual development of children has become better understood as intimately connected with emotional development (Freud, 1975; Kleine, 1993; Rogers, 1988; Winnicott, 1982); however, the manner in which understanding has transferred to education, in pedagogy and at the institutional level is inconsistent. Engagement with group improvisation in music and drama has the potential for undifferentiated intellectual and emotional learning, engaging the 'whole-self' through embodied activity. Improvisation is not just *learning about* intellectual-emotional development, but forms experiential intellectual-emotional *learning through doing*. Acknowledging the emotional and intellectual working together, as unified experience, has now become better understood, and Flow contributes to this. 'Flow' theory (Csikszentmihalyi, 1991) is an optimal state of unified high-level functioning through immersion in activity, the 'quality of experience as a function of the relationship between challenges and skill'. Improvisers commonly refer to such an experience as being 'in the zone' or 'in that place'. A number of studies have explored Flow as a feature of improvisation in jazz (for example, Hytonen, 2010; MacDonald, Byrne and Carlton, 2006). Improvisation's open form provides for this expression of intellect and emotion, the 'whole-self'; in this way intuitive understanding is valued, together with musical skills and other knowledge, in a unified manner (see Chapter 8).

It is within the 'socio-musical' setting (Lewis) that free improvisation forms learning: without an external score people improvising create through developing and negotiating relationships in the group, the choices made lead to the music. As the socio-musical process of improvisation is found in different ways across cultures, within idioms and styles throughout the world, this has profound, far-reaching cultural implications for broad educational aims. Pervasive, adaptable socio-musical improvisation can reflect the complexity of cultural identities within contemporary pluralistic societies. In the current cultural, political contexts arising through globalization, improvisation provides a vital educational resource. But how is improvisation realized within the social-musical setting? *'[...] those musicians themselves who are extraordinary – extraordinary not for the usual reasons, or in addition to the ordinary reasons; they've been together for a long time, they are a community, they come out of the community, they're very generous with each other [...] their music was the place where you're supposed to have these generosities'* (Lewis, p. 14, l. 5). The description is of an improvising ensemble and Lewis highlights the ethical propensity of improvisation. *'The next step here was to realize that it was about personal transformation – you would have to come to the improvisation as a changed individual and that you transformed yourself as the kind of human being who can operate in a large space and a lot of that was quite prosaic and obviously, if everyone's playing all the time the textures are not going to be that diverse. So that means, realistically, in a large group you're going to spend most of your time listening'* (Lewis, p. 10, l. 2). The description provides a useful framing for conceptualizing the activity in educational contexts – learning here takes place, principally, through group activity. Group learning through collaborative creativity becomes an important theme for improvisation-as-learning and a number of theories support this. Psychologist Lev Vygotsky (1987) describes the *development of learning as a social process* – a fundamentally important proposition for the organization of education and one that is realized in improvisation activity. So too, Sawyer has written about the nature and value of creativity that is developed in groups and the relation of this to improvisation (Sawyer, 2008, 2011). The idea of 'distributed creativity' (Glaveanu, 2014; Schroeder, 2012) for education, rather than creativity as 'individual genius' provides a helpful articulation of free improvisation as learning activity: creativity is located in the group activity, between participants in the environment, over time. The benefits of group activity as learning question the assumed reliance upon individual competition as an overriding, determining educational strategy. Describing the process of learning in improvisation as distributed creativity helps to move from the need to emphasize a single composer's 'work' and to acknowledge the potential of the socio-musical process at work.

Improvisation-as-learning is embedded in Nicols' interview. She emphasizes the importance of John Stevens' role in free improvisation's development in London. '*John [...] was one of the founding pioneers of free improvisation in Europe. You could almost look at anybody in the European improvised music scene and they've been influenced by John, if not directly by playing with him then by playing with people who did play with him. And all the musicians played with him – Evan, Derek [Evan Parker, Derek Bailey] [...] he was just phenomenal, he really was. He took rhythm in particular to a whole new area. Previous to that you would hear drummers who had fantastic time, you know playing metrically, and they'd throw it all over the place, but as soon as you took the meter away they'd often sound like beached whales, you know floundering about on dry land and John devised ways to keep that (sings: bip, ba, bip, bap, clap, bap) that thing that you hear that is so kind of [...] people take for granted that kind of, that rhythmic feel in free improvisation, but really it was not that usual [...]*' (Nicols, p. 3, l. 14). As a kind of peer mentor, Stevens informally shared knowledge, encouraging and influencing others – the sort often found in jazz and other music (Berliner, 1994), reflecting the apprentice model and learning 'on the job'. In this way Stevens' innovations in free improvisation influenced musician colleagues and others who subsequently played with those musicians. Nicols describes a central aspect of Stevens' innovative approach, concerning understanding of time in music. '*[...] if you think of Ornette [Ornette Coleman] time – no changes, that whole thing of taking away the harmonic and exploring what it would be like to play free, with time, but still keeping an actual pulse, then John and people like John saying, OK well what would it be like to take everything away. It's an evolutionary process, and I suppose classical music has its own evolutionary process. Free improvisation, coming from the jazz tradition, is a natural evolution coming from the different periods in the history of jazz*' (Nicols, p. 4, l. 16). Developments in free improvisation extend the understanding of time beyond reference to the metronome alone. Interpreting time more fluidly, as qualitative time, (or kairos), offers further musical possibilities, for example, in education, building pieces by focusing entirely on creating an imaginative *soundscape* (Paynter, 1970) rather than, say, prioritizing pitch and meter. There is a 'push and pull' between meter and the more fluid interpretation of time in creative music. Innovators John Stevens (SME) and Eddie Prevost (AMM, 1997), both drummers, also retained their more conventional 'jazz' playing in different ways alongside their personal developments in free improvisation in which the approach to rhythm departed from 'playing time' or principally adhering to strict meter.

Developing Improvisation-as-learning

The link between improvisation's musical, creative, social features and learning is a rich opportunity for formal education. However, as Bailey suggests: 'Improvisation [is] [...] the most widely practised of all musical activities and the least acknowledged and understood' (1992, p. ix). This effectively describes a disparity between what is practised in music and what is taught in formal education. As traditional education has not acknowledged improvisation's potential in music, a cyclical self-perpetuation has occurred through which those who pass through music schools, and elsewhere, have done so without gaining experience and knowledge of improvisation practice. The interviewees' development as improvisers has largely been through autodidactic practice (Chapter 9), 'learning on the job' and non-formal means. Several interviewees pointed to shortcomings in education's understanding of improvisation. *'Some years ago I was asked to give a sort of lecture demonstration to the* [name removed] *for their new Improvised Music Module. That was run by* [name removed] *not an improviser, of course, they usually aren't. And they were interested students and they knew a bit, but what I found amusing was that to get their credit for the module they had to write a graphic score, which was then assessed by the tutor, you know this was the improvisation module [...]'* (Butcher, p. 14, l. 19). Clearly, institutions require the benefit of experienced, knowledgeable practitioners – but more than that an embedded understanding of improvisation needs to be reflected by the structure of courses and staffing decisions (for example, as it has been at Mills College and University of California San Diego). The extract illustrates an over reliance on text as an indication of achievement in improvisation activity. The idea that the improvisation module is assessed by means of an assignment to write a graphic score, while tautological, also points towards what may be perceived as the greater difficulty of assessment of improvisation in education. This is sometimes offered as a reason for improvisation's absence. Assessment is a highly emotive topic, particularly for creative practices. However, this 'difficulty' reflects pedagogical inexperience rather than an innate problem to do with the assessment of improvisation activity. All educational institutions concerned with creative processes address assessment. For example, numerous, respected fine art schools in the UK are known for their histories of developing experimental practice and, of course, all apply assessment procedures in order to meet institutional requirements – through the grading of students' work in degree shows and so on. Assessing creative practice is always contentious and ongoing debate is not only desirable but essential, however *experienced practitioners with pedagogical expertise* have knowledge in order to apply appropriate criteria that are sensitive to the group and individual processes at work (Mills College, Sonic Arts Research Centre, Ramapo College, Newcastle

University and others have used formal assessment procedures for improvisation activity). Criteria for the assessment of improvisation can be developed with the acknowledgement that, beyond solo, it is a group activity and how, within that, individuals contribute to the group's activity and organization. Assessment needs to acknowledge the ongoing *process* and employ dialogical forms that include self and peer assessment. With the danger of assessment becoming a 'blunt tool' and of 'grade chasing' running counter to authentic learning, it is also necessary to reemphasize the place of trust in the process of free improvisation that supports the experiential group learning. For this reason it is important to ensure that the design of assessment supports and does not counter the process of improvisation's development.

Experienced practitioners teaching in academia have the capacity to transform perceptions of improvisation. However, there is a shortfall between the need for experiential learning in improvisation and the necessary skills and experience within the faculties for its implementation. '*So when I left my home town and went to school, went to* [name removed] *they had a music improvisation class, and that was the first time I encountered the notion that there was a thing called improvisation that you could study, in a systematic way and the class was utterly dreary and boring and it immediately became the class that it was hard to drag yourself to. And then Anthony Braxton came and taught a workshop and it was a revelation and I thought OK this is what I want to do – my first encounter with improvisation in any rigorous or systematic way was this horrible class, where the guy who taught it never improvised at all*' (Ostertag, p. 12, l. 1). The two accounts of academia (Butcher, Ostertag) in the UK and US represent experiences that are decades apart, yet both reflect institutional inadequacy in addressing the true potential of improvisation. Ostertag's description demonstrates how experienced and pedagogically aware practitioners can effectively bridge the gap between formal education and the practice of improvisation. The knot presented in a number of the interviews by the relationship between formal education and enacted improvisation is cut through with the inclusion of genuinely experienced, practitioner-improvisers in places of education.

For Honsinger the discovery of improvisation comes in high contrast to his former experience of formal music education. '*I went to New England Conservatory back in 67, 68. It was a disaster*' (Honsinger, p. 7, l. 7). '*So we get to this* [theatre] *space and I said well what do you want us to do? And he said I don't know just do something. I said OK, so we start and it was: 'Wow'. I said I guess I'm going to leave this classical business behind – from one moment to another I decided, yes this is my life. So just a little understanding made me decide, yes this is what I do, so … I discovered my life, which is quite amazing*' (Honsinger, p. 7, l. 45). But why is there such a gulf between the experience of music in formal education and that of improvisation? Improvisation's openness can provide for the creative expression of individuals, groups and movements, as a vehicle for 'voice'. This is very dissimilar to the traditional educational focus on the composer and the work and concomitant thinking that frames the role of musician. The legacy of 'classical' music has dominated educational thought and practice and has been heavily supported in terms of educational and artistic funding (in a way that does not reflect its minority status). But there are also numerous accounts of improvisation as an important practice within 'classical' music's development (Barnhill, 2006; Goehr, 2004; Berkowitz, 2010), as Mitchell puts it: '*all the great composers improvised*'. With the prizing of authenticity, rigour and truthful interpretation in 'classical' music, the absence of improvisation is inconsistent. Goehr's account of the development of the fixed work's dominance helps explain improvisation's marginalization, as do the developments towards music copyright and music as fixed reproducible consumer product (Attali, 1985; Benjamin, 1936).

Education's institutionalized resistance to improvisation is compounded by the influence of the music industry's predominant concern for fixed product. The goal of encouraging a limitless consumption of music as product leads to a complex relation with the process of improvisation – one in which improvisation has been fundamentally marginalized. The broad concerns of the economy for product and consumption have been increasingly reflected in education – Michael W. Apple has put it in this way: '[...] freedom in a democracy is no longer defined as participating in building the common good, but in living in an unfettered commercial market, in which the educational system must be integrated into that market's mechanisms' (1998, p. 146). Educational disinterest in the social process of improvisation is, in part, an outcome of the way economic aims have become reflected by educational practice. In the UK for example the increased 'corporate' ethos in education is evidenced by the 're-branding' of schools as 'academies' and incentives for industry involvement, the growth of 'accountancy culture' in educational planning, the increased emphasis on vocational courses and business studies in schools and so on. However, improvisation-as-learning's value for music in education lies in its process; in much the same way as drama employing improvisation has been successfully employed as an educational tool. The 'socio-musical location' is the site of learning in improvisation: that which transpires between participants provides the focus for developing work and learning.

Although many kinds of music feature improvisation, it is often conflated with, and thereby limited to, 'jazz' and this can lead to a confusion and misunderstanding for education. Improvisation is a broad phenomenon and, reflecting this, *free* improvisation does not rest on one style of music; its development can encompass many practices and styles. The experience of jazz provides some lessons for free improvisation in education. Jazz education tends to focus on a narrow band of music (typically developments in the 1950s and 1960s) and in practice tends to not represent the breadth of even that music (for example, early jazz, free jazz). Prouty (2008) describes jazz improvisation in education in this way: '[...] formal instructional systems in jazz improvisation are frequently criticised for leading to just the opposite result, limiting individual improvisational choice and having a stultifying effect on performance [...]'. Mantie's (2008) study of jazz in education in the USA is also critical of the way improvisation is situated, describing improvisation as '[...] a neglected aspect in jazz education [...]'. While considered important, the idea of originality and experiment associated with improvisation troubles 'The codification requirements of the educational system [...]'. Mantie identifies inadequate teacher training and 'codification that distorts' as problematic areas of jazz education. But, in relation to improvisation, are these causes or symptoms of a deeper institutional resistance to the music's improvisational nature and characteristics? Henry Threadgill (in Fischlin, 2011) explains it in this way: *'I'm gonna get ahead of your question because this all goes to the idea of the word "jazz", and to what has happened in schools and universities that try to perpetuate jazz because they've forgotten the complete history. That history has something to do with the aesthetics of the art. When you go back to the very beginning of so-called "jazz" it's an independent thing created by each individual and that's the way it's supposed to be made. If you go and study music in India there's a way it's made; in Bali there's another way that it's made; and there's a way that it's broken down in Europe. That's the way it's made – and yet we brought the European method over to America and tried to impose it on so-called "jazz music", which is dead wrong.'* A significant part of the way jazz is created stems from the openness to improvisation. This, once again, illustrates the disjunction between successful practice in the world and what is taught. Prouty writes, 'Power, in the narrative of jazz "learning" of the language of the music stands sharply at odds with institutional study'. In this way it is little wonder that education 'sanitizes' (Nicols) jazz through standardization and repetition. The parts of jazz that appeal to traditional educational aims and structures become emphasized – large groups reading parts, grading instrumental technique and so on, with consonance and sophistication being prized. The downplaying of improvisation in jazz education narrows that music's broader creative educational potential. There is a danger that the preservation of existing educational practice takes priority over what can actually be addressed and learnt in the process of improvisation. Butcher's account of the graphic score for assessment of free improvisation illustrates how readily education can similarly 'distort' a form to suit its ends. Improvisation throughout the world is also far more diverse and complex than that suggested by the jazz/education dichotomy alone (Nettl and Russell, 1998; Bailey, 1992). The consideration of improvisation in its broader sense, as a human interaction, informs and questions the nature of successful learning and teaching across the curriculum. In this way improvisation and its features can be a tool for critiquing the nature of broader aims in education, for example: How is emotion being situated and valued in teaching? How is the inescapably social dynamic of activity being actively engaged and reflected upon? How are cultural differences becoming acknowledged through practice in education? And, indeed, how creative is the learning activity?

As we have seen, a criticism of jazz education is that it has contributed to a standardization of practice, emphasizing reproduction of a limited part of that music's history, privileging what Anthony Braxton (1985) describes as 'stylization'. A challenge for free improvisation in education is to retain its vital heterogeneous character by remaining open to different practices and cultures. *'... an improvisation course at music school and they were playing FMP and Incus* [record labels specialising in improvisation] *and that's how he first encountered it and it was part of their course of instruction ... I heard his first record, which was him with a tenor player and a drummer and it sounded like Tony Oxley, Derek Bailey and Evan Parker. It's really odd putting out your first record sounding so much like other people because in our day that's the last thing you'd attempt to do. You'd be mortified to think that anybody would think you sounded like anybody else. For them it was kind of an aim'* (Butcher, p. 16, l. 17). One obvious but important difference between jazz and free improvisation is FI's absence of a stock set of 'tunes' with which jazz musicians develop approaches and perform – the 'standards'. Without this shared repertoire there is always the opportunity for something new, generated between the players. There is an increasing body of exemplary free improvisation recordings (on, for example, Emanemdisc, Incus Records and a large number of other labels); however, it is the process generated by individuals in group playing that provides the focus for education and *learning by doing* – the opportunity to make something new, together. A perspective of the history of free improvisation is necessarily balanced by an acknowledgement of the importance of individual voices in the development of the music. In any creative field, awareness of what has been done previously provides useful information, but the creative work is in producing, rather than reproducing, as in fine art in which *practice* is tacitly understood to be very different from the study of its *history*. The idea of 'voice' is complicated, as effectively instrumental techniques and playing approaches can be traced across communities and cultures and all musicians have influences. Free improvisation was initiated by players within a field of collaborative activity who developed adaptable instrumental approaches and techniques that were responsive within the music's openness. Examples are Derek Bailey: guitar, Evan Parker: saxophone, John Stevens: drums, Tony Oxley: drums, Han Bennink: drums, Peter Brotzmann: saxophone, Barry Guy: double bass, Hugh Davies: built instruments, Paul Rutherford: trombone, Keith Rowe: guitar, Eddie Prevost: percussion, Jamie Muir: percussion, and there are numerous others. As with all music, significant innovations become part of the pool of knowledge, and learning in free improvisation balances an awareness of what has gone on previously in the field with personal, individualized development. For education, grounding free improvisation activity in inclusive, creative group learning activity provides the orientation in which participation and group development is prioritized. In this way the socio-musical focus leads to a living aesthetic, rather than a concern for reproduction.

Improvisation and Teaching

Improvisation raises good questions about the role of the teacher, for example: if the activity is described in terms of a self-organizing system, a laudable educational aim, what are the implications of this for teaching? The focus for teaching in improvisation is with creating the conditions for learning activity to occur rather than prescribing the content. Issues of direction and accomplishment exist in balance with autonomous creative participation through which musical decisions are made – allowing for the emergent within improvised music activity is a pedagogical aim. In Chapter 6's example of improvisation in basketball, self-organized interaction is functional for the development of group learning: *'we'll let them work it out'*. The point at which the team is losing becomes an opportunity for the development of group learning. Planning for content and method that is not overly directed or determined by a coach, leader or teacher can require a shift in understanding of the role. This requires acknowledgement of the potential ability of all those involved in guiding the process together, through interaction, developing flexible frameworks in the process. This also requires thinking that is attuned to 'allowing learning' to occur (Rogers, 1988) and this is approached through trust: '[...] trust that they are going to do the right thing and that you don't really have to do anything [...]' (Lewis, p. 6, l. 16). The absence of intervention by the coach, or teacher is informed by awareness of the developing socio-musical activity in a session. Importantly, activity utilizing improvisation involves an '... expression of trust in their ability to work it out for themselves'. Trust forms a mutual contract through which activity develops.

The role of the teacher is therefore one of supporting and guiding the autonomous group learning process with its distinct cultural/inter-cultural identity and relationships. 'There is something phenomenal about a group of different experiences, making really strong performance in music' (Nicols, p. 10, l. 14). Groups can be nurtured through the introduction of frameworks and, retaining the autonomous character of the activity, these are also best developed collaboratively '[...] there was a big emphasis on getting people to go inside of themselves [...]' (Mitchell, p. 5, l. 17). For example, individuals can be assigned the task of introducing a simple idea that will ignite activity – a signal, an image, a piece of text, a video, a piece of artwork, a story, a timbre, a pitch, a rhythm, a feeling, an action and so on, with the aim being to initiate whole group engagement. Simple ideas communicated well provide the freedom for response. As the process of improvisation successfully unfolds, these ideas may become elaborated, or not, having served their purpose. The group's playing provides information for how future pieces may be initiated or directed. In educational contexts there is the danger that, as writing may become involved, the framework's importance overtakes that of the group improvisation activity – the process of learning by doing. Of course, teachers require evidence of learning and the written contributes to this. However, audio and video recording provide for reflective learning and may contribute to assessment – as Berliner (1994) points out, recording has been a formal educational tool since 1917.

There are a number of accounts of developing free improvisation in higher education contexts, including Lewis (2000); Schlicht (2008); Ford (1995); Allen (2002), and in these the underlying principles of improvisation are relevant for different settings. The approaches and exercises found in Stevens (1985); Oliveros (2005); Schaffer (1992); Paynter (1972); Agrell (2007); and Dennis (1970) can be interpreted across age groups and levels of experience. While a resource of ideas creates confidence, in my experience it is misleading to suggest that the improvisation activity can be carried out by means of a guidebook, or stock set of exercises. Each group is unique, and it is this that provides the source material for learning and teaching in improvisation – remaining true to the self-organizing potential. A handbook, by its nature, will tend to suggest a generic approach. In the example of educational exclusion in Chapter 3, I embraced and encouraged improvisation with spoken word and decks, as well as a range of other instruments, incorporating the musical interests of those involved. This led to successful activity, in a formal context, employing improvisation – the ideas found in Oliveros, Stevens and elsewhere were not used in that setting. The mode of operating is indicated by the cultural interest and character of the group; overly prescribing a way to teach improvisation can, paradoxically, lead to a denial of the central autonomy of free improvisation. The self-generating activity in the process of improvisation is both the means and the end. For teaching, thinking about the social dynamic and cultural context of activity is rewarding – identifying and encouraging the potential of all those involved enables the process. As Murray Schafer (1977) has suggested, '[…] don't try to shape a philosophy of music education for others, shape one for yourself'. So too, Heidegger's (1968) idea of a holistic, educational 'open-space', in which the learner's engagement is prioritized over pre-specified teaching, is reflected in the realization of improvisation activity. Importantly, the teacher's *lived experience* of improvisation provides insight and confidence for its implementation in learning.

In 'Psychological constraints on improvisation', Jeff Pressing describes how in improvisation:

> the knowledge base will include musical materials and excerpts, repertoire, sub-skills, perceptual strategies, problem-solving routines, hierarchical memory structures and schemas, generalized motor programmes, and more. It is a cauldron of devices collected and fine-tuned on the basis of optimizing improvisatory performance. One task of pedagogy is to systematise these elements, but this systemization can never be complete; individual differences in sub-skills and orientations to artistic output require that programmes of optimal operation be individually tailored.
>
> (Nettl and Russell, 1998, p. 53)

There is a logical appeal in the list of skills and knowledge that suggests these may be discreetly addressed in order to improvise. But what does this really mean for practice and teaching? While to 'systematize these elements' will appeal to conventional educational thinking, does any of this hold true for teaching that seeks to address the true diversity and breadth of practices found in the lived experience of free improvisation? Evan Parker has rightly suggested that improvisation can be carried out, or thought about, but that you cannot rehearse improvising. The dividing of the whole can negate the experience. Improvisation questions an inherent problem in much educational thinking, one of fragmentation (Small, 1977). Human beings don't improvise in a broken down manner because it is not possible. Of course, it is possible and useful to reflect on the parts of a performance, but that is a separate activity from improvisation. Tonight I perform with a quartet – we have never played together. While I am intrigued by the individual's approaches, the group music will emerge through a commitment to 'crossing the line' that is to participate in the activity, at one time, together, and by remaining in that mode for the duration of the concert. Only through 'jumping in' will improvisation become experienced. For this reason the group activity is the primary social, pedagogical vehicle. I'll return to this theme later in the section on Activity Theory.

Participation in large group activity is instrumental in the structure of daily school life: sports, daily school assembly, swearing allegiance to the flag and so on. Free improvisation's *'Nurturing what you do with others'* (Mitchell, p. 7, l. 33) provides an opportunity for large group participation: one that embodies autonomous creative expression rather than competition or subservience. Its characteristic autonomous participation significantly reverses 'top-down' models still found in much education, as improvisation requires and values individual's contributions. With the offer of responsibility, free improvisation can contribute to a more democratized education, with students as 'participants rather than recipients of curriculum'. In this way students' develop a conception of *learning as autonomous action* as they determine the development and outcomes of sessions. The 'ownership' of learning through the use of improvisation processes can also be highly effective for inclusive education. *'Let's say if you've got a kid and you don't expose them to all kinds of music and everything when they're growing up, and they're just left to tune into what the going product is, a lot of times people can get lost'* (Mitchell, p. 3, l. 2). Additionally, the experience described in Chapter 3 suggested that stress and anxiety in education can become diminished by the improvisation learning process that calls for assertive decision-making on the part of students. A World Health Organisation (1986) study showed how stress is linked to the absence of control in the work processes. As improvisation empowers learning it can also contribute to improving self-esteem.

The idea of using improvisation in the classroom may be daunting for inexperienced teachers; for some, improvisation activity may evoke images of a class 'out of control'. However, in terms of what is referred to as 'classroom management', or the concern for behaviour, the pedagogical process introduces autonomous decision-making in an integrated group fashion – this itself forms group self-management. The example provided in Chapter 3 is of extremely challenging students who began to find success in learning with the help of a pedagogical approach employing improvisation in a number of ways. The group developed a cooperative work ethos through the activity. The activity valued their ideas and action and all had chosen to participate – in other words, they had 'a stake' in it and this was central to the process. Productive work and 'behaviour' followed from this shift in responsibility. Employing improvisation offers a deepening understanding of the teacher-student power relationship. The shared willingness to allow for the unknown in improvisation engenders trust in the group. It is an open opportunity for individuals to take responsibility for the development and successful outcome of the lesson, together, and this can be a big stride. For example, a teacher may effectively make use of silence and discover how students create with reference to that silence. In school contexts, in which students as obedient recipients of instructions is often the norm, encouraging students to take responsibility for what happens in the room can be profoundly empowering – particularly when taking place in an ongoing, developing manner. Unsurprisingly, as an enhanced sense of responsibility is sustained, this carries over to other lessons and personal life (see Chapter 3).

Improvisation in education aligns with the broad term 'Activity Theory' (Vygotsky, 1987). AT encompasses the complexity of social processes, rather than reducing phenomenon to its parts and thereby distorting it. For improvisation in education AT reflects the entire situated group learning process and the different overlapping musical and social systems that are inevitably entailed in the activity. In other words, for education, this perspective acknowledges the simultaneous aspects of improvisation activity – which includes group and individual accomplishment. Within this perspective, Vygotsky's (1987) theory of *social processes as originators of mental processes* clarifies group improvisation's potential for education. The context for learning in free improvisation is group activity. *'[…] it was one of those situations where there was a oneness in the group and somebody came up to me afterwards and said: "You don't really need an instrument do you, it just sort of seeps out of your pores",* (laughs) *and there was something in that, that the oneness with the group came out in a oneness with the instrument and when I think, I was using my voice and my body in a way that just communicated, whatever I did, and that was the moment'* (Beck, p. 11, l. 8). The challenge of collective music making through not-predetermined free improvisation involves inter-subjectivity whereby the inter-mental is internalized by the individual. The not-predetermined character of the form and the inter-subjective, group-learning process provide a pedagogical axis. In improvisation, learning takes place by collaboratively creating music in 'real-time' and it is this that provides the teacher with the form and material content of the lesson. Additionally, Vygotsky's Zone of Proximal Development (ZPD) theory: the 'space between' participants' developmental and potential developmental level, can offer a conceptual mapping of how sequences of sessions may progress. For example, a group that has established a way of successfully working together can then be given the challenge to find new ways of creating music, developing fresh ideas and different strategies, extending knowledge and understanding of how the group may operate together. The addition of new players or combination introducing contrasting experiences, can provide such an impetus for group development.

The teaching activity has a reciprocal improvisatory character. Adaptability, responsiveness and creativity are valued features of teaching – knowing how to guide and contribute to the autonomous learning process and when to remain quiet, to 'let learn'. While the focus here is with teaching and improvisation in music, the implications created by this can be interpreted at a broader level, for pedagogy as a whole. Within their day-to-day practice, teachers are required to improvise. Livingstone and Borko (1989) found that experienced teachers improvised in every class. Being alive to the possibilities thrown up by students' responses, each day, in all subject areas leads to 'good practice' – teaching benefits by valuing its improvisational dimension. Students' responses essentially contribute to not only the here and now, but also forthcoming lesson design and schemes of work. Rather than conceiving teaching and learning in separated ways, they can be more productively understood as interrelated, dependent systems (Bateson, 1979; Maturana and Varela, 1987) linked in the process of improvisation (see Chapter 8).

Sawyer (2007) describes the four areas of common knowledge found in experts (doctors, lawyers, architects, scientists and so on) as: *deep conceptual understanding, integrated knowledge, adaptive expertise* and *collaborative skills* and identifies these descriptors as those required by improvising musicians. The development of expert skills and knowledge in different professional domains employs learning environments (inquiry, problem and project based) that are improvisational in character. Rather than compartmentalized, de-contextualized knowledge, Sawyer argues, education needs to focus on collaborative, open-ended problem solving through which students gain the four areas of common knowledge found among experts. Sawyer also argues for the improvisational character of such learning to be reflected in the pedagogical approach to teaching across subject areas.

Learning from Performance

Sharing an *'unrepeatable moment'* (Butcher) is a special experience for both performers and audience. For learning, witnessing how the process of improvisation unfolds for those with experience contributes to developing understanding. *'I learnt so much from going to gigs. You know I was free improvising before I knew there was a scene. There was just something in the air. You know I was trying to copy the weird bits off* Mothers of Invention *records with my brother. Or copying bits of Stockhausen electronic music. What I realized I was kind of doing was free improvising. I'm talking about when you're 16, 17, 18 this sort of thing. And then through listening to jazz in London – I listened to people like Derek* [Derek Bailey] *and realized there were people who dealt with these issues in a very profound way. And it all came through gigs'* (Butcher, p. 17, l. 23). The uniqueness created by the unrepeatability of the improvisation event has been reflected by attitudes to recording in the early days of free improvisation. At that time the notion of recording the music was debated and there were those who vehemently believed that recording was an inappropriate denial of the extent and possibilities offered by the form's unique commitment to 'the moment', in a particular space, with a particular group of people (from a conversation with Philip Wachsmann). While learning about any music can be aided by the experience of hearing and seeing musicians play in real-time, witnessing musicians *create* the music at the point of performance helps develop a deeper understanding of the process. When I first attended free improvised concerts, I was taken aback by the very silent, almost church-like reverence of the audience in the upstairs room of a pub (at that time I was more familiar with rock audience behaviour where talking doesn't interrupt very loud performance). Gradually I became more aware of how that silence was an outcome of the attentiveness to the shifting detail within the unfolding musical events, of an active, participatory audience involvement. Ranciere's (2011) account of theatre and it's 'spectators' describes the audience as similarly active: 'It requires spectators who play the role of active interpreters, who develop their own translation in order to appropriate the "story" and make it their own story. An emancipated community is a community of narrators and translators'. The audience in free improvisation experiences the players' unfolding negotiation in performance while creating music in real-time. As the music becomes revealed, audiences become engaged in a more participatory manner and this can contribute to the continuum of learning.

Improvisation and the Developing Musician

The ethos embodied in the music business is so intransigently concerned with music as consumer product that the process of improvisation, although it may lead to such product, is given little credence. However, improvisation makes a significant contribution within different forms of music making. Butcher describes the way in which improvisation has been important in commercially successful music. '[...] *in the last say fifty years of popular music making, improvisation has been an important element. What that's been used for through rehearsal, studio work to develop a finished product which doesn't contain much improvisation. But the process of making it from The Beatles up to hip hop music, improvisation will be a part of arriving at the end result*' (Butcher, p. 5, l. 42). Mitchell describes the benefit of being able to respond to difference within each performance of a written score, working with awareness of how: '[...] *every night's different, every minute is different*' and the need to respond to circumstances that continuously change (Mitchell, p. 13, l. 34). For the developing professional musician, pragmatic, vocational concerns understandably come to the fore, but the idea that improvisation is unimportant for those with ambition in different music is misguided. More than being a special skill, improvising is a fundamental facility that will inform the developing musician's overall approach to playing and performing in different spheres of musical activity, improvising ability contributes to extending the musician's prospects. The ability to explore possibilities, 'find parts', adapt, contribute individuality, play inventively and fluidly without a written score, find ways to work confidently with diverse others and their music, as well as a deep conceptual awareness of how to be creative at the point of performing are all elements of improvisation and assets for aspiring contemporary musicians. Such knowledge and skills are developed through the experience of free improvisation. The ability to adapt to new circumstances at each performance also contributes to the resilience that is required of a working musician. Composers' increasing awareness of improvisation's potential within their work further demonstrates the need for the integration of improvisation within music education planning.

Improvisation, Resistance and Education

The themes arising from improvisation's link to marginalization, subjugation and exclusion have been repeatedly played out in education in different ways. Chapter 3's account provides an example of educational exclusion and the agency provided by improvisation. 'We are necessarily working against myths that deform us. As we confront such myths we also face the dominant power because those myths are nothing but the expression of that power, of its ideology' (Friere, 1996, p. 26).

Improvisation's exclusion from dominant education practice can be read as a means of preserving the status quo, thereby supporting hegemonic power, but the history of improvisation also demonstrates a close association with resistance, providing for the expression of subjugated groups that forms a challenge to such power. Examples of the link between improvisation and such 'struggle' include: Black Power and free jazz developments (Carles and Conolli, 1971); the Women's Movement and the Feminist Improvisation Group (Smith, 2004); the Association for the Advancement of Creative Musicians and African American self-determination (Lewis, 2008a); 'jam bands' and 1960s counterculture; Amon Düül and the renewal of post-war German identity (Amon Düül, 1969). The fluidity and adaptability of improvisation can provide for need, for expression that has not been formally legitimized in education. In this way improvisation's inclusion can contribute to furthering aims of education, and improve the quality of experience for all.

The African American experience provides a history of resistance and self-determination. The development of African American music, and its increasing popularity from the early 1900s, initiated the need for a more fundamental reassessment of improvisation's role in music, the influence of which can be traced through to the current wide range of research interest in improvisation (Chapter 2). The sociopolitical dynamic embodied within improvisation and composition in the USA is explored in George Lewis's important article: 'Improvised Music after 1950: Afrological and Eurological Perspectives' (1996); this work is a landmark in the field. It describes important historical themes of improvisation and has influenced the delineation of subsequent improvisation research and writing. '[...] the AACM's revision of the relationship between composition and improvisation lies on an unstable fault-line between the new black music and the new white music'. Contrasting accounts of the work of Charlie Parker and John Cage, Lewis explores the manner in which the social and institutional positioning of improvisation and composition reflects inequality and prejudice: 'new white music' being historically assigned as 'serious music', and 'art music', while 'new black music' has been assigned as 'jazz'. This theme is echoed by Anthony Braxton's reflections on negative criticism of his citing European influences such as Stockhausen in the development of his music, while at the same time it remains unquestioned that white musicians should be influenced by, for example, John Coltrane: 'I see it as racism'. Chicago's Association for the Advancement of Creative Musicians (AACM, with the motto: 'Great black music') has, for many, provided an exemplar of commitment to collective music practice, and Lewis' 'A Power Stronger Than Itself: The AACM and American Experimental Music' (2008) extensively documents this history of self-assertion, as Muhal Richard Abrams explains: '[...] we intend to take over our own destinies, to be our own agents, to play our own music' (Lewis, 2008). Improvisation's capability for representing different voices, made clear through the African American music of the twentieth century, has characterized its re-emergence.

'Articulating Perspectives of Improvisation for Education' (2008)

The final section of this chapter is a 'play-within-a-play': it broadens the discussion of improvisation and learning by outlining findings of the research project: 'Articulating perspectives of improvisation for education' (2008). This research explores accounts of improvisation in music for education. In the course of analysis, the unifying quality of free improvisation emerged as an over-arching theme. In this way the features arising from engagement with free improvisation point to what is described as *being*. *Being* is adopted as a preferred way of encapsulating these features of free improvisation. *Being* linked all of the emergent features for education and retained an emphasis upon their individual characters, without distortion through further categorization. The following four features: *Awareness, Unknown, Play* and *Social* emerged from accounts of professional practice in free improvisation for the purposes of contemporary educational practice. Anonymity was the norm for these interviews.

The method of inquiry and analysis within this section's research (2008) was Grounded Theory (Straus and Corbyn, 2007). The inquiry examined the process of free improvisation and synthesized ideas for development in education. Participants were improvisers, audience members, students, teachers and promoters. Participant observation and fourteen semi-structured interviews took place in conjunction with performance and rehearsal activity in the Bay Area, California, and while touring in the UK and Finland. The participants were asked to describe their perspective of free improvisation and a set of prompts was on hand; interviewees were supported in taking the interview in the direction they wished. Participant observation related to twenty performances that ranged from solo to improvising orchestras (including one with over one hundred and fifty performers). The Grounded Theory method involved three stages of analysis of the interview transcripts and diary of participant observation. These stages: *open coding, axial coding* and *selective coding* established features and themes of improvisation for education. The theme of *being* informed the phenomenological approach of the further, in-depth study of free improvisation (2013) that forms the basis of Chapters 5 to 9.

Awareness was referred to consistently in the interviews (2008). Different aspects of awareness were associated with free improvisation. There is that which has been described as of the 'moment' and the 'here and now'. The 'moment' can be seen as the place where free improvisation occurs: K: '*What I like is that you have to be there – and the music exists just then and there – that's the finest thing of it*'. Others described actively extending this awareness by different means: daily listening; meditation; developing a deepening of awareness; or practising t'ai chi through which: F: '*[...] the moment can be perceived as intensely as possible*'. While for some 'perceiving' was described as within the context of enacted free improvisation, for others this thinking extended towards the idea of 'body as instrument'. Developing, or 'heightening' awareness was seen as beneficial for the process of free improvisation. The emphasis on awareness is a response to the challenge of making music without predetermined structure. This includes descriptions of intuition's importance: J: '*Transcending the rational thought process, that's where it happens for me – being in that completely intuitive space*'.

The free improvisation form is not-predetermined and the music becomes realized in the process of playing together. Openness and the willingness to allow for possibilities is a central feature. Several interviewees emphasized this not- predetermined, or *unknown* aspect as important: T: '*I keep the unknown dimension first*'. In this interview, the 'unknown' was foregrounded, and the musician's role interpreted as that of conduit, to '*make the unknown known*'. For T the mystical connotation of this was inherent in the practice. But even without the mystical interpretation, in order to participate in free improvisation, openness towards working with the not known initiates the activity. This unknown quality was both a challenge and seen as an '*exciting and attractive feature*' (Rose). The agency offered by such an approach, that, through this unknown quality forms learning by doing, engaging intuitive understanding, emerges from analysis as a strong feature for education. Improvisation's unknown quality is reflected by MacDonald and Wilson's (2006) description of a 'mastery/mystery dichotomy', whereby jazz musicians identified soulful, ineffable qualities as important. The tension between this and other approaches to making music was expressed in different ways, for example: T: '*If you have a road map that tells you how to get somewhere then fine – when you get there leave the map and go and do your business – why I'm going there is for some kind of relationship whether with nature or with some people now that's the heart business. Leave the map we're going to do the heart to heart*'. 'Leave the map [...]' suggests improvisation and intuitive human interaction and the written plan a strategy that can negate the '*heart to heart*', the deeper level of human communication. For T the '*heart business*' is the purpose of such interaction. The 'unknown' feature of free improvisation can challenge expectations in learning. One interviewee described their attempts to include free improvisation within a university music course. H: '*They don't see it as a way of taking the shackles off and exploring what the relationships might be [...] They want a product [...] within a recognizable genre and form and that sort of thing [...] The notion of doing something that would be ephemeral, that would be interesting and give food for thought, in terms of an event which happens between people, is kind of too insubstantial, all too flimsy and naff for them to do with any degree of commitment [...] So I dropped it [...] and then some people said so why can't we actually do it!*'. Here, undergraduate students unfamiliar with the approach to music and learning reject the chance to engage in free improvisation. However, the theoretical re-introduction to improvisation leads students to want to '*actually do it!*' For university students in a different setting '*taking the shackles off*' was precisely what they were seeking through engagement with free improvisation: S: '*[...] an opening up of a cage I felt I have been in with classical music [...] a way for me to finally break out – a kind of release*'. And, O: '*[...] natural ways to make sound and make music [...] the frustration makes you want to break out. I think that's how all music started, as this kind of playing*'. Here the language used suggests a celebration of the potential of autonomous playing and also a return to something that relates more readily to the human condition. The freeing aspect was echoed by another interviewee's comment on music conventions: J: '*Sometimes you get stuffed up with the different rules, you know, that people before us have made up*'. Improvisation can also offer an alternative to orthodoxy.

Play emerged as a significant characteristic of free improvisation for education. The following interview extract comes from an internationally respected veteran improviser/composer. While the professional performance of music by means of free improvisation was regarded with great seriousness, the element of play was understood to provide for the process. J: '[...] *like being in a playground, you have some toys you can play with and you have some instruments you can use – it's like a game and many times it's like [...] to have fun'.* Saxophonist Ornette Coleman also referred to the significance of play: '*I didn't know you had to learn to play. I thought you had to play to play. I still think that'* (2007). When well understood in an integrated context, *play* engages participants' collaborative creativity in improvisation. Winnicott (1999) describes play's fundamental importance: 'It is play that is universal, and that belongs to health [...] playing leads into group relationships'. And, it is: '[...] creative apperception more than anything else that makes the individual feel that life is worth living and the opposite is more compliance'.

Drama in education demonstrates the broad utility of a process that integrates play and improvisation for learning – typically, drama games are employed within thematic work and of course performing drama with character and story forms 'a play'. Additionally, the music process' inclusion of play can offer accessibility for those who have not experienced success in more traditional academic ways. Play also provides an engaging introduction for free improvisation activity. For educational aims, the feature of *play* combines with the feature of *awareness*. With participatory activity comes a natural progression towards the focus upon listening and further developing experiential understanding of the group composing process. With judicious guidance, *play* and *awareness* can continue to work in tandem. There is a view, associated with Montessori education and elsewhere that very young children in their absorbed state of play are in a condition akin to meditation. Culturally it is our habit to move the child on to the next thing or activity; however, within this view, allowing the child to remain for an extended period encourages the development of the facility to learn. Extended, focused *awareness* and *play* lead to the facilitation of learning in the act of free improvisation. To this end, some interviewees also cited meditative practice as additionally helpful in furthering practice.

The *social* nature of free improvisation emerged as a significant theme for education: T: '*Does it include me or does it not – we're gonna feel that so you can't fake it [...] do they really care for me as a human being. See, that's what I want to know'.* The 'not-predetermined' character and the absence of a fixed norm allow for the openness to others; the form is inclusive regardless of cultural orientation and musical experience: M: '[...] *in a hospital context – so people come down from the wards [...] to get a chance to find out what is improvisation. Let's look at the very simple signs – so everybody play a long note – any note you want but play a long note [...] really place it in the context of everybody else'.* The inclusive social feature of improvisation activity was described as having the potential to provide extraordinary possibilities. C: '*The best thing about contemporary improvisation is its incorporative ability – its ability to handle difference – its ability to handle remarkable and drastic difference between performers, between groups and you have the potential to accept the difference while maintaining your own position which is completely outside – in a manner that's constructive and not debilitating to the other people [...]'.* Valuing the importance of the group and individuals' voices within that, being heard and at the same time shaping the group identity through playing, embodies an ethical approach. D: '*Have your music but allow other's music to exist [...] you have to make room for it and understand that they need to have their own music, I think that's important*'. Repeated examples of this inclusive/ethical aspect were also identified in the parallel participant observation research activity reflecting performances in a variety of improvisation settings. Q: '*[...] the music has a function of how to be a social being*'. Connections between the act of free improvisation and broader educational aims were voiced. One interviewee, working within higher education, articulated the process as being precisely about social interactions with the music as a '*mirror*' of that: H: '*[...] it's a way of thinking about relationships and how the people in the room are relating but the mirror side of that is that there might be a piece of music. And so you say these relationships are the way in which we make a piece of music*'. Through the features of *Awareness, Unknown, Play* and *Social*, free improvisation provides for the development of autonomous learning. With the need for decision-making, in order to 'make it happen', participants introduce their own parts, 'scores' and 'scripts', reflecting the experience, cultural orientation and preference of those involved; individual and group identity is reflected in the social process and musical outcomes.

The development of musical knowledge and skills in the process of improvisation is significant: many highly regarded musicians, known for distinctive and influential musical developments, have emerged through free improvisation activity (see Chapter 9 *Approaches*). It is also clear from the study that the significance of free improvisation for education goes beyond the learning of discrete music skills. The activity forms social and personal development and is relevant across educational settings. A specific application of free improvisation is in the development of listening skills. The theory and practice of successful listening, as a key ingredient in successful learning, across the curriculum, can be developed through free improvisation activity. Within the experiential, autonomous learning activity, work with the *unknown*, or not-predetermined offers self-determination that contributes to the broad development of the successful learner.

Although free improvisation is occasionally found within education, this has been the exception rather than the rule. However, teachers have been seen to highly value creativity within their role and at the same time young people are generally unafraid of improvisation (MacDonald and Wilson, 2005). Opportunities for trainee and qualified teachers to gain experience of free improvisation, exploring the potential for themselves, will contribute towards alleviating the negative cycle created by what some have described as their fear of improvisation.

Chapter 8

Body

Improvisation and the Embodied Mind

The body is a condition of improvisation. The theme of the *body* emerged from the interviews through ideas of listening, the physicality of playing, movement, spatiality and embodiment. This theme connects the other themes: *Process, Learning* and *Approaches*. Experienced performers 'inhabit' their activity in the development of practice, engaging the whole self. The theme of the body is central for grasping improvisation's potential in practice and education. While aspects of music are rightfully studied at a conceptual level, embodied practice takes place through enacted improvisation in which perceptual, motor and conceptual activity are not separated. As our bodies' presence is encompassing, the 'be-and-end-all' of our existence, discussion of the body, like being, is not without difficulty: it can be too easily essentialized. For this reason, for practice there can be wariness of theorising 'the body' and its academic connotations (for example, film director and artist Steve McQueen [2014] in discussing his films: *Hunger, Shame* and *Twelve Years a Slave*). However, for improvisation, better understanding the theme of the body leads to a truer picture. But what is the embodied mind in improvisation?

Oliveros's practice is informed by an advanced understanding of how the body perceives and responds, before the thought has taken place: '*[...] you're sounding before you know what you're sounding – there is delay [...] about half a second*' (p. 4, l. 40). '*In any sensory experience the body takes one tenth of a second. If you take part in highly specialized training it can be reduced to one eightieth of a second [...] Lester Ingber [1982] was my teacher for some time [...] It's really essential, it's really important. It's what is*' (p. 6, l. 6). Oliveros has developed in-depth knowledge of auditory processes and the characteristics of human response, and a systematic approach to developing understanding of the body's listening and responding abilities (Oliveros, 2005). '*As we sit here there's a lot of sound going on. It's about modes of attention: inclusive attention and exclusive attention and being able to negotiate both at once. Your focal attention is only momentary, it's only brief but then it can be sequential. But the sequence of focused attention, we're getting waveforms but we're also getting packets [...]. You have a kind of smooth analogue way of processing and you have digital packets. But exclusive attention when you are trying to narrowly focus on some detail, to understand speech for example, your attention is focused on the speech, in order to detect it, understand it, interpret it, all of those things. But sometimes we are focusing in that way and also it can be expanded to include whatever else is happening around*' (Oliveros, p. 6, l. 36).

The different kinds of listening, or *'modes of attention'* situate the body's importance in improvisation. *'The body knows what to do [...] this is a very important aspect to improvisation [...] allowing the body to lead'* (Oliveros, p. 5, l. 1). The refutation of the Cartesian mind/body divide initiated an opening in which the embodied mind has been theorized and better understood in different fields. Heidegger's (1962) phenomenological exploration of being, as undivided being-in-the-world, led to the need for better understanding of the body's nature. Although Heidegger's work resituates the body's centrality for understanding being the body per se is rarely directly discussed. Subsequently, Merleau-Ponty (1962) addresses this question by examining the phenomenology of what it means to perceive in *lived experience*. More recent developments in cognitive science, through neurology, form a connection to the phenomenology of Merleau-Ponty (1962) – opposing the mind/body divide and pointing towards the unified embodied experience of being.

In order to study the lived experience of improvisation in music, the phenomenological precept is: 'To return to the things themselves', in so doing the body is acknowledged as a condition of experiencing improvisation. Merleau-Ponty (2009):

> To return to things themselves is to return to that world which precedes knowledge, of which knowledge always speaks, and in relation to which every scientific schematisation is an abstract and derivative sign language as is geography in relation to the country-side in which we have learnt beforehand what a forest or prairie or river is.

In this way improvisation becomes understood through the body's experience. This is reflected by Oleyumi Thomas' idea: 'why I'm going there is for some kind of relationship whether with nature or with some people, now that's the heart business. Leave the map we're going to do the heart to heart' (2008). Rather than lost without a map, its overreliance can lead to a distancing from *what is*, or, the things themselves. Merleau-Ponty describes how it is the body that grasps the world; rather than the mind's development of concepts and rules *it is the body that organizes experience*. The focus on *embodied* improvisation leads away from the over-emphasis on the cerebral and inadvertent denial of our 'whole-self' and true capability.

The nature and significance of the embodied mind is becoming more fully understood in different ways. Lakoff and Johnson (1999) cite three studies of 'neural modelling as an existence proof for the embodiment of the mind'. These studies by Regier (1996); Bailey (1997); and Narayanan (1997) show how it is possible that parts of the brain used for perception and motor control can, in principle, be used for reasoning.

> The embodied-mind hypothesis therefore radically undercuts the perception/conception distinction. In an embodied mind, it is conceivable that the same neural system engaged in perception (or in bodily movement) plays a central role in conception.
>
> (Lakofff and Johnson, 1999, p. 37)

The embodied mind is also supported by the theory of autopoiesis. 'Autopoiesis' (Maturana and Varela, 1987) was coined as a way to describe the self-producing systems of bio-chemical cells. Through autopoiesis cognition is understood as an enacted process of embodied mind interrelating with environment, through which realities are constructed (rather than an objectified reality being understood by a detached mind). Autopoiesis contributes to understanding embodied improvisation as a feedback or self-organizing system (Chapter 6). The biological theory of autopoiesis has also been theorized in sociology, complexity theory, philosophy, psychology, education and elsewhere.

Embodied improvisation counters the belief in the cerebral as the source of all truth regarding existence, what Hubert Dreyfus (1991) referred to as the 'myth of the mind'. Dreyfus challenged early models of artificial intelligence (AI) by drawing from the understanding of being-in-the-world found in the work of Heidegger and Merleau-Ponty. Early models of AI reflected an outdated concept of reason, ignoring later developments in twentieth-century philosophy in which existence became understood as embodied. In free improvisation the absence of the predetermined score and the agency of embodied, autonomous action surpass the 'myth of the mind'.

The body's significance in improvisation can also be framed in a different manner: Foucault's (1972, 1980, 1991) explorations of power and knowledge situates the body's sociopolitical significance. His studies of sexuality, madness and political systems of control describe the body and its assignations. In this way the body in improvisation links to the themes of 'voice' and struggle within hegemonic power structures (Chapters 3, 4 and 7). Foucault has continued to influence a range of theorizing in which the body's sociopolitical contexts and meanings are central, which include feminist theory; gender studies; queer theory; and post-colonial studies, and these have also formed connections within improvisation studies in different ways (Tucker, 2008; Waterman, 2008; Boehmer, 1993; Butler, 1993).

Physicality and Spatiality

The theme of the body and improvisation also arises in the interviews in a pragmatic, workaday manner. '*I'm trying to create something that's of interest to the people sat in front of me, basically, and myself. If I see a bunch of bored faces, I've failed, you know. I normally bring a theatrical element to my playing, something a bit visual. I mean I don't overdo it but I mean I don't stand there like a statue and play and twenty minutes later step from the spot when I've finished, I don't play like that, I try to use the space*' (Tomlinson, p. 5, l. 46). For Tomlinson the music is also interpreted in a physical/visual manner – the '*theatrical element*' is unabashed in the communication of the performance. Tomlinson favours a pragmatic view that reflects decisions regarding professional performance practice and a working musician ethos. This contrasts with others, for example, as well as embodying performance Oliveros' perspective is highly analytical and conceptualized, through listening in particular ('Deep Listening') and, of course, both views reflect particular socially situated histories. And so the theme of the body emerges in different ways. While the discourse of free improvisation in the UK has often reflected an 'art-music' approach to performance, the 'seriousness' of which tends to elide the body in discussion, within free improvisation practice there are also broad connections to performing arts elements through which the place of the body has been acknowledged (for example, through the work of improvisers Lol Coxhill, Hugh Metcalf, Maggie Nicols and Paul Burwell).

The theme of the body in improvisation in music is grounded by the common use of spatial metaphors reflecting our 'grasping' of the world through the body (Lakoff and Johnson, 1980). Berliner's (1994) extensive study of 'thinking in jazz' is imbued with repeated reference to metaphors of spatiality and embodiment. He describes the process of negotiating harmonic development in improvisation as 'dancing' through the chords and how: '[…] veterans commonly experience the basic structure itself as stationary and themselves as moving through it. The form's successive harmonic chambers seem distinctly multi-dimensional […] the passage through has about it the feeling of time and space, as artists absorb and negotiate the aural features of their changing surroundings'. The common use of the term 'feel' in music in non-formal contexts, reflects embodiment and elsewhere Berliner emphasizes the way the music is grasped through 'feeling' suggesting a kind of proprioconception, or locating the body via the music in space. This reference to physicality and space was similarly present in Honsinger's description of the process of developing as an improviser: '*I do open my mouth and do very odd things. He's immobile, he was* [Derek Bailey]. *I'm very mobile in the sense of that's who I am, what I am*' (p. 4, l. 27). '*People were laughing. And I don't remember what I was doing but I'm sure it wasn't Derek they were laughing at – but it was just what I was doing in my movement that cracked them up […] When I discovered improvisation I also saw a retrospect of Buster Keaton […] and I'm absolutely sure that he influenced me completely […] from the beginning I was influenced by the theatre*' (Honsinger, p. 5, l. 5). The physicality of Honsinger's performance, his instrumental approach and his use of voice asserts: '*[…] that's who I am, what I am*'. The implicit action of Honsinger, Tomlinson and Johansson's musical physicality is demonstrated in movement and spatiality as well as awareness of the sociocultural context of their music performance. In these three cases awareness of this physicality, the implicit action, also leads to a challenge to expectations in the performer-audience relationship. The knowing physicality of Johansson's performance practice plays with ambiguity that hinges on the question of how movement relates to the sound's production. Johansson's performance creates a '*visualization of musical sound*'. '*A piano player has to stick to his instrument but my instrument is here, there and everywhere, more or less so I have to move a bit, and they say it is theatre but it is, I have nothing against it but […] I do visual acts but for me it is also music. I have a rubber cymbal. And people hear a big cymbal in their heads, sometimes and they see the cymbal. Not hearing, but they see the sound. I play with this seeing and hearing and turn it sometimes backwards round […] the visualization of musical sound – in some parts*' (Johansson, p. 8, l. 18). Exploring the spatiality of sound in this way also questions audience expectations as the effect of this additional level of communication leads to a commonly asked question: Is it music, theatre or something else? While the rationales differ there are nonetheless similarities to Honsinger's reference to movement and doing '*strange things*'. Through improvisation Johansson and

Honsinger have developed personalized responses to the performing situation, by way of their instrumental roles, as they extend their musical exploring to physical, visual, vocal and movement aspects in performance. Here *musical gesture* includes the physical/visual, extending the music's interrogation in performance. These extended physical aspects of embodied musical performance practice have developed through decades of playing in a wide variety of contexts. The inclusive openness to 'other' aspects in performance is also reflected in Nicols' practice, described in Chapter 6: '[...] if there's a baby, or if there's a bird, just be open to whatever's there is in that moment, in those unfolding moments, yes' (Nicols, p. 7, l. 41). In these accounts, music practice doesn't stop at the sound, it is not separated but acknowledges the spatial and environmental aspect of performance. While this is not for everyone, the open process of improvisation leads to this less bounded approach to performance.

Embodied Learning

The term *somatic theory* is associated with writers in whose work the body is important, for example: Merleau-Ponty, Lakoff and Johnson, Wittgenstein, Foucault, Austin and others. Somatic theory is also associated with Stanislavski's (1988) influential 'memory of emotion' technique for actors emphasizing physical action.

Somatic theory provides a common theoretical link between different strands of thought and practice that inform improvisation: in arts, psychology, philosophy, cognitive science, education, biology and linguistics. In discussion with dancers and theatre practitioners, *somatic practice* is commonly referenced, and research in improvisation in music can also benefit from a broader recognition of music as somatic. As we more fully understand the embodied nature of improvisation in music, so too the modes of studying and researching music can reflect embodiment's centrality. For practice, David Sudnow's (2001) self-study of learning to play jazz piano is, in effect, a case study of embodiment. The phenomenological study retains a focus on the 'first-order knowledge' of experience. In the process of learning, he examines the body's 'grasp' of things and for this reason the influence of Sudnow's phenomenological 'construction account' goes well beyond the study of music. For music it is also worth considering the particular instruments relation to embodiment. Moving from guitar to saxophone, I found the embodied relationship with the instrument to be the principal difference. Practising the saxophone involved a different kind of activity and attitude than when playing the guitar. Breathing produces the music and is the music, resulting from the changes in the internal contours of the player's body. While the sound producing mechanics of, for example, a piano are distanced from the player (the key activates a hammer that hits the string) the saxophone and the breath are more simply and directly connected. For better or worse, there is a different embodied dimension to playing a saxophone. Embodiment via the instrument becomes reflected in a variety of ways, for example, while Keith Rowe's (2001) innovative laying the guitar flat was, in part, a way of creating distance from his body, for some 'electronics' players a challenge can be to involve the body in a meaningful way that isn't 'distanced', disembodied or negated by the technology.

'*Because I'm a wind player it's something that is going to be quite naturally centred in the diaphragm area. So there's going to be feeling coming from that centre of my body, there's sort of, of a grrrrr! that really gets me and that's really what I want to do*' (Beck, p. 6, l. 27). Beck's extract describes the visceral aspect of his improvising as significantly motivational. In analysis and academic discourse, the joy arising through the physicality, or embodiment of playing, is easily overlooked, and here the emotion derived from the playing is clearly expressed: '*It's the speed and the speed is part of the excitement. To be able to do things almost ahead of yourself, that's really fucking exciting. I love that*' (Beck, p. 7, l. 19). The enjoyment experienced in improvising needs no justification; it is a worthwhile cause in itself and of course for education and learning this is an invaluable source of motivation.

The learning by doing found in improvisation is also termed *kinaesthetic learning*. '*I really feel space and energy in space, movement as well as sound. I'm less visually oriented*' (Oliveros, p. 4, l. 40). Views vary on the significance of what has become known as 'multiple intelligences' (Gardner, 2006) and the separate although connected 'learning styles' (visual, audio, kinaesthetic). However, kinaesthetic learning is under-acknowledged as education tends to be designed with a predominantly visual/audio bias. While research surveying the 'families' of learning styles (Learning Skills and Research Centre, 2004) is circumspect regarding direct applications for pedagogy, it suggests that 'a knowledge of learning styles can increase students' self-awareness regarding their strength and weaknesses as learners'. This contributes to learners' 'lexicon of learning' and their *metacognition* of how learning progresses by different means. Rather than over-emphasizing a 'style' of learning, acknowledging the capacity for learning by more than one means is more beneficial for learners and pedagogy. For example, soon after entering formal education, pupils typically experience a slump in creativity (Gardner); increased teacher awareness of kinaesthetic learning's potential may well improve this picture.

Improvisation develops knowing through doing within given contexts. In the theory of *situated cognition* understanding and reasoning are not separated from but tied to these specific social, environmental contexts. Via situated cognition the theme of body in improvisation links to Chapter 5's description of environment: '*[...] you're creating an environment, you're also interacting with one – so you have to pay attention*' (Lewis, p 1, l. 6). Knowing, as a verb, is interrelated with doing within an environment. This study acknowledges the intercultural community of practice of improvisation and examines knowledge of improvisation that has developed through its situatedness. In other words, knowledge of practice, represented in the interviews, is not divorced from the embodied, sociocultural context from which it has emerged: embodied improvisation that is enacted within an environment. Similarly, in the description of learning and improvisation in Chapter 3, the process develops within the specific environmental context of educational exclusion in East London. The situated nature of cognition deepens understanding of the need for wariness of generic, one-size-fits-all approaches to improvisation in education; rather, approaches can be developed that relate to the specific, situated context. Descriptions of 'jam sessions' in jazz histories in which the less experienced participate with advanced players in specific sociocultural contexts, performing in front of an audience, reflect situated cognition. Berliner (1994) describes how jam sessions could go on for days and tunes could be played for an hour. 'Sitting in' similarly encapsulates situated learning: *'The time I played with Coltrane, when he came up to me and said come up and play, and just shook my hand. To me that was just like, without a word being spoken, I got so many messages from that you know [...] I mean after the first set I was like trying to get packed up and get out of there. He said no, no, come on back, let's play some more [...] Like I said, I grew up in an environment where all you had to do was to show someone that you were interested in what they were doing and they would teach you'* (Mitchell, p. 9, l. 1). Developing understanding of how musicians learn needs to acknowledge the situated nature of this learning. It is not simply a case of adopting aspects that suit formal education and replicating these in that completely different context. The music itself is a response to the situated environment. The problems associated with the qualities of academic jazz and its relation to improvisation (Chapter 7) illustrate this through the lack of acknowledgement of the situated way in which the music evolved. Improvisation develops within its situated context.

Improvisation, Decision-making and Emotion

Working with immediacy engages intuitive responses. The term *intuition* is used here as the drawing on knowledge gained from experience without recourse to reasoning; intuition is a part of rather than separate from knowledge and we draw on intuition when immediate decision-making is necessary, when improvising. The relation of reasoning and emotional response is central to the discussion of the body in improvisation in music. The *'more emotional fields'* (Beck) and the role of emotion in music is often either celebrated or distanced. Attitudes stemming from traditions in European 'classical' music prioritize 'seriousness' – the legacy of this carries over into much experimental practice, although the nature of this 'seriousness' is most often not fully discussed. While emotion is often deemed counter to rational decision-making, this section describes how the reverse is the case.

Through a series of studies, Damasio's *Somatic Marker Hypothesis* (2000) describes how reasoning and decision-making processes are intrinsically connected with emotional response; describing some of this thinking helps illuminate the important connection between this and improvisation. Somatic markers are physiological signals that connect reasoning to emotion, informing and enabling decision-making. Damasio describes how without this connection to emotion, effective decision-making is not possible. There are two pathways for somatic markers: the 'body loop' in which the emotion is experienced and the 'as-if loop' in which the mind anticipates bodily changes in the process of decision-making. While emotions are often demoted or separated out as having a lesser importance, evolutionary emotions are sophisticated and reflect the complexity of our social being. We can better think of ourselves as having two overlapping evolutionary systems: the emotional survival system overlaid with our cerebral reasoning system. Through understanding of the interrelatedness of emotion and reasoning, the theory resituates the importance of the wide range of emotions. The legacy of the mind/body split has led to emotion becoming mistrusted and eschewed in much research, although more recently there has been a growth of interest in emotion and its significance is increasingly acknowledged across disciplines.

Damasio describes emotions as changes in both the body and brain in response to stimuli – physiological changes take place becoming emotions that tell the brain about the stimuli. Emotions become associated with outcomes informing decision-making, both consciously and unconsciously. But why is this important for improvisation in particular? The required immediacy of embodied improvisation takes us directly to the body's decision-making processes and the somatic markers are in the 'first line' of decision-making. Unlike written composition, with the possibility for ongoing revision and so on, unmediated improvisation calls for effective decision-making from moment to moment and the Somatic Marker Theory explains how this is possible. While Oliveros' understanding of '*the body first*' occurs in the discussion of the nature of perception processes, listening and response times, it is equally relevant for the discussion of the cognition/emotion connection in decision-making. Not-predetermined improvisation is realized through the embodiment of the two overlaid systems: the cognitive and emotional systems working together. This is not a call for the emotional to have free reign in improvisation, but an acknowledgement of the importance of this interrelatedness in the immediacy required in improvising. Damasio puts it in this way: '[…] there is no such thing as a mind without emotion […] we are not thinking machines, we are feeling machines that think' (2000).

The Group and Embodiment

As the experience of improvising occurs with others, the nature of embodied group activity is significant: '*[…] the other bit of metaphor or idealism is what it felt like to be in a group where a sense of musical oneness which can go beyond music […] a oneness was being created […] it's stepping aside from that logico deductive space into more emotional fields I suppose*' (Beck, p. 3, l. 17). '*[…] the oneness with the group came out in a oneness with the instrument […]*' (Beck, p. 11, l. 9). The embodied experience is also *inter-subjective* (Husserl). Our being-in-the-world is simultaneously with others being-in-the-world (*mitsein*), experienced here as participation in the act of free improvisation. The term *inter-subjectivity* helps by acknowledging the complexity of social free improvising interaction. The term has multiple connotations; in phenomenology inter-subjectivity is described in terms of empathy (Stein, 1989) and psychological give-and-take – improvising develops from empathic, inter-subjective willingness in the act of creative music making together; a number of subjectivities co-exist, simultaneously influencing the course of events through embodied action. The inter-subjectivity of embodied improvisation is important for creative group music in education (Vygotsky, 1987). Group learning and knowledge has a particular character, for example: In the study of large ship operation in which five to ten members of the crew are responsible for navigation, Hutchins (1995) has shown how there can be knowledge that resides within a group and is not attributable to any one member of that group – Hutchins develops a cultural rather than computational model of cognition. So too, children learn through group activity in ways that they cannot when alone. Durkeim (1951, p. 310) writes: 'when the consciousness of individuals, instead of remaining isolated, becomes grouped and combined, something in the world has altered'.

As our bodies *are* ourselves perceiving, a condition of experience, without which there is no world, recognition of this aspect helps describe embodied improvisation. Creating a not-predetermined autonomous music, without focus upon a score, our means of contributing and communicating is through the 'flesh' (Merleau-Ponty, 1962) of ourselves with others, it is *inter-corporeal*. Through 'flesh' we perceive and interact with the world and each other. 'Flesh' defines our physical presence in the world as well as the perception of the world. While inter-subjectivity reflects social, psychological processes between people, inter-corporeality describes the bodies' presence in space and the collective embodied perception. The unmediated experience of performing improvised music draws attention to 'the things themselves': our bodies' inter-corporeal experience, in time, within a particular environment.

Creating music through improvisation is an *intervolving* with others and the world. Merleau-Ponty describes the painter's 'style' – the point at which the hand and the painting meet demonstrates for him the nature of existence. The act of listening in improvisation is equivalent to the painter's eye, perceiving and realizing the world through imagination. Through improvisation's intervolving, the theme of listening (Fiumura, 1990; Ihda, 1976; Oliveros, 2005) is twinned with the theme of silence (Picard, 1963; Cage, 1961; Jaworski, 1997) reflecting two perspectives of being-in-the-world. There are different approaches to listening with different emphasis. For many, listening is integrated within the embodiment of practice – through playing, alone and with others. Listening can be approached via systematized 'ear training' through which, for example, the skill of identifying musical intervals is developed. Additionally, emphasis can be with a more holistic attuning of the body, focusing on aspects of perception and awareness with the aim of increasing facility. Attention, awareness, listening, being present and consciousness are all terms that describe a desired state for improvisation.

Consciousness

The theme of listening and response leads to questions of consciousness. *'Creative consciousness – but it's not necessarily from the conscious mode that it comes. Different modes of consciousness: body consciousness is faster than thinking consciousness'* (Oliveros, p. 5, l. 19). One of the reasons improvisation has attracted wide research interest is that the complex human, social processes involved and their implications are not fully understood.

Improvisation raises fundamental questions about how humans function and the true nature of our capabilities. This includes the need to better understand the nature of consciousness. The desire to find a unified concept of consciousness is often tied to revealing some essential meaning in life, often via religious beliefs. Through the later work of John Coltrane in particular, links have been made between improvisation, consciousness and the mystical, equally, others have eschewed such associations. Regardless of these views, for improvisation the body is a condition of its experience and with this comes the evolving understanding of the nature of consciousness. Damasio's (2000) work explores the neurobiological mechanics of consciousness as a function within embodiment and this can help illuminate improvisation. He describes how we are beginning to understand a neurological architecture of consciousness, an anatomy with specific areas of the brain. Within this view there is 'core consciousness', the sense of self in the here and now, and 'extended consciousness': '[...] the capacity to be aware of a large compass of events, i.e. the ability to generate a sense of individual perspective, ownership, and agency, over a larger compass of knowledge than that surveyed in core consciousness [...]' (2000, p. 198). Damasio also describes how consciousness and emotion are not separable. The phenomenon of music activity can reflect our sense of self, our extended consciousness and our way of interpreting the world - whether this be a mothers' musical talk with her baby, the experience of a music festival, a crowd singing at a football match, a group of improvising musicians, my daughter's whistling while getting ready in the morning or any other form of music activity.

The Relation of Embodiment and Discussion

This chapter concludes by exploring the relation between embodied practice in improvisation and discussion. Ideas of embodied mind, body first, inter-subjectivity, inter-corporeality, the body as a condition of improvisation, and learning by doing lead to questions about the role of discussion for the development of practice. Experienced improvising musicians have an intuitive understanding of the benefits of not allowing the activity to become overly analysed prior to performance. In this way, the not-predetermined form emerges by allowing the body to lead, Oliveros' remark *'the body knows'* is a helpful axiom for developing free improvisation. The 'body knows' is tacitly acknowledged, consciously and unconsciously, in physically located arts such as dance, drama and performance art. Musicians who share no common spoken language can play together successfully without a score and produce profound music through embodied interaction in improvisation, demonstrating sophisticated understanding of the other's intentions. '*[...] working methods: first play, listen to it, then talk about it. Translating something that is embodiment – embodied sound making, then translate it into spoken word after the fact, which is really the right order*' (p. 2, l. 1). Oliveros' delineation of the relationship between music and discussion is significant. Our verbal or textual response to sound or music, however clear, is separate from the experience of music. Embodied sound first and spoken word second is an important descriptor for improvisation practice and one that is relevant across the themes of *Learning, Process, Body* and *Approaches*. '*[…] we discovered something very important […] if we talked about improvisation before we did it, it usually fell flat, but if we sat down and improvised and then recorded it, and then talked, then it was interesting and we advanced our practice. […] you're communicating with one another directly […] spoken conversations don't have to happen before you play […]*' (Oliveros, p. 1, l. 43). '*[…] we understand that we mustn't talk about it* [before playing] *[…] you're going to kill it if you do*' (Oliveros, p. 2, l. 15).

The following extract further explains the role of discussion through the example of working with an improvising orchestra. '*Oh, and I forgot to mention, an important part of the process – we had some extensive discussions, we actually did more discussing than playing […] we'd play and then we'd talk about it and critique what we were doing […] We're playing, we're critiquing. At first people would say things like: "I can't just stop what I'm doing and start talking", and I'd say: "Well why not? You're already talking* [laughs] *– of course you can". It's just that they had a self-conception of this is my playing and this, my other life. This is my heightened consciousness, awareness and this is about my conscious life and so to mix those up and break up that romantic conception of the improviser made it easier […]*' (Lewis, p. 14, l. 9). While describing the importance of discussion for the process, Lewis concurs with Oliveros' point: '*[…] we'd play and we'd talk about it […] We're playing, we're critiquing*'. The account goes on to describe the group's progress through the approach of playing and critiquing and how: '*[…] some felt they were being heard in the group for the first time*'. This occurs through skilful guidance of playing activity in combination with the subsequent, constructively organized discussion. The relation between the embodiment of playing and discussion in improvisation in music is nuanced. For the successful development of learning through improvisation the balance is always important. For example, while a student may successfully perform music, this is not necessarily accompanied by successful spoken articulation, and, however good the theory, as Oliveros says, talk first can '*kill it*'. Education shows a strong bias towards text and analysis, and 'doing' is often afforded low status – improvisation reverses this picture. The purpose and communicative power of embodied improvisation lies in action, drawing on pre-conscious, unconscious and conscious thought processes and so discussion that supports embodied improvisation aids the development of practice.

Chapter 9

Approaches

Improvisation as Strategy

All humans have musical faculty and there is debate about how this evolved – theories include music as a feature of reproductive display; music as a behaviour associated with group identity; and music as a by-product of the facility for language, a spandrel. There is also debate about whether music or language came first (Levitin, 2007). Our musicality is expressed and suppressed in different ways. Problems arise in the interpretation of this musicality, or its 'ownership' – and, particularly, how the concept of music has become co-opted, through formal, institutionalized processes. In this respect improvisation, in its broadest sense, remains an accessible means and provides for the human need to be creative in a way that is not addressed by other approaches. Improvisation is itself a strategy: an open activity that is endlessly available and flexible. Beck's description of his development in music becomes a case study of how improvisation provides for the need to be musical. *'[...] we had a piano in the house, when I was a child and I used to spend ages, improvising, experimenting'.* SR: *'What age were you?'* Beck: *'Er, as soon as I could remember, 3 onwards anyway. And I do remember I used to sing as well. Probably to everybody's chagrin and eh typical kiddies stuff. I've no idea what the melodic lines were like, but they were ideas about puppy dogs (laughs) and all sorts of things. And then on the piano I do remember loving the generation of chords, and leaning on the black notes and just making a lot of racket. And so my folks said would I like piano lessons when I was 6 or 7. And I said yes, please, and as soon as I started them, it killed it stone dead'* (p. 1, l. 5). Beck's memories of early musical experience contrast starkly with the introduction of formalized expectations. His joy in music is temporarily extinguished. Chapter 8 referred to 'serious music's' ambivalence about emotion and reflecting this the teacher doesn't recognize or value the initial intuitive musical engagement. *'I laboured on with that system for a number of years always feeling frustrated and a bit bored with it [...] in parallel to that I'd started playing the ukulele when my hands were not big enough to play the guitar, in skiffle groups, and that was more fun. And then I decided that I'd make some recordings of myself playing the piano and thought: that sounds just like I'm playing a typewriter – and I gave it up'* (p. 2, l. 8). *'I fell in with a group of people at school who were interested in things moving towards jazz, some of it was jazz'* (p. 2, l. 26). *[...] I had a few lessons and decided, because I'd had the experience of the piano, I thought well I'll just go it alone. So that was what I did with the saxophone'* (p. 3, l. 3). Beck's formative experience of music education informs future decisions about how to develop. An outcome here is the adoption of the *autodidactic* approach common among improvisers. It is clear how motivation, participation, self-determination and the human need to play music are ill addressed in the example of the formal approach Beck encounters. From early childhood to adult life, improvisation provides a vehicle through which musical expression is possible. Improvisation provides a means that becomes a musical end in itself.

Autodidactism

Regardless of how slowly or quickly formal education responds to the potential benefits of improvisation, thereby improving the quality of experience found in education, the practice of improvisation continues to flourish. Autodidactism, or self-teaching, is what free improvisers do. In Beck's case, and in other interviews, it is a choice that is clearly informed by the shortcomings of the formal approach. In this respect, the term acknowledges an approach resulting from need, as people 'did it for themselves', without the assistance of formalized structures, and the term reflects improvisation's characteristic self-determination. But the autodidactic approach is also more than a 'fallback position' compensating for shortcomings within formal education. Improvisers involved in a *'lifetime of learning'* (Mitchell) are necessarily largely engaged with a self-directed process. What the term doesn't reflect, with its focus on the self, is the important relational, inter-subjective social aspect of improvisation. *'[...] we're self-teaching, we're learning from each other [...] We do an autodidact process, with the outcome of which we don't even know (laughs). So we're teaching ourselves to do something that we don't really know what it is. We're just looking for an outcome and we'll know it when we see it, and that's a part of improvisation too'* (Lewis, p. 14, l. 36). The term *autodidact* suggests solitary activity, such as practising on an instrument; however, the self-learning process also occurs together. Improvisation is the flexible medium through which participants' different learning agendas are realized simultaneously, together. For this reason improvisation needs to be not-standardized, that is allowed to remain open to truly differentiated learning: *'[...] we can't really learn anything from people that are all the same'* (Mitchell, p. 10, l. 38). While a criticism of 'academic jazz' education is the pull towards the standardization of approaches and playing, improvisation, as a process rather than a style, is open to the diversity of practices and with that the opportunity to incorporate a wide range of strategies – for this reason there is no single way of approaching improvisation. Within this picture autodidactism enables the development of individual creativity, a process that can continue over a lifetime. While autodidactism is a practical approach, it is also a philosophical, creative one characterized by responsibility and dedication. In Lewis' description of working with an improvising orchestra, the autodidactic approach and the group process coalesce. The processes of working alone and in group contexts are interrelated, informing one another – the demands of the group setting provide useful information regarding what may be developed individually, while the material generated through individual's practice contributes to the group pieces, simultaneously providing information for others. Individual development through autodidactic improvisation practice takes place alone and in group settings.

Within the autodidactic, self-led practice, the term *assessment* may not be much used; of course, the term is usually associated with institutional processes such as grading (see Chapter 7 *Learning*). However, with autodidactic modes of furthering practice as something of a norm in free improvisation, informal self-assessment inevitably takes place – although this may not necessarily be overtly acknowledged. In everyday life we continuously analyse, make choices and act upon decisions, identifying 'where we have got to' and 'where we might go'. Musicians work with awareness of sound that involves ongoing analysis and assessment of the sound environment in order that informed decisions can be made about how to participate. Contextualized by Oliveros': '[...] *first play, listen to it, then talk about it*' and Lewis': '[...] *we'd play and then we'd talk about it and critique what we were doing*', assessment can inform the future direction of a session, both for the individual and the group. It can indicate how far intentions have become met and provide reflection about what has occurred in the process. At the same time, while individual aims may be clear, a plausible aim for one may not be necessarily shared; the need of others, their experience, preoccupations and development in improvisation may well be dissimilar. As Butcher described previously: '*if it's group playing, it's a collaborative process involving often contradictory creative input of other people. Things that you wouldn't have thought of yourself [...]*'. As individual intentions differ, the process also calls for acknowledgement of this.

Technique

Typically, improvising musicians spend a great deal of time practising, developing and maintaining facility and technical ability. The musical demands of improvisation benefit from the acquisition of fluent technical ability that is contextualized by the creative, collaborative aim. Within the orthodoxy of formalized development, in which technique is prized, there may have been little or no regard for the idea of creative music making. Unsurprisingly, the relationship between instrumental technique and improvisation is therefore less than straightforward. Strong associations between the acquisition of formal technique and the denial of improvisation have occurred, exemplified by the classically accomplished instrumentalist who, while at the 'top of their game', may well eschew improvisation through a lack of exposure to practice and its potential. Regardless, it remains the case that among experienced improvisers notably high levels of technical application are commonplace. Mitchell's view of the development of practice offers a framework and is repeated as it provides a thematic motif: '*[...] what I've done and continue to do is try to improve all the time so that I'm able to speak in any kind of situation. And that's what you want to be able to do, you want to have enough technique to be able to present the ideas that you're hearing in your head. You keep working on your technique, so you can present more ideas and then continuous thoughts, because it's also a thinker's game*' (Mitchell, p. 6, l. 28). This quotation describes improvisation's potentially unique relationship with learning and the question of technique is well contextualized in relation to ongoing creative and professional need.

Discussion of 'technique' can usefully retain mindfulness of improvisation's availability, regardless of experience or level of expertise. In this way the elitism that some formal education has encouraged in music becomes questioned. Additionally, improvisation is an activity through which developing instrumental approaches and techniques have become birthed, subsequently influencing different forms of music. For Tomlinson *good technique* was emphasized as enabling of the particular demands created by improvising, in the example of his solo trombone performance. *'[...] I try to acquire as good a technique as I can and I try to bring that to bear upon improvising. When I can't think of anything to play I can rely on technique. I think I've got strong chops. Physically I've got strong chops and I can play a solo for half an hour without falling flat on the floor'* (p. 2, l. 22). Tomlinson's attitude towards technique aligns with conventions associated with the 'workmanlike' or 'no-nonsense' attitude common among professional musicians – as a highly regarded instrumentalist, the approach has held him in good stead.

Improvisation's testing of boundaries and forms is also found in the way instruments are used and explored and is particularly evident in European contemporary improvisation. Free improvisation is often characterized by its particularly wide range of 'other' ways of playing, or 'extended techniques' – the phenomenon's exploratory, creative nature is reflected in the approaches to musical technique. The 'extended technique' term is broad and tends to suggest additional, innovative ways to use an instrument in order to develop sound producing, musical possibilities. It has led to idiosyncratic adaptations in playing and alterations to the instrument itself, for example: Removing parts of a trombone, or the mouth-piece of a clarinet or saxophone; introducing 'false fingerings' on a wind instrument; playing a guitar laid flat; bowing the body of the double bass; incorporating sound altering objects and electronic devices, and so on, all of which extend the instrument's creative potential. In the process the instrument itself can becomes less bounded and its use more fluid: An electric guitar's 'pedals' may become an instrument in their own right; the lid of a piano takes on a percussive role; the strings of a bass below the bridge provide a new area of exploration; the direct use of a piano's strings and 'inside' mechanisms changes the role of the keyboard, and so on. There is also associated extra-instrumental activity: exclusively employing, or incorporating objects or 'junk' alongside conventional instruments; placing objects between the strings of instruments to alter the sound possibilities; using software with an unpredictable or faulty element in its programme; employing chance radio tunings; as well as self-designed and built instruments. Such innovation is a result of the exploratory process – one of personalized active discovery through which novel developments may occur.

While some creativity is overtly obvious, through self-designed instruments, the use of 'table-top' objects and so on, this same investigative intention occurs with instrumentalists who employ the limitations of traditional instruments to explore creative possibilities by 'looking inward'. Interrogating the playing possibilities of a chosen instrument is characteristic of activity in free improvisation. The same drive for ways to be creative is reflected elsewhere through the multi-instrumental approach, for example: Anthony Braxton has, at times, included a huge collection of saxophones, clarinets and flutes; similarly the Art Ensemble of Chicago sometimes performed with a vast array of instruments.

With the aim of composing in real-time, 'spontaneous composition', improvisers typically demonstrate high levels of skill and practising remains at the heart of preparation. Rather than bypassing practise, the obverse is the case; improvisers are likely to maintain extensive practising schedules. Mitchell reflects how survival depends upon personal development. *'But it's only the people who went on to develop themselves are the ones who remain. So, um, music is, in the end, 99.9 per cent work'* (p. 12, l. 29). Beck directly referenced the importance of practising: *'I think there is something about music, sophisticated motor skills, in one way or another, whether it's manipulating a lap-top or an acoustic instrument and the way you develop motor skills is largely through practise. So to me I couldn't care less whether somebody has learnt a particular theory but I think they're far more likely to generate some interesting music if they've done a lot of practise [...] the key thing is whether they are motivated to practise at all, I mean spend time, because it requires the development [...]'* (Beck, p. 12, l. 10).

Faced with something as illusive and fluid as improvisation activity, we readily turn to the more concrete, for example, the acquisition of technique as something more tangible to grasp. This contributes to the activity but is also not the activity. People improvise in music together in order to play and express, regardless of expertise, and an attitude of *allowing* in improvisation forms part of the approach as it enables the process. For this very reason learning in improvisation requires consideration, an attitude, that goes beyond assumptions through which, for example, the regard for technique becomes synonymous with an exclusive activity. As musician and composer Dom Bouffard pointed out in conversation, improvisation is like being given permission, knowing that your choices are what is required. Of course allowing for that which transpires will not be aided by too rigid an approach, the 'agility in the term' (Lewis) calls for flexible thinking. This *allowing* approach can also be understood more analytically. Beck's interview referenced his other role as a counsellor, using a psychotherapeutic approach, he described working with that which is not fully understood in a counselling session: *'[...] that's the bit about being in the moment, there might be some things going on and you think: Oh I don't know what the fuck this means and what that is, but don't try and struggle to understand it too much, just go with the flow and say and do things which are just instinctual and it might reveal something to you immediately but it might take a couple of sessions for you to think, ah, when this was going on it was probably a reflection of this that or the other'* (Beck, p. 14, l. 42). Too easily theorizing and overbearing analysis can suffocate that which is ephemeral, instinctive and necessarily undefined, or indeterminate. The contingency of participating creatively in 'the moment' of free improvisation as it unfolds is not the same as reflective understanding of what is occurring in the overall composition: *'[...] your reflections about how something may feel later on may lead you to a different interpretation of what is or was happening, which can be very informative to both the counsellor and the client*' (p. 16, l. 1). Part of 'being in the moment' is the acceptance that not everything can be fully understood as the music unfolds. At each moment we are also essentially contributing to the overall picture that may be better understood later, allowing for that which is not known is a strategy that becomes skilfully developed through the act of playing; this takes us back to Oliveros': '*[…] first play, listen to it, then talk about it*' (Oliveros, p. 2, l. 1).

Solo

If improvisation is formed through adaptability in collaborative contexts, how does solo performance fit within this picture? Can solo performance be improvised? Of course, in unmediated solo playing it is possible to play in a completely predetermined fashion. However, it is telling that solo players *choose* improvisation in order that compositional decisions about content are made in the course of performance in each new setting – the properties that improvisation can offer often make it the preferred approach. The proliferation of improvisers who perform solo as part of their practice attests to the attraction of the improvisation approach. Mitchell refers to playing solo as a necessary part of the total development in music.

In Anthony Braxton's first solo performance, he found he'd used all of his material within five minutes, leaving him, alarmingly, with nowhere to go. His subsequent influential solo recording *For Alto* (1970) is, in part, a response to this initial experience. He chose 'areas' of the saxophone to explore, for example, the extremely high register; lyrical lines; bebop inspired material; staccato playing and so on as a compositional strategy that addressed the problem he experienced in solo performance using improvisation. Braxton's compositional approach, informed by his negative experience of running out of material, also leads to a formalized kind of improvising. This is one approach among many: material is needed and solo playing is, initially, a very challenging prospect. It's a personal preference and it depends what the aim is. However, putting a kind of 'set list' of compositional ideas together provides a different focus than working with open improvisation's broader potential. Preferences reflect musical interests and Braxton's written compositional output demonstrates his particular interest in formal composition that, in part, explains his choice of approach on *For Alto*. Evan Parker, with over twenty solo recordings on tenor and soprano saxophones has described his practice as a slowly evolving music, in which material and music has continued to develop over decades. His interest is in how improvisation forms music in changing ways across a large time scale, in a more incremental organic way. Rather than solo playing negating improvisation it reveals that improvisation remains a compositional approach regardless of the lack of collaboration with others, and for those who are interested in improvisation's potential, it is a preferred approach.

The Question of Spontaneity

Spontaneity is commonly associated with improvisation as essential to practice and tends to be referred to uncritically. However, the questions arising from spontaneity lead to a range of interview responses through which other important themes emerge; this section discusses these different interpretations. '[...] what I'm striving for is to be able to create spontaneous composition. And I think that this helps me know how composition works and then you can apply these principles during an improvisation' (Mitchell, p. 1, l. 8). The idea of 'spontaneous composition' has also been expressed by the approaches of the groups Spontaneous Music Ensemble (SME) in the UK and Instant Composers Pool (ICP) in Holland, and improvisation as real-time composition is increasingly referred to in music and dance. Mitchell's use of spontaneity is contextualized by studying composition. '[...] people want to say they're "in the moment" of the improvisation. Knowing how composition works helps. If you're improvising with somebody and they're playing eighth notes all the time and you want to add some counterpoint to what's going on, you may think, well maybe I should play some triplets here, you know. But of course people ought to be aware that all they're doing is playing eighth notes. There's nothing wrong with that if you put it in context [...]' (p. 7, l. 7). Here the discussion of spontaneity is linked to compositional knowledge; developing an analytical approach develops musical awareness for improvising. 'I've spent a lot of time when I was teaching workshops and improvisation [...] noticing what inexperienced improvisers were doing and figuring out different ways to address the problems [...] if you listen, a lot of inexperienced improvisers, all they do is follow. Following is like being behind on a written piece of music, in other words, you know your part, I don't really know my part so I'm listening to see what you're doing and by the time I've waited to see what you're doing I'm already behind' (Mitchell, p. 6, l. 40). For inexperienced players there may be, understandably, some sense of 'safety in numbers' in large group improvisation; however, a 'following' approach to playing foreshortens musical development. To this end, participation in large group improvisation can be balanced by experience in the more transparent small group and solo settings through which the compositional effect of decision-making in practice, by all the members, can become better understood.

How does spontaneity in improvisation relate to a musician's familiar material? Experienced players in particular will inevitably know their material and techniques very well, in light of this how do they view spontaneity? '[...] everyone's trying to avoid the familiar and stick with the spontaneous. The problem is most of the time what spontaneity produces is the familiar (laughs)' (Lewis, p. 17, l. 6). Citing studies of the music of Charlie Parker and John Coltrane (Spence, 2009; Owen, 1974), Lewis elaborates: '[...] how did the impression arise that Charlie Parker was so spontaneous or even John Coltrane, you hear the same things over and over, but what accounts for the power of it, it's not in the spontaneity that's for sure, there's something else there'. SR: 'What is it?' Lewis: 'Well, I don't know, but let's take out all the things that obviously don't work (both laugh) and start there, you know one of those Sherlock

Holmes things, once you've eliminated all the obvious things then however improbably, this is the truth (laughs)' (Lewis, p. 16, l. 30). This squarely challenges presumptions about the place of spontaneity. The example also raises the secondary question of the similarities and differences between jazz, improvisation and free improvisation. Bebop influenced saxophonist Gilad Atzmon described how a 'fair player' will know fifteen patterns, a good player will know fifty or more. For the free improviser such an approach to patterns can be problematic as these idiomatic habits will tend to be included and as Ryle (1997) describes: '[...] response is necessarily partly novel. Else it is not a response'. There's a push and pull here between being able to respond openly and having material or 'knowing your part'. As the development of motor skills is necessary for playing an instrument, acquired through the development by practising and learnt behaviours, habits exist in balance with the facility for adaptability within immediacy and this balance can be developed through group playing. A distinguishing feature of a mature free improviser is the confidence they place in their material and judgement in how to make use of these resources in a fluid manner within settings that will differ. At the same time, the ongoing development of such material is part of a life's work. *'[...] I kind of felt that spontaneity is overblown, most people aren't that spontaneous, they're doing mostly the same thing, there are all kinds of little rituals that people do, you know that they do every day, just to get through their everyday lives, and they use the same version of those repetitive rituals when they play music'* (Lewis, p. 15, l. 15).

Beck refers to a strategy for improvisation aimed at encouraging spontaneity: *'[...] another approach which is that I'm going to let my mind go as blank as I can and let random sounds emerge and see if they suggest anything. And the problem with that is that what will tend to emerge is the clichés that you've been rehearsing with yourself for any number of years'* (Laughs) (Beck, p. 9, l. 43). Beck echoes Lewis' view – spontaneity paradoxically leads to the familiar; in this case there is also a negative connotation of clichés. If what individuals produce is reliant upon what they have already developed, does this question the idea of the 'not-predetermined'? How 'open' is free improvisation? Lewis describes the process in this way: *'[...] you revel in the combinations, which are potentially infinite'* (Lewis, p. 16, l. 19). Creativity arises through interaction and the music develops from the ways individuals and groups combine what they do. Free improvisation is creative through the *choices* at the point of performance. Rather than dependent upon individual spontaneity, although part of the picture, how those involved choose to simultaneously interact, play and respond, leads to the composition of the music. The opportunity for creativity presented by *'the combinations, which are potentially infinite'* is a singular feature of the open free improvisation form.

The theme of *the known and the new* was directly discussed in Mitchell's example of Art Blakey in which the importance of *exploring* was introduced. *'I mean even Art Blakey would tell musicians; OK, you've got this down, I don't want to hear it again tomorrow night, I want to hear you reaching for something else, I want to hear you exploring. I'd rather have you up there making a mistake, you know, trying to do something, than finding some area that you're comfortable with and doing it over and over again'* (Mitchell, p. 12, l. 34). Although hard-bop and free improvisation are often discussed in terms of their dissimilarity, there is clearly shared purpose in 'reaching for something else', in other words seeking to create at the point of performance. Exploration is a valued component that is necessary for the music's success.

For Honsinger, the question of spontaneity requires understanding of the broader context of improvisation: '[...] when you start thinking about it, the complexity of, of, let's say a concert, all the things that are influencing you, the audience, the place, whatever, I think has a great deal to do with the outcome [...] and I suppose the only, the only thing is to be prepared for this complexity. I would say that it's [...] and of course spontaneity is part of this complexity, I would say – so, I think it comes down to experience and really being part of this complexity offers a possibility that [...] that this complexity transforms into some kind of simplicity. So if you have the confidence to realize the complexity, then you can become simple, I would say. Because it's kind of like, seeing, that, you are just a crumb [picks up a cigarette end from the ashtray] you're just like that in the complexity, but if you understand that [...] then you can offer simplicity. And I would say, spontaneity is maybe another way to express the same thing, but I would have to say that spontaneity is overrated' (Honsinger, p. 11, l. 24). Theorizing improvisation via the interviews aims is to reveal the true nature of practice; it is not that spontaneity should be negated but that the contribution of spontaneity become clarified. Honsinger echoes the description of improvisation operating within a larger feedback system. Within the entire system of things and events spontaneity is but one part within this 'bigger picture'.

Presuming spontaneity to be an over-riding aim in improvisation is common in music and beyond. Some years ago I had the opportunity to attach sound sensors to the saxophone that were triggered by movement; I'd been considering such an approach for some years and was excited by the idea. However, at that time there were difficulties with the technology and a lack of control over the sound and it wasn't possible to develop musical ideas through playing. Afterwards I explained my misgivings to a researcher who responded: 'What's all this about control! You're supposed to be an improviser'. One way of describing facility is as developing an increased ability to work with an instrument; musicians become effective creative collaborators by means of this. Confusion between the development of the facility needed to improvise effectively and the perceived need for spontaneity can obscure creativity in improvisation. Uncritical spontaneity can be traced to some popular mid-century thought. In Johnson's (1987) influential book on drama and improvisation, there is a lengthy chapter titled 'Spontaneity' in which spontaneity is conflated with creativity and imagination while the meaning of 'spontaneity' itself is not explored. Rightly or wrongly, spontaneity is presumed to be a desirable aim, inevitably creative but, in addition, it is suggested as a means of accessing 'unconscious' truth. For Johnson, spontaneity is a way of releasing our oppressed, hidden selves, a source of creative potential. The idea that spontaneity is inevitably valuable is not borne out by the interviews. These assumptions lead from thinking that is very much a product of the time in which much education could be very oppressive – for example, corporal punishment was still practiced, and class divide and gender discrimination were maintained by the structures of education. At the same time, popular Freudian theories associated with the unconscious were very influential. In Johnson's examples, which illustrate his approach in drama, the embodiment of oppressive forms of education is overcome through a kind of Freudian-Jungian influenced approach to creativity (in the same way as word 'association' is put forward as a means of releasing the unconscious through 'Freudian' associations). While such exercises and games are useful for stimulating potential in drama and can be highly engaging, positive creative qualities are attributed to spontaneity in an unquestioned manner. The lack of discussion about what spontaneity actually means has left an assumption that it can lead to freedom, away from oppression and towards unquestioned creativity; in other words, if it's spontaneous, it must be good. Whilst developing immediacy is necessary, and a fun activity, collaboratively improvising with someone whose goal is to be constantly spontaneous can quickly negate the creative process. The newer perspective provided by Berlin's Echtzeitmusik scene has in some ways resituated, or rebalanced, spontaneity in improvisation. With an initial focus on reduced materials, Echtzeitmusik sought to create distance from the earlier developments in free improvisation, in particular 'hyperactive' playing. In its development Echtzeitmusik demonstrates openness to a diverse range of compositional strategies, rather than highlighting spontaneity, different kinds of creativity emerges in different ways while improvisation remains central.

Collaboration and Improvisation

Butcher further clarifies the question of the relation between what we already know and seeking to create anew at the point of performance: '[...] that's what I think improvising performers do, we do have vocabulary and ingredients but they are malleable enough if not to be ever changing then really fluid at the true moment of creation' (p. 6, l. 20). For Butcher, playing in a wide variety of contexts, or combinations has characterized his professional music practice. Discussion of musicians often celebrates instrumental expertise, and many highly regarded improvisers are known for exceptionally developed personalized technical ability while the equal facility to work in different contexts can be less celebrated. '[...] perhaps the most unique thing about this practice is that if it's group playing it's a collaborative process involving often contradictory creative input of other people. Things that you wouldn't have thought of yourself, things that you may not agree with, things that will force you to operate in a way that you weren't expecting. And I find that very intrinsic to the improvising process and what makes it, when it works, almost the most interesting music you can get'. SR: 'I think that's one of the particular features of your music, having heard you in different settings. I commented to Mick Beck on the duo that you did, I said I really like the way John seems to be able to latch onto the other thing that's going on, and then, you seem to be able to turn and extend [...] in many different contexts'. Butcher: 'It is my particular interest. It is this thing of how to maintain your own personality, yet use it to make musical sense with the people you're working with and to accept their intentions to be as important as your own' (Butcher, p. 7, l. 21). Butcher's articulation of this 'personal interest' is particularly clear and it delineates the collaborative aspect of the process. It is not the individual's instrumental ability alone but the additional facility to work musically with diverse others that creates this successful approach to making music. Identifying that: *'[...] perhaps the most unique thing about this practice is that if it's group playing, it's a collaborative process [...]'*. Butcher's instrumental approach has developed a characteristic adaptability. Lewis similarly identifies others' intentions as important in the process of improvising. *'[...] when you are trying to play with someone, whatever instrument or whatever they're doing, you're interacting with them, you're not even playing with them, it should come to you at a certain point, some sense of their intentions, it should come, and maybe people could be tuned into that and could allow, tuned in as a question of method'* (Lewis, p. 5, l. 14). These articulations of the collaborative nature of the approach resonate with Nicol's perspective of improvisation as *'social virtuosity'* (Chapter 5) or the social-intelligence expressed within the musical relationships. True creativity occurs in improvisation through the fluid use of materials in response to the possibilities on offer in each collaborative setting.

The theme of collaboration extends to community in Mitchell's description of the AACM. *'I think it's important to establish lasting relationships with musicians and I've been fortunate from that point of view, to have come along at that time when there was a group of people who were interested and had a vision about how they wanted their destinies to go. In terms of not just their music but their philosophy and the way they were thinking they were going, to have some control over their lives'* (Mitchell, p. 2, l. 10). These *'lasting relationships'* also form a context for the development of strong, creative individuality: *'I'm just talking about the way they represented their own individuality onto the music, I mean if you look at and study the AACM you'll see that although we are all there together, none of us are the same. Because there was big emphasis on getting people to go inside of themselves and come up with their own text [...] That was the general philosophy of the AACM. I mean if we just look at the different people. If you just look at the saxophonists: Anthony Braxton is not like me at all; Joseph Jarman is not like Anthony Braxton. Henry Threadgill is not like ... John Stubblefield is not like any of us, you know on and on. That's why I consider myself fortunate to have been put into a group of people like this'* (p. 5, l. 13). The collaborative relationships can nurture the development of outstanding creativity. In the AACM this took place through the total study of music: improvisation as well as the development of approaches to analyse and written composition.

The relationships in improvisation are a condition of its practice: *'[...] you revel in the combinations, which are potentially infinite'* (Lewis, p. 16, l. 19). But what does the 'combinations' mean? What are the relationships? Different discourses from different fields can help illuminate improvisation and this section continues the inter-disciplinary comparison to developments in contemporary art. Nicolas Bourriaud (2002) describes globalization and the growing 'urbanisation of artistic experiment [...] this system of intensive encounters has ended up producing linked artistic practices: an art form where the substrate is formed by inter-subjectivity, and which takes being-together as a central theme, the "encounter" between beholder and picture, and the collective elaboration of meaning'. This relational description reflects improvisation in a number of ways: Chapter 2 described the emergence of improvisation in music during the 1960s as part of a much broader movement of artistic expression, with concurrent links and the mirroring of different artistic practices. Recently, there has been a large international growth in improvisation, or free improvisation activity. It seems the activity forms a response, or meets a need in current times: although we are swamped by information and obsessed by screens, we are also able to make connections with one another in an unprecedented way. And, the 'encounter' of improvisation can offer the inverse of technological overload – the creative immediacy of improvisation forms an inescapably human exchange. The introduction of the ideas presented by *relational aesthetics* (RA) initiated a debate that itself reflected the ambiguity of diverse artistic practice in the globalized context and, moreover, illustrated the need for the relational aspect to be more widely acknowledged. RA represents diverse practice and, like free improvisation, the term is not without problems. However, the idea has successfully drawn attention to the nature of developing practice that centres different kinds of relationships in its production within the contemporary global context. For these reasons, in addition to the more generalized term 'participation', it helpfully describes improvisation.

I've referred to different art practice and theory in the course of the chapters' discussion of improvisation. In many ways writing about art is in advance of much writing in music. It is more encompassing and agile in its acceptance of 'other' practices that disregard disciplinary boundaries, and boundaries are less defining of practice within the art world; different approaches and media are given comparable status. For these reasons it's worth considering how the idea of Relational Aesthetics developed. Bourriaud introduced the term to describe a tendency in artistic practice in the 1990s in which diverse new work was created through the use of different ideas and approaches that effected different kinds of relations. The term *relational aesthetics* moves away from theorizing and practice that separates aesthetic and ethical concerns. The work of Rirkrit Tiravanija, Philipe Parreno, Vanessa Beecroft, Maurizio Cattelan, Jes Brinch and Henrik Plenge Jacobsen, Christine Hill, Carsten Holler, Noritoshi Hirakawa, Pierre Huyghe and Liam Gillick reflect this 'relational' tendency. Bourriaud's influential idea opened an area of debate about the nature of artwork that is created with and through the relations that are developed: Claire Bishop (2006); Julian Stallabrass (2004); Grant Kester (2004) and others have critiqued the relative merits of the idea. Bishop's article 'Antagonism and Relational Aesthetics' proposed a more politically direct form of installation art and draws from the examples of Thomas Hirschhorn and Santiago Sierra in which, for Bishop, the relations involved more clearly enunciate the politics of the work. Chapter 2's description of improvisation's various connections within the lineage and breadth of socially orientated artwork going back to the 1960s and Bishop's (2006) writing on participation reflects this history. However, that critique of relational aesthetics does not acknowledge Bourriaud's own critique of postmodernist failure – the inadequacy of postmodernism to address the global changes that have occurred since its theoretical inception nearly forty years ago. As Bourriaud puts it, 'Too often, people are happy drawing up an inventory of yesterday's concerns, the better to lament the fact of not getting any answers' (2002). Views of participation and relational art are highly contested and artist and writer Liam Gillick (2006), whose work Bishop is particularly critical of, has challenged what he views as Bishop's misrepresentations and inconsistencies in describing to the actual work involved.

To clarify the relational connection, I will reiterate how I am articulating free improvisation. It is not used to denote a style of music – I am not opposed to style, but the potential of the process of improvisation is simply more encompassing. Rather, improvisation, and free improvisation as a guiding term for the activity, can become realized in 'infinite' ways. Bourriaud: 'As part of a "relationist" theory of art, inter-subjectivity does not only represent the social setting for the reception of art, which is its "environment", its "field", but also becomes the quintessence of its artistic practice' (2002, p. 22). It is the relational practice of musical interaction that forms the music through improvisation, regardless of style (or whether the outcome is jazzy, noisy, electronic, rocky, minimal, reduced, laminal, influenced by contemporary classical, and so on). For improvisation, grounding discourse in the relations that emerge also addresses a recurrent problem in improvisation theory, that of the limited usefulness of the categories that can lead to circular debates about, for example, whether something is really 'non-idiomatic', free jazz or free improvisation, or original. Discussion of improvisation that is dependent upon fixed or limited categorization often does little to truly illuminate the process, hamstrung as it is by the need to shoehorn the diversity of what actually goes on into an inadequate framework. Focusing instead on the indeterminate *relations* alleviates the need to over-categorize and more truthfully locates the music in the specific, unique relationships of each encounter. While the histories of improvisation are important, the 'moment' and emergence is the concern in improvisation and this occurs through the '*infinite combinations*' that result from its relations.

More recently theorizing of developing relational practice in contemporary art has been extended through the focus on *use* through which further alignments to the practice of free improvisation can be made. Ideas and practices associated with *usership* have been furthered by theorist Stephen Wright; Alistair Hudson, Middlesbrough Institute of Modern Art; and Charles Esche, Van Abbemuseum. Usership is a principle of practice that counters notions of the expert, authorship, spectatorship and profit. It opposes the influential post-Young British Artist art market ethos through which fashionable artists seek to 'make a killing'. Wright (2013) describes: 'breaking down the long standing opposition between consumption and production' via the rise of networked culture 'not just a form of opportunity-dependent relationality, but a self-regulating mode of engagement and operation'. By way of comparison, this also mirrors what improvisers in the globalized context, working in diverse new constellations do. *Useage* speaks to the practice of free improvisation within the economy. Developing technology has let the genie out of the bottle for the music industry – free reproduction is common practice, undermining the consumer/product paradigm. While the music industry and musicology seek to maintain past paradigms that do little to address these changes, improvisation remains consistently flexible and continues to develop. Free improvisation was initiated through a bypassing of industry's primary commercial concerns and sustains as a process of relational practice.

Relational aesthetics, participation and usership provide a helpful inter-disciplinary means of reading improvisation in music and elsewhere. While we readily accept conventions of disciplinarity in discourse, we can also recognize how current practice within other disciplines share a great deal across disciplines – more than tends to be acknowledged. Activity may differ, but within the intention, purpose and relations of practice and outcomes there is much in common.

Chapter 10

The Capacity of Improvisation

Life

This chapter begins by looking outwards towards improvisation in different areas of life. Philosopher John Gray (2011) has referred to the need for 'the spirit of improvisation', rather than the reliance upon redundant 'grand narratives' that stem from the prevalent legacy of humanistic faith in the West, and its unrealistic assessment of history. Gray challenges this legacy in Western thought as a catastrophically inadequate way of thinking about the world and our coexistence within it. He points to the myth of human 'progress', illustrated by repetitious holocausts and the reluctance to acknowledge and respond to devastating environmental impact resulting from human activity.

> I think this spirit of improvisation is really what we need, rather than imagining great grand narratives of progress which then gets disrupted as people panic and then turn to extremism it would be better if we just had confidence in our own powers of improvisation [...] and confidence that we can actually prevent some of these terrible downturns or at least mitigate or prevent their worst aspects if we see them as normal, if we see them as not a completely inexplicable thing that happens out of the blue – but it's sort of normal for markets to go mad, it's normal for capitalism to be unstable, it's normal for politicians to sometimes be crazy. All human institutions are infected by insanity from time to time because the human animal is not and never will be fully sane and if we understand that maybe we can guard against it.
>
> (Gray, 2011)

What Gray describes as 'the spirit of improvisation' is an acknowledgement of the human capability to respond creatively as need arises. The capacity to act adaptably to inevitably changing circumstances is presented in preference to the over-reliance upon structures that have been shown to repeatedly fail, with disastrous results. Of course there is a need to more fully understand the nature of this 'spirit of improvisation' through the further examination of what improvisation can mean in the context of action within and between states. There is also a need to understand improvisation at a day-to-day level, and these two aspects are linked: the 'spirit of improvisation' occurs between people, in kinds of interaction, in its knowledge and adaptability that is socially rooted.

While improvisation is identified as a disciplinary activity, it is also a human capability. Chapter 3 describes the practice of improvisation in music and drama as a successful method for developing learning; the agency of improvisation extended beyond the musical discipline and was reflected by strategies within the teaching approach. Utilizing the agency of adaptable improvisation at the point at which students create music informed decision-making, future planning and implementation in the teaching process, creating a productive cyclical exchange. Operating in the variety of situations, across experience, involves engagement with the emergent, something we all do (although we may not direct our conscious thought to this). Enacted improvisation is available in the everyday and in 'day-to-day' terms we can understand improvisation as a capability. Improvisation can be 'about' music; however, for educational purposes learning through improvisation is transdisciplinary – the features offered by improvisation in music within the themes of Process, Learning, Body and Approaches transmigrate to the broader social context of education. The history of drama in education, in which improvisation is a central pedagogical tool, is a transmigration – the agency of improvisation moves from one area to another – from theatre to education, drama becomes active learning.

Improvisation is a large part of how we do things – telling us about the truer nature of our being-in-the-world, and this doesn't necessarily fit neatly within any particular discipline. So too, most music activity hasn't developed from music-as-discipline. Improvisation research itself has been initiated from within a multiplicity of disciplines of which music is only one (and, in fact, the practices and modes of study within much disciplinary music are resistant to improvisation). This not-necessarily-disciplinary characteristic tells us about improvisation's nature. It is tempting to use the adjective *undisciplined*, but, while improvisation can resist effectively, this word too strongly ties, and therefore limits, to the oppositional. Improvisation is also not entirely *post-disciplinary*, as disciplinary approaches contribute to understanding aspects, if not the entirety. In these ways, improvisation holds a kind of 'shape-shifting' quality – when needs be, appearing in the diverse areas of human activity, often unrecognized, and like a superhero with the ability to save us in dire situations. But 'shape-shifting' is also too romantic an image that pulls away from the more day-to-day essential usefulness of improvisation, for example, that musicians demonstrate in their practice and described in the later sections on law and film. Through improvisation's fluidity, its potential to cross the constructed disciplinary boundaries, multiple meanings can be represented simultaneously. The variety of activity and emerging relations arising from improvisation in music is an under-swell, an outcome of the music's 'not-predetermined' form. Acknowledging the 'agility in the term', improvisation needs to be re-described in a more encompassing way that includes and at the same time goes beyond the dominant reference to music. In uncertainty we prefer to move to a state in which things are resolved and ambiguity can be the enemy in academic discussion. Regardless of this preference for certainty or hope for reassurance, ambiguity or multiple meanings (rather than vagueness) is a feature of lived experience. To accept that meanings are intrinsically ambiguous is not easy – we resist it, however, improvisation's meanings are several and interrelated and only become clarified through their contexts.

Lyotard (1984) described the fallibility of our 'grand narratives' and introduced the term 'postmodern'. However, the narrative of postmodernism in art has always been largely a Western-orientated idea (Bourriaud). Although attempts have been made to apply the term 'postmodern' to improvisation in music, the process of improvisation's evolving character has never quite fitted the mould. While diverse free improvisation is without a grand narrative, it is also not postmodern. As well as being ageless, the relations that are formed in the activity of improvisation in music are encompassing, broad, humanly structured and diverse. For Bourriaud (2010), *altermodern* describes contemporary art in which the globalized context, rather than Western perspective, provides the arena for creativity. So too, improvisation's multiple, simultaneous interpretations are better served by acknowledging its more encompassing, global context.

Chapter 2 described the growing range of improvisation research that includes pedagogy, philosophy, psychology, sociology, anthropology, law, urban planning, literature, architecture, post-colonial studies, gender studies, human-computer relations, emergency response, fire-fighting management, negotiation, sport, architecture, medical surgery, management, marketing, entrepreneurship, the military and of course drama, dance and music. With improvisation occurring at the level of evolution, and the call for improvisational responsiveness in global organization, the need to better understand the capacity of improvisation is clear. Sawyer (2003) writes: 'empirical studies have shown that all social interactions display improvisational elements. Many of these studies focused on emergence and collaboration in classrooms and in families'. Many people who haven't considered improvisation are, in fact, highly skilled improvisers themselves. For example, within families there are very often members who respond creatively to the inevitable changes that occur and are able to communicate effectively with others, fostering collaboration, in different ways.

The association between improvisation and human survival informs the nature of the capability. Improvisation is commonly linked to emergency because in such situations of need innate aspects of the capability become apparent. 'Thinking on our feet', acting with immediacy, working at a high level of perceptual and conceptual engagement, engaging trust and risk, employing creative strategies that may be unexpected in addressing a given problem, need compels us to draw on this capability. In Chapter 6, connections and comparisons were made between the processes in evolution and those found in improvisation, through self-organizing systems. From an evolutionary perspective, this ability to respond to emergence defines survival; successful adaptation to environment leads to the continuation of life.

Technology increasingly mirrors our ability to work in adaptable ways; real-time processing and the mobility of communication provide current examples. The possibilities offered by technology fundamentally challenge older systems of communication and organization, at many levels. As activity once tied to a single site by means of older technology is now networked and mobile, and as new modes of communication and procedures emerge, the validity of organizational structures, once taken as 'given', is increasingly questioned. Within this picture the understanding and development of creative processes, including improvisation, is being linked to success or failure, and of course this is a call for education to respond. The contemporary preoccupation with 'real-time' functioning mirrors improvisation's embodied temporal condition of being. Technological systems that offer the immediacy of 'the moment' affect the organization of relations from the intimate to those between states. Rather than acting compliantly in deference to fixed systems tied to outmoded technologies and hierarchies, responsiveness and adaptability is a new imperative. As the ways in which we operate and organize develop, there is a need to further acknowledge the human capability for immediacy demonstrated by improvisation.

Within this bigger picture of improvisation, the particular can tell us about the universal. In San Francisco, in 2008, a conversation with Deborah Daniloff, an experienced practising lawyer led to an impromptu interview describing Daniloff's understanding of improvisation in the legal processes and the development of law.

'One of the main places where you see improvisation is in the courtroom. [...] you have to be aware of all these parties around you and respond to how they are reacting to what you're saying and that's where the improvisation comes into play. I really believe to be a good trial lawyer you have to be flexible and you have to improvise – it just happens all the time [...]. I was so tired after working on a trial [...] and I started forgetting things, I wanted to ask the judge if I could move something from the middle of the courtroom that had a lot of exhibits on it – it was a cart with wheels on it: it's called 'the cart', and I couldn't for the life of me think, in that moment, remember what the thing was that I wanted to move, so I said: 'Your honour, may I please move the, er, er, the table with the rolling wheels on it' and just the fact that I was tired and I couldn't remember the word and it came out kind of funny, just made everyone laugh and the jury included and really lightened the moment and it can sometimes make you seem more approachable to those that – to the whole group of people in the courtroom [...] There are a lot of examples of improvising in the courtroom for myself [...] I prepare, I have a theme, and then usually I throw the stuff that I've prepared out of the window when I'm in the midst of it [...] But the real stellar lawyers probably also do the same thing but will think probably more in terms of themes and adjust how they are presenting these themes as they go through rather than walking in with a script or a set outline of what they are going to say or do. You will definitely have some improvisation from the bench itself, from the judge because they're responding to the parties or the witness or the jury – juries that may have to learn, may have their own issues, have their own questions. And I know the judge is always thinking: Is my ruling going to be appealed? – and they have to often think on their feet – to say something on the record that the court of appeal isn't going to frown upon – there's not a lot of planning for much of that' (private conversation).

Daniloff locates the agency offered through improvisation quite precisely within the legal procedures. It is not only a case of recognizing the performativity and theatricality of the courtroom: its presentation; rituals and role playing; the tragedy and comedy, but within this precisely how, why and with what potential outcomes improvisation occurs as it affects the relations and processes at work. She explains how skilful improvisation, responding to parties' reactions, will depart from 'the script' and how awareness of how relations in the courtroom are emerging influences the development and outcome of cases.

Skilfully improvising to good effect means recognizing the human potential as it occurs, and elsewhere she describes how the ability to improvise while working with a hostile, 'misogynistic' judge eventually leads to a successful appeal and just outcome. Significantly, Daniloff also described improvisation as part of the process of developing law.

'Besides the trial there's probably improvisation in the development of the law or defining what is the rule [...] for example a lot of your intellectual property decisions [...] to the extent that there's not anything out there, it's kind of a new subject. One that comes to mind is Brown versus Board of Education [1954]. It's the one that said separate was not equal in the US. So you couldn't have separate facilities for minorities and for whites and that was a law that said that can never be equal [...] they must have pulled from the basic concepts of equality, but that was new. This was a particular decision that came from the US Supreme Court that broke new ground [...] that was a breaking decision. 'Roe versus Wade', [1973] that's the famous decision that said a woman has the right to decide on whether she has an abortion or not and that comes from the belief that there is a right to privacy [...] by the way the right to privacy isn't written into our constitution, they had to derive that right from other rights that were written in there, and the way society has developed – all the things that were happening socially – and so there's another piece of improvisation by the court – they had to break new ground and improvise'.

Of course established structures and procedures are very present, but within this framing improvisation is significant – it is important to acknowledge improvisation's creative presence when it appears, how and why the capability is used and to what effect. Too often a false opposition is presented of structure versus improvisation, or chaos versus order. Improvisation plays with structure and also creates structures, and while chaos could result from improvisation, it is certainly not tied to improvisation. Advanced engagement with improvisation means deciding on its effective purpose for different contexts and a similarly precise use of applied improvisation can be found in different areas. Film, television and theatre director Mike Leigh (2008) is frequently referred to as making great use of improvisation. Leigh's use of improvisation is systematized and integrated within the entire process that results in screenplays and play-scripts bearing the author's name. His process has entailed initial work with actors in isolation, giving them tasks aimed at initiating the development of character, building a detailed history, over several months, and exercises include being in character in public. He then creates situations in which characters interact, in the studio and public places. Significantly, it is through this lengthy collaborative process of discovery that the narrative and its thematic content emerge. Leigh's method of using improvisation questions the role and meaning of the term 'director'. More accurately, he is devising, writing and directing while collaboratively making films. Once more the engagement with improvisation leads to a kind of transmigrating that redistributes creativity.

Film director Alejandro González Iñárritu's collaborative approach to working with drummer Antonio Sanchez led to the acclaimed improvised solo drumming score for the film *Birdman* (2014). When Sanchez was commissioned to create the score, he composed drum themes for each of the characters and submitted it to Iñárritu, his response being: 'it was exactly what I didn't want'. They subsequently met and discussed the inner workings of the main character (played by Michael Keaton) and Iñárritu encouraged Sanchez to improvise to the dramatic development and movements within each scene, with the aid of hand signals. The results were recorded and tested in the actors' rehearsal (*Vanity Fair*, 2014). In this way the film score was developed and performed through a highly attuned process of improvisation. By contrast, Iñárritu (2014) has also described how in the process of shooting the film 'nothing was improvised' by the actors, 'every turn of the head, every phrase was choreographed'. The many, very long shots often encompass multiple mini-scenes, the result being that lengthy sections were recorded one at a time, negating the need for, or possibilities offered by, editing. There are debates about what constitutes the creative performance and for some, good music always retains an essential improvisational element: seeking to create anew in the moment, in the space, rather than aiming to repeat – as Mitchell describes working with or without a written score: '*each night's different, each moment is different [...]*' The performances of the *Birdman* ensemble are collectively successful in a way that feeds the creative process; it is the constrictions provided by the approach, and indeed the claustrophobic sense of space within the back-stage theatre setting, that aids the chemistry in which you can see the thoughts and emotions come alive through interaction. To paraphrase Stravinski: the greater the constraints, the greater the creative freedom.

While improvisation is available throughout our day-to-day lives, its application can be made in a specialized manner. Many improvising musicians are renowned for high levels of knowledge and skill, this doesn't pull away from the availability of improvisation, rather it demonstrates the breadth – children are often recognized as natural improvisers, for example, the entirety of a busy playground forms an effective self-organizing system. But improvisation is also an available, applied choice – as with the solo improvising musician, who could employ a score – frequently improvisation is a preferred way, offering the fruits of creative immediacy.

In fundamental ways there can be an overreliance on 'the plan'. All the messages my partner and I received prior to our daughter's birth, from pre-natal classes and books, told us to wait as long as possible before going into hospital for the 'delivery'. Apparently it is common to have to return home again as these early signs may not lead to the actual birth and this will be dispiriting. We were encouraged to have a script. On the day, with early signs, my wife was very relaxed and not 'put out', and when I returned from a busy West End of London laden with baby equipment, I telephoned for an ambulance. An experienced paramedic was quickly with us and extremely surprised to find these inexperienced prospective parents still at home as the three-week early baby was 'crowning'! A further ambulance with two crew arrived and the paramedic explained that we couldn't move until the midwife had arrived and given consent – such is the hierarchy of the procedure. Forty minutes later the midwife arrived, dropping things from her bag as she climbed the many, narrow stairs to our apartment, making it to the room she produced a stethoscope with one end-piece missing that she looked at quizzically. We looked on expectantly. Eventually, after a hair-raising journey to the hospital, my daughter was born within the hour.

Despite the best intentions of the pre-natal classes, the books and so on, what was missing in this plethora of advice was the need to accept and trust in *what is going on* and, of course, the essential need to respond accordingly. The growth industry surrounding childbirth and the plethora of books, equipment and courses too easily exploit the inexperience and anxiety of prospective parents. We needed to be accepting of what was *actually happening,* the emergent baby, rather than being overly concerned with the plan. John Lennon's phrase: 'life is what happens while you're making other plans' is a good fit. Our misplaced trust in the birth plan distracted from our capacity to respond, informed by our perceptions of what was occurring. Additionally, the reliance upon hierarchical procedure (waiting for the midwife) jeopardized the situation – organization research shows how 'flat structures' (Belasan, 2000), that is those without hierarchical dependency, are 'more agile, flexible, efficient, productive and adaptable', as they engender creative responsiveness. The fundamental experience of birth is a good place to start acknowledging our human capacity to respond creatively as events unfold.

Learning

Improvisation is significant in the development of successful learning. Chapter 7 included two contrasting examples: the improvisational approaches of 'high-level learning' and improvisation's role in offering equality of opportunity in education. Through improvisation education can focus on collaborative, open-ended problem solving through which students gain the four areas of common knowledge found among experts: *deep conceptual understanding, integrated knowledge, adaptive expertise* and *collaborative skills* – these are also features found in improvising musicians' practice (Sawyer). Necessarily, the improvisational characteristics of this learning are mirrored in the pedagogical approach that will respond to emergent learning knowledgeably and supportively, regardless of the subject areas. As an activity that engages and develops through the process of group interaction, improvisation reverses 'top-down' models of learning. Enabling 'voice', improvisation draws essential value from the expression of distinct difference. Encouraging different voices to create at the point of performance rather than seeking to repeat will question education as cultural reproduction: while the aim of repetition narrows creative options, improvisation calls for creative decision-making in its processes. There can be resistance to improvisation. Too readily education's failure to grasp improvisation's significance, as a profound learning process, is projected as a failure of improvisation rather than, more accurately, a reflection of inexperience and limited educational thinking, training and design. So too, institutionalization is problematic as it can obfuscate the potential human capability of the improvisation phenomenon, thereby preventing the inclusion of practices that extend knowledge.

Chapter 3 described improvisation's important relationship with ideas of inclusion; the implications of this are far reaching, not only for good educational practice but for improvisation as a relational arts practice and beyond. The philosophy of educational 'inclusion' in the UK, stemming from the 1980s, aimed to provide equality of opportunity. However, the term 'inclusion' has become co-opted by 'arts-funding-speak' (Bishop, 2006). Furthermore, the New Labour government exploited the connotations offered by reference to inclusion to further much broader political goals (Mulderrig, 2012). With this in mind, reference to inclusion needs to be made with awareness of its abiding social significance for education.

In a 2008 interview, reeds player Oleyumi Thomas describes his attitude to collective music making as a call to 'Bring your stuff [...]' – the invitation to express a particular, individual contribution within the collective experience. Skilfully facilitated, the improvisation process will value and engage difference. The diversity of improvisation that is potentially present, the 'infinite combinations' (Lewis) forms the foundation of the pedagogical process, giving rise to the collaborative, creative activity. The example of working with those who had been excluded from education showed how improvisation encourages the development of diverse social relationships while contributing to the aim of inclusion. The development of trust is nurtured through the process, and this supports the teacher-learner relationship. By means of expressive participation, the students in this difficult setting developed the sense of an owned, autonomous culture of education that carried into other lessons and subjects: the sense of worth in the value of the contribution enhancing the sense of self.

Academic structures can too easily overshadow the very social nature of learning in school and with it the essential need for the development of social intelligence. Traditions have valued compliance and disciplined hierarchical structure over learning that is informed by its social context. For example, ethics is sometimes taught, paradoxically, without reference to the existing group context, and the nature and quality of the group's communication in which that teaching is taking place, or indeed the larger social structure of the learning community. The active processes of improvisation foreground the ethical, social dimension in education. By this means, the creative, collaborative character of improvisation develops 'social-intelligence'. The implementation of improvisation in music and elsewhere is an opportunity for what Lewis refers to as *personal transformation [...]*. Collaborative skills are necessary for effective learning in all subject areas. Collaborative learning is, arguably, one of the most useful forms of contextualized educational practice that can become developed – the social, adaptive nature of the process of improvisation serves this development. Employing improvisational learning strategies develops a more socially aware educational arena in which collaborative learning is valued and developed, regardless of the subject, engaging and advocating the human capability for creative, adaptable responsiveness. As learning is necessarily a social process, one in which people naturally support one another and become supported, the denial of the collaborative aspect is difficult to justify. Contrasting with the culture of competition in education, encouraged between individuals and institutions, Chapter 7 discussed the under-articulated importance of group learning – taking place through inter-subjective processes. Knowingly or not, competition in education simultaneously appeases 'traditions' and helps service the competitive economy. Unfortunately, this becomes compounded when governments try to use education as an opportunity to gain political favour. For example, too often an increased focus on competition in education is promoted as the way in which the left can 'prove rigour' while 'driving up standards' and, similarly, the right can offer reassurance to their supporters by reference to 'good old-fashioned methods'. Rather, group learning is an essentially important aspect of development in education. For education, improvisation's 'unique' aspect (Butcher) is the activity's combination of collaboration occurring in diverse social contexts married with personal development.

We can understand the importance of improvisation for education in a day-to-day manner: in action in Music, Drama, English, Citizenship and so on, potentially transmigrating across the range of subjects in the curriculum – necessarily mirrored by the responsive, adaptable creativity of the teaching itself. We can also understand the place of improvisation in education at a meta level, as a response to the truer indeterminacy of life. Luhman (2002) describes:

> There should be a pedagogy that prepares the offspring who need education for a future that remains unknown. The unknowability of the future is a resource, namely, the condition for the possibility of making decisions. As a consequence, learning and knowledge would have to be replaced by learning how to make decisions, that is, how to take advantage of not-knowing.

The construct of education itself, in many ways, expresses adult doubt and fear of indeterminacy; presenting young people with an over-protective narrative of the world is a poor preparation for life. Rather, improvisation proposes active, responsive learning that seeks to creatively negotiate indeterminacy.

The Phenomenology of Improvisation

To look at the nature of the phenomenon of improvisation we also need to consider how phenomena are perceived and become conceptualized; the examination of improvisation is only in the context of our understanding of how meaning itself is achieved, and what that meaning making leads to. Merleau-Ponty's relevance is in the exploration of the means by which we create understanding of the world: the examination of the phenomenology of perception – that takes place through our bodies.

> The real is a closely woven fabric. It does not await our judgement before incorporating the most surprising phenomena, or before rejecting the most plausible figments of our imagination. Perception is not a science of the world, it is not even an act, a deliberate taking up of a position; it is the background from which all acts stand out, and is

presupposed by them [...] When I return to myself from an excursion into the realm of dogmatic common sense or of fiction, I find, not a source of intrinsic truth, but a subject destined to the world.

(Merleau-Ponty 1962)

Recognizing the essential subjectivity and inter-subjectivity of improvisation, within being, leads to the need to describe the act in ways that reflect its changing and temporal dimension. In order to avoid limitations, *describing* rather than seeking to *define* is a more helpful strategy in the development of meaning.

Improvisation is characterized by its openness that mirrors our perceptual openness to the world. The not-predetermined leaves the improviser 'open', allowing for creativity in all of its different contexts, in whatever ways it may arise. In creating at the point of performance this inherent openness seems obvious, but for practice it is nurtured through sophisticated, experiential understanding. '*[...] that was the great lesson that I learned, you know, that every night's different, every minute is different. If you can get yourself in tune with how things are flowing you fair better, because then you're relaxed, you're totally open, you know, and then you can take yourself out of the picture of trying to control everything and then you find the flow, and then you get into that flow and you let the music reveal itself. That was an important lesson for me to learn [...] to me this is a very important factor – to make sure that you're open. And that you're relaxed and that you've come to that realization, you know – wait a minute, this a different space than I was working in last night. And that's half the situation*' (Mitchell, p. 13, l. 36). Mitchell's description is important; it delineates the essential value of the ability to respond. Being open is realized by allowing the development of the music, not trying to control it, but being aware of how things are different on each occasion, in each moment. The description also suggests Taoist thought (Lao Tzu and Lau, 1964) of becoming effective by removing the controlling self in order to '*let the music reveal itself*'. This 'open' attitude informs how we relate to others; in Chapter 9 Butcher described the creativity of accepting others' intentions and Lewis suggests how '*tuning in*' to others intentions can become part of a method. '*[...] I'm trying to direct my attention to particular features in the given environment that I think I can use or work with [...] when you are trying to play with someone, whatever instrument or whatever they're doing, you're interacting with them, you're not even playing with them, it should come to you at a certain point, some sense of their intentions, it should come [...]*' (Lewis, p. 4, l. 42).

As not fixed, mutable, evolving, adaptable, fluid, not-predetermined, shifting, flexible, developing, responsive and available improvisation's phenomenological openness leads to its special quality as a social, group activity. This gives rise to questions of community, best discussed through specific examples. Places of education develop their own communities and are part of community. Chapter 3 described the education of young people in East London through the perspective of music, drama and improvisation. The interviewees' too are members of a 'community of practice', connected through the shared professional activity of improvisation in music. By way of its process, improvisation holds inter-cultural agency – enacted group improvisation functions through self-determined difference;

improvisation engenders different approaches to music making. Retaining openness to different events characterizes the potential in improvisation and this aspect simultaneously describes its potential and difficulty for education. Education tends to favour and reward the fixed standardization of approaches; it is less good at acknowledging how enacted, creative processes enable the development of learning. This disjunction may contribute to explaining why many high achieving adults, examples of which can be found in politics, arts, sport, business, academia and elsewhere, have not achieved well at school: in short, and at the much broader societal level, potential capability for human development is not being acknowledged by education. The reductionism leading from an institutional desire to meet targets can easily produce a blind-spot concerning the capability for different, adaptable, creative responses in learning and this works against more over-arching educational goals. Through the example of music we can see how the process of improvisation's openness to difference, its positive potential, regardless of the setting, means that it is available for different 'voices': those with different musical-cultural orientations, as well as for different kinds of achievement.

Key to conceptualizing improvisation is the notion of embodied mind. Although ever present, cultural ambivalence about the body reflects uncertainty and confusion regarding its essential significance. For example, while idealized body images are ever present across media, diseases associated with body image are also common. Reflecting this conflicted picture, it is no surprise that understanding of the body's fundamental importance, and in this case the connection to improvisation's potential, is out of step. Increased knowledge of the embodied mind underscores the need for continued research in *enacted* arts practice. Meaning in improvisation is embodied and socially situated and so the *lived experience* of improvisation provides the focus for discussion. While this has extended out towards various areas of theorizing, these only become meaningful when contextualized by improvisation's lived experience.

Within the phenomenological approach of 'going back to the things themselves' the ten interviewees' experiential understanding of their practice is prioritized. This experience exists in the world, not separate from it, and is reflected in improvisation.

> I cannot conceive myself as nothing but a bit of the world, a mere object of biological, psychological or sociological investigation. I cannot shut myself up in the world of science. All my knowledge of the world, even my scientific knowledge, is gained from my own particular point of view, or from some experience of the world without which the symbols of science would be meaningless. The whole universe of science is built upon the world as directly experienced [...] we must begin by reawakening the basic experience of the world of which science is a second-order expression [...].
>
> (Merleau-Ponty, 1962, p. ix)

The immediacy required for composing in the process of performing calls for a particular presence in time within engagement in the world, an intervolving. Each experience of improvisation in time is potentially unique. Rather than a fixed object of study, the experience of improvisation is ongoing, and continuously changing through its processes. Improvisation, tied to time in the present (rather than fixed in the written form), is experienced, rooted in and existing within our human, social situations. Through the temporal explorative engagement with music and sound, improvisation is indivisible from being and time: '[...] *this unrepeatable experience [...] That's a rare thing in our society – Western societies [...] To have a sensory experience which is only going to happen in that moment is very unusual'* (Butcher, p. 19, l. 34). Improvisation turns us towards the specific circumstances of the present. While musicians' histories are heard in the music, through improvisation the music occurs inescapably in the now, telling us about the present. Butcher's comment also reflects how reproduction and repetition has come to dominate culture; the performance practice of improvisation is unusual because it operates outside the dominance of repetition.

The themes of improvisation, *Process, Learning, Body* and *Approaches* are non-linear and form, simultaneously, a number of strata of improvisation that create their own registers. They are also, of course, interrelated, or imbricated, acting in ways that support one another and the body is a condition of improvisation through which the themes of improvisation are experienced. There are a number of terms that partially reflect this aspect of improvisation: gestalt, holism, multiplicity, oneness, co-presence, but none of these quite captures the breadth of changing possibilities in improvisation; each brings connotations that limit the conceptual openness and availability of improvisation. The working together of the themes of improvisation also reflects our intervolving with the world of things and others. So too, the relational nature of improvisation is itself unifying, mirroring the coexistence of its themes. Improvisation's potential for sociality is inclusive; it offers a trans-disciplinary process across experience; creatively responsive; simultaneously a part of and creating the environment; engaging the whole self. When we go 'back to the things themselves' we find improvisation. What can become highly developed among musicians is the ability to attune to emerging possibilities, but the opportunity to respond creatively within temporal emergence in life also occurs across our experience. Improvisation is a condition of being-in-the-world and the human processes found in improvisation in music are reflected in other contexts as the experience of improvisation is present in different activity. Our response to being truly alive is to act with what is, the world of time and things, through which we improvise.

Part 3

The Interviews

Roscoe Mitchell

SR: What is the place of free improvisation in your practice?

RM: I think that I study composition and improvisation as a parallel because what I'm striving for is to be able to create spontaneous composition. And I think that this helps me know how composition works and then you can apply these principles during an improvisation. So I go back and forth. I may have a period where I'm doing concerts that are totally improvised and then I may have a period where I'm doing concerts that are compositions and improvisation mixed as a form – a way to study how the whole process works.

SR: What's the difference between composed and improvised for you?

RM: Although improvisation has been around for a long time, I don't want to say it is a young form but ... if you look around at the great composers, I mean they all improvised. So I just feel it's important, for me, to study music as a whole because there are so many things that happen in music that I find interesting. An improvisation may inspire a written composition. I believe it's important also to leave some music behind for people that might be interested. You know, like after you're gone, and so on – or even while you're still alive actually. So, for me it's been helpful to formulate my ideas. To be able to actually put them down and then move on to another source of study. If there's something in an improvisation that I'd like to learn more about then I may write some things out to help me do those things, to help me think about them, in terms of where do I want to come in. Do I always want to come in on 1? Perhaps I don't always want to come in on 1. Maybe I want to come in on the 3 or the quintuplet or the last part of the quintuplet, all these different questions, how do I want to place these beats inside of a metric unit. Perhaps if there are 8 notes, I might want to come in on 7. All of these different questions and for me it's been helpful to do these things in real-time, so that I am aware of them when I am improvising. I mean write a composition out that addresses these problems.

SR: So the writing is part of the practice.

RM: I kind of feel like for me to be a good improviser, and to be able to improve your skills as an improviser, it's worked out that I've studied composition and improvisation as a parallel. The concert with Muhal Richard Abrams was completely improvised (a duet concert a week prior to the interview). But there again I think it's important to establish lasting relationships with musicians and I've been fortunate from that point of view to have come along at that time when there was a group of people who were interested and had a vision about how they wanted their destinies to go. In terms of not just their music but their philosophy and the way they were thinking about, they were going to have some control over their lives. And that when people sat down and they looked at the lives of some of the great masters, that came before, you know, how things turned out for them, by being not organized and being loners and things like that.

SR: Are we talking about people like Charlie Parker?

RM: Absolutely, all the greats. I mean some people – well Charlie Parker had what, two European tours in his whole life, or something. Of course some musicians moved to Europe where they were more accepted. And I think that's because Europe has a longer standing tradition of supporting art and, well, here just recently, jazz is accepted in the States on a broader basis. For me growing up though, my parents were always aware of everything, there wasn't this separation between this age group and that age group. But then I came up in a time when you were exposed to all kinds of music and also there was also a lot of live music right in our neighbourhood, and everybody had access to it, I mean, the very young could experience it by going to the movie theatre. You'd have a movie and after that it might be Count Basie's big band, Duke Ellington's big band, Ella Fitzgerald and so on. Now we've gotten kind of away from that, things have moved into a category of the large corporations controlling art and putting emphasis on the part that makes them money. Let's say if you've got a kid and you don't expose them to all kinds of music and everything when they're growing up, and they're just left to tune into what the going product is, a lot of times people can get lost, whereas for me it was different. A radio station might play a very wide variety of music throughout the day, there was something for everybody. You could go to a restaurant or something like that and they had those juke boxes that you put a nickel in and the programme was very wide. Whatever was popular, jazz tunes or, all that was right there so people were able to listen to all kinds of music and make their own decisions about what they liked and didn't like.

SR: I've read that the AACM was very involved with composition as well as improvisation. Composition can be funded whereas improvisation has difficulty with funding …

RM: Some places had a better time accessing funding than others. For instance if you look at the BAG [Black Artists' Group] organization in St Louis, I wouldn't say it was easy but they had an easier time than people in Chicago. In St Louis you had lots of people applying for funding and they were inspired by the work that the AACM was doing but they had smart people there: Oliver Lake, Julius Hemphill and all these people. They were able to get funding pretty rapidly, not only for their organization but they had a building and all these different kinds of things. In Chicago, a larger city, you had more people applying, so the AACM didn't really start out getting grants and things right away. I mean the organization was mostly funded by members paying dues, citing different projects that we wanted to accomplish. Eventually we got some space in the Abraham Lincoln Centre, where we could have our rehearsals, and have our schools and so on. I mean that's the other kind of thing that's not around that much anymore, these community centres. When I was growing up there were community centres where our kids could go, like after school, to programmes and so on and so forth, The Abraham Lincoln Centre in Chicago was one of those. So from that point of view that made a difference. Now the notion of the composition thing, Muhal had a band that he kept together at that time that he called The Experimental Band. And we were encouraged to write for the band, you know write for the band and bring in compositions and get them played. And listen to them and see what you did right and what you did wrong and have the opportunity to change things if you needed to.

SR: Where were these people coming from who were writing music?

RM: Well, Muhal encouraged us to do that.

SR: Was that coming from Muhal?

RM: That was coming from Muhal Richard Abrams. He always encouraged.

SR: Just write something down.

RM: Absolutely, absolutely, you know, write down your idea. I mean when we'd get out of school we'd go right over to Muhal's house. We'd get there at something like 1.30 or 2 in the afternoon and oftentimes we wouldn't leave until 9 o'clock at night, and then next day same thing. We explored a lot of different things together at that time.

SR: What age were you then?

RM: This was 1961, I guess, so I was 21. I was 21 years old then, but we explored all kinds of things, all kinds of things. We'd go to art museums and maybe spend the whole day looking at different art, all these different things. It was kind of like a total world of learning … what I've seen of people that are particularly talented, they usually can do almost anything in art, they have to decide which way they're going to want to go. Because out of that group of people we had Lester Lashley who is a very talented artist, although he still plays, you know, art became his real focus. So, like I said it was a whole pool of learning, I mean you could learn things from all these different people and certainly the compositional process was very interesting. Each person has their own take on it; the concerts were all different because each person would have their own take on that – I mean you were inspired.

SR: You mean a different way of writing?

RM: A different way of writing – their own personalities. I'm just talking about the way they represented their own individuality onto the music, I mean if you look at and study the AACM you'll see that although we are all there together, none of us are the same. Because there was big emphasis on getting people to go inside of themselves and come up with their own text. That was the general philosophy of the AACM. I mean if we just look at the different people, if you just look at the saxophonists: Anthony Braxton is not like me at all, Joseph Jarman is not like Anthony Braxton, Henry Threadgill is not like … John Stubblefield is not like any of us, you know, on and on. That's why I consider myself fortunate to have been put into a group of people like this. So I learned early on. Well I think a lot of those people they kind of had that going – I mean that's probably the reason for the coming together of the AACM. People had had a look at the scene to see what was happening. There was a new license for the clubs that started to come down where, you know if you had a trio, you only had to pay this much for a license. If you had anything other than a trio then it was this other amount of money that you had to have. A lot of the clubs would hire a trio to play and then there were sessions. We saw the emergence of the DJ starting to come on. And people didn't want to do that, they wanted to move their music to a concert setting that featured individual members, in their own compositions and so on like that, so it's a whole world of thought that evolved, that you're starting to deal with.

SR: How did that work in relation to the competitiveness within music: people … I'm thinking of the 'cutting contests', that kind of atmosphere. I also wanted to ask you how you developed your saxophone voice: what do think about technique and ideas?

RM: Technique is an important thing to have in order to express your ideas. For me if I'm listening to a saxophonist, the first thing I'm listening to is the sound, that's primary for me. If I hear a saxophonist who doesn't have a sound I'm not that interested. And about the sessions and so on, there were sessions in Chicago and it's true you know. You go to a session and someone calls something you don't know and you come home and learn that and come back next week and they call something else you don't know, so there's definitely that competition element in it, which is healthy. In my mind music has its own laws – you don't abide by those laws you loose. So all of these different things are important and it's no different with improvised music. Certainly there are levels and degrees among improvisers, so what I've done, and continue to do, is try to improve, all the time, so that I'm able to speak in any kind of situation. And that's what you want to be able to do, you want to have enough technique to be able to present the ideas that you're hearing in your head. You keep working on your technique, so you can present more ideas, and then continuous thoughts, because it's also a thinker's game. So you want to be able to have the long-range thinking. Certainly studying composition helps you develop that because you know how things develop and so on. And I've spent a lot of time when I was teaching workshops and improvisation and all that kind of thing, and noticing what inexperienced improvisers were doing and figuring out different ways to address the problems and so on, because, if you listen, a lot of inexperienced improvisers, all they do is follow. Following is like being behind on a written piece of music; in other words, you know your part, I don't really know my part so I'm listening to see what you're doing and by the time I've waited to see what you're doing I'm already behind. So working on different methods that actually get you up to speed, that are in the moment, like people want to say they're 'in the moment' of the improvisation. Knowing how composition works helps. If you're improvising with somebody and they're playing eighth notes all the time and you want to add some counterpoint to what's going on, you may think, well maybe I should play some triplets here, you know. But of course people ought to be aware that all they're doing is playing eighth notes. There's nothing wrong with that if you put it in context, if you want to have an improvisation that doesn't use anything but eight notes, you can also do that. Sometimes, working with music you can take one small element and then really have a real look at it, and then it starts to reveal itself to you in another kind of a way. What I found is the only thing that helps you with music are the things that you really learn, the things that you don't really learn they're already out there haunting you, until you really decide to really learn them. So it's all of these different things that play into the picture.

There's nothing wrong with nurturing what you're doing with others. I mean you can go back further than the AACM to the big bands and so on. People are like families, that's why they played so well together. Wow, and if you think it's nothing go out there right now and try to keep a big band together and working. You know that's very difficult. When I was coming up there were established big bands that were playing and so on. And to me the only way to have a really good big band was to keep it together for a while. It doesn't matter if everyone is a really good musician, until they really learn how to play together, you start to establish a real sound, inside of the big band. We had a big band in the AACM and smaller groups.

SR: So there is a comparison to Ellington, in that he was writing for these individual voices.

RM: Oh, absolutely, yes. I mean if I think about the AACM, there are people in there that not only have their own ideas about how they want to play the music, they have instruments that nobody else even has. So the palette for composition is a very wide palette. Not to mention having all this experience of playing together for so many years. To me that's very important because

I knew that when I got on this track in music I was there for the long haul because it doesn't stop. A lot of people thought oh, it's going to stop and that's going to be it and nothing else is going to happen. What people have seen over the years is that this really doesn't stop. Actually, to try to accomplish what I'd like to accomplish in music I'd need more than one lifetime, to accomplish that because music itself is so vast.

The time I played with Coltrane, when he came up to me and said come up and play, and just shook my hand. To me that was just like, without a word being spoken, I got so many messages from that you know. Like we might shake somebody's hand or something like that, or squeeze your hand or something like that, you know. When Coltrane presented his hand to you, oooh, I'm a musician, it felt like, none of that, I'm totally at peace with myself – I have no fear of anyone else with a saxophone in their hand. You know all of these different kinds of things, without a word being spoken. Totally open, totally at peace, totally putting you in a very relaxed mood, you know. I mean after the first set I was like trying to get packed up and get out of there. He said no, no, come on back, let's play some more. It was because Jack DeJohnette, when Jack DeJohnette was in Chicago, he and I played together all the time. And when Trane came through with that band with Jack DeJohnette and Rashid Ali and Jimi Garrison, Alice Coltrane and Pharoah Sanders. Jack DeJohnette was the one that told Coltrane, oh, have him come up and play. I'd really just gone down there to hear it, to hear them. So I mean for me, and back then I couldn't even imagine what it would be like for someone to ask you what your name was and you said John Coltrane, you know. For me that was too big of an overwhelming thought to entertain anything like that. So, it's amazing how you can run into things in life where not a word needs to be spoken, not a word needs to be spoken. Like I said, I grew up in an environment where all you had to do was to show someone that you were interested in what they were doing and they would teach you. There was one guy that used to be out in the park every day with his saxophone, and he would be out there morning till evening, standing by this tree running nothing but all these scales and arpeggios. Over and over and over and over again. I mean these are the kinds of experiences that I grew up with and they have made a lasting impression on me. And I know that if you stay true to your music, you know, usually music will take care of you. And for me I mean one great thing that happened for me, sometimes you worry about money and you worry about this and that, I think I'm going to stop worrying about this because it always works out anyway … And once I did that I was clear, you know, I was clear. Stay on your music, there's a lot in music and you need your time. Periods of study are wonderful. And like you said, there's more things starting to happen here and there's more things starting to happen there. Just be ready for when things start to happen. Being depressed or, oh there's nothing to do, that doesn't bode well, not for anybody. The best thing to do is to use your time wisely and keep working on your music so that when something does happen, you're ready. And in terms of writing – write! Even if there's nothing happening. So somebody calls you and, OK, I need a piece for this and a piece for that. Go in the drawer and here it is. It's already written. All these different factors are important and sometimes you can make your best achievements in the down times.

A lot of classical trained musicians are becoming more interested in improvising. People from all different fields of music are stepping out of the category, I mean, Charlie Parker wanted to study with Varese and someone else too, but who knows what Charlie Parker would be doing today if he was alive. What we saw from him was a constant growth in his music. The same with Coltrane, you know, you saw a constant growth in his music. And these were individual people also. Charlie Parker when he was young, he studies Lester Young, they don't sound anything alike. You had music evolving with Charlie Parker way back from when he was with Jay McShann [bangs fast rhythm on the table] like that kind of beat. And what he was playing was far removed from that. So I think most serious students of music, they're always in there trying to learn more and develop their music and achieve their visions for their music. We've had many different eras in music, some of the great classical music interpreters are gone, and they're not going to be replaced. Horowitz for instance, there's never going to be another Horowitz. It's not the same, it's totally different. What we don't want to do is get people to be like other people because then we start to lose their individual approaches as to the way they do things and then we're missing out on a lot like that. Because we can't really learn anything from people that are all the same. I think that's one of our most prized possessions, that we're all individuals and this is where we learn.

I think there's several different avenues of study. Also, like if you're in the field of improvisation you need to study solo work too. Because you need to have the sense that you are able to walk out there and present a solo concert of your own ideas and that strengthens your ability to present your ideas and that gets carried over into the larger ensemble, so you have to be able to function on your own and you have to be able to function with a large group of people and certainly you can put your different emphasis on different things. You can start your session with different things, you can start your session with finding out what is the dynamic of this group. A lot of times that's based on what's the softest dynamic you have there. OK, so you want to work at that to try to get the balance, to get everyone to sound like one. So everyone can hear what the ensemble sounds like and then setting what instruments are there and different combinations of different things. How you can think together as an ensemble. I mean what excites me most is when you hear an ensemble improvising and you can actually hear them thinking, you know, you know that they all know that they are in a certain place and they still have this option of having several choices to make. What ruins an improvisation is when there are no choices. Another way to circumvent copying is to … maybe you played a really nice idea, I heard it, I don't have to play it right after you, I can play that later on, you're going to be somewhere else by then … All these different things are just methods of learning. With improvisation it's just the same as anything else. As if you're practising scales to learn. There's the scales of improvisation as well, that one needs to practice. So that they have been incorporated into the vocabulary.

SR: What do you mean by scales of improvisation?

RM: You have to figure out different ways you want to practice your improvisation. Some of the things we're talking about right now: large ensemble balances, knowing what the dynamics are, knowing what the soft things are. And of course that doesn't negate that the loud things can get really loud, that's another colour in the palette. Sometimes the softer instruments can go, sometimes the louder instruments can go, sometimes you can have this combination, the red with the blue, the green with the yellow, all of these different things. The same sorts of thoughts that you would have if you were actually sitting down writing composition for this particular ensemble. All of these things have to be evident in the improvisation and for me what I do is I study all of these elements in order to gain freedom. All of us have our own individuality that we bring to the improvisation but you still have to work on that. Otherwise you are always doing the same thing all the time. I mean that's what I found fascinating about the 60s for instance. When people finally decided to make that move and trust themselves to move and step over into these other areas of music, it was very exciting. You had all these different people's personalities and so on going on. But it's only the people who went on to develop themselves, are the ones who remain. So, um, music is, in the end, 99.9 per cent work. There's that small fraction where some nights you can't do any wrong. But still … most of the time you're out there working, and that's what's exciting about it, you know. So, being able to explore it in that way. I mean even Art Blakey would tell musicians: OK, you've got this down, I don't want to hear it again tomorrow night, I want to hear you reaching for something else, I want to hear you exploring. I'd rather have you up there making a mistake, you know, trying to do something than finding some area that you're comfortable with and doing it over and over again. So, it's all of these different things.

Each night is different – where I fall down, (laughs) if I did something good the night before and then get up there and try and do the same thing.

SR: Try and repeat the good bits.

RM: Right, right. Just kind of observe what's going on in the evening and try to get into the flow of that. Then you get the best out of it, you know. It never works, trying to take music by the collar. That just doesn't work out. Find the flow, get into the flow and just let the music reveal itself ... even written composition varies from night to night, depending upon the mood. And then if its improvisation, that shouldn't be the same every night, you know, the improvisation should not be the same every night – there should be a different take on it.

SR: So there's allowing for spontaneity around the composition?

RM: Absolutely, absolutely. I mean that was the great lesson that I learned, you know, that every night's different, every minute is different. If you can get yourself in tune with how things are flowing, you fair better, because then you're relaxed, you're totally open, you know, and then you can take yourself out of the picture of trying to control everything and then you find the flow, and then you get into that flow and you let the music reveal itself. That was an important lesson for me to learn. If I'm touring and I'm working within certain confines, of some areas that I'm trying to have more control over. It becomes very exciting if I'm playing every night because I'm constantly thinking: Oh what did I do last night, what should I do to move forward on that or I shouldn't have done that or I won't do that again. All these different kinds of things. A lot of times if I'm doing that, usually after the concert I have to have a wine just to calm myself down. So I can let the mind shut down, so I can relax and pull myself away from it, you know. But that to me is a very important factor... to make sure that you're open. And that you're relaxed and that you've come to that realization, you know, wait a minute this is a different space than I was working in last night. And that's half the situation. I mean even if you're working on a composition, or whatever, that is going to be different every night and a lot of times the way you play the composition will influence the way you approach the improvisation. There are all these minute details that define these areas.

Maggie Nicols

SR: I want to ask you about the place of improvisation in your practice. How did you start improvising?

MN: Well, apart from the improvising that we all do as children – which I do feel we are all born to be improvisers, the actual first official improvisation I did was with John Stevens and it all happened [pause] because I went down the Old Place, Ronnie Scott's. I'd been doing jazz standards, bebop, cabaret and all sorts, rock bands, soul bands and I heard Mike Westbook and I think it was John Surman, I can't remember who was playing, and it was all instruments and no voices and I remember thinking, oh, wow, feeling, I think I could hear a voice in here! I'd love to hear a voice in here and somebody saying, well John Stevens works with voices. So I went up to the Little Theatre Club and heard him with Norma Winston and I think Derek was playing that night, Derek Bailey, Evan Parker, I can't remember if Trevor was playing that night, Trevor Watts. But anyway, I was so absolutely blown away and I went up, you know quite shyly, said I would love to do something like that and John just said yes and then I didn't have the courage, and I bumped into Trevor somewhere else, and he said come up this Saturday and I did and it was amazing. John set up this piece, which I use in workshops to this day – the Sustain Piece (Stevens, 1985) where you just take a breath and sing or play any note. I did it with GIO (Glasgow Improvisers' Orchestra), I do it with everybody really, and the most amazing thing happened: it was Trevor playing the alto and John was just playing overtones on a gong and we just kept our notes for a while and then me and Trevor just started bending towards each other and just went into this incredible, blissful experience, it was just phenomenal, and I was hooked from then. I worked with John's Spontaneous Music Ensemble (SME) for some time. So that was in 1968.

SR: What were you doing prior to that? You used to dance didn't you?

MN: Yes, I was a Windmill Girl. My first singing job was when I was sixteen in a strip club in Manchester after the Windmill closed, because I was fifteen when I was at the Windmill. From there I started singing with jazz musicians, firm functions, that sort of thing, lots of jazz musicians did that for a living but as long as people could dance, in those days, you could pretty much do what you liked, you could play anything as long as people could get up and dance and it would be a quick step, or a foxtrot the sort of things you hear the live band doing on Strictly Come Dancing – I used to really love that – I mean I learnt so much – and then I worked with this bebop piano player called Dennis Rose in pubs, and he just taught me everything really – that was the first thing I did after the strip club – and I went on to sing with these other musicians in these functions. And so suddenly going from that to free improvisation in 1968, it was just brilliant.

SR: That's a massive leap as well – they're like different worlds aren't they?

MN: Yes.

SR: The Windmill or a strip club in Manchester and then …

MN: I suppose working with Dennis, although Dennis was a revolutionary in his own era – Dennis Rose – because he was one of the pioneers of the bebop in Britain. Nobody knows him, really, except musicians, who actually were unofficially trained by him, I mean so many of us served apprenticeships with him, you could put it that way, which is how it used to be, isn't it, in the music scene, there wasn't formal education in that way except with classical music, so most jazz musicians learnt through playing with other musicians and Dennis mentored loads of musicians. So in some ways he was a revolutionary, so in that sense, he was the spirit of bebop, not as a style which it became, obviously it fossilized and became a little bit just going through the motions, but the way Dennis played it, it was truly experimental. And then to go from that to John Stevens, although musically it was very different, the spirit was very much the same. John was a pioneer, was one of the founding pioneers of free improvisation in Europe. You could almost look at anybody in the European improvised music scene and they've been influenced by John, if not directly by playing with him then by playing with people who did play with him. And all the musicians played with him – Evan, Derek … he was just phenomenal, he really was. He took rhythm in particular to a whole new area. Previous to that you would hear drummers who had fantastic time, you know, playing metrically, and they'd throw it all over the place, but as soon as you took the meter away they'd often sound like beached whales, you know floundering about on dry land and John devised ways to keep that [sings bip, bap … bip … bap, clap, bap] that thing that you hear that is so kind of – people take for granted that kind of, that rhythmic feel in free improvisation, but really it was not that usual. I have this theory, because John had this place he could play he found called the Little Theatre Club, which was up about five flights of stairs, very narrow stairs, and I have a feeling that one of the reasons he developed such an amazing approach was that he just didn't want to carry a full kit up all those stairs. So he devised these weird, amazing, small, very interesting sounds, in the little kit. And I think that's part of the reason [laughs] well, since he died I've thought that, I wonder if he just thought I must get something smaller that I can carry up all those stairs. He did certainly – he used things like temple blocks, he used lots of sounds that took him somewhere else.

SR: What about the relationship to the United States. There is a different reference to jazz there – have you any thoughts on that?

MN: Yes, of course. Well I do feel things are revolutionary in their time and if you really think about it, what jazz is in its essence, before it becomes stylized, mannered and sanitized, it is improvisation, a true jazz musician is inspired. It's not just a question of scales, obviously scales are part of what you learn, but a true jazz musician transcends that and uses the scales as a stepping stone to explore and experiment. And each development in jazz – if you think of Ornette, time, no changes, that whole thing of taking away the harmonic and exploring what it would be like to play free, with time, but still keeping an actual pulse. Then John and people like John saying OK well what would it be like to take everything away, it's an evolutionary process and I suppose classical music has its own evolutionary process. Free improvisation, coming from the jazz tradition, is a natural evolution coming from the different periods in the history of jazz. In the same way as, I can't speak from the classical perspective because I'm not a classical musician but I'm sure that people like Joelle Leandre who would talk about the work with John Cage and I'm sure Pauline [Oliveros] as well, that newness has a similar thing as well, probably negating what has come before but also a growing out of what has gone before. I think each new movement replaces but also embraces what's gone before. Firstly you have to replace, when you are learning a new language but then you also embrace. So working especially with Irene and Joelle is a joy because Irene comes from a jazz tradition and Joelle comes from the classical tradition, I come from jazz but also soul, blues and also cabaret, theatre and you know we have both learnt the new language of the more abstract free improvisation but also can integrate the different roots and histories, our own personal musical histories as well, so I do feel it is a beautiful contraction, you embrace what's gone before and replace it.

SR: You bring all these different aspects: dance, talk, singing, rhythms, stories, voices into a single performance …

MN: Exactly, to me the source, the universe is improvisational, so if you're drawing on that source you are drawing on something that is multidimensional, you can't get more multidimensional than the universe can you … I'm not talking mystically particularly now, I'm just talking about the history of humankind and before humankind, if you're drawing on that then it's infinite, it is multidimensional – like you say a child, whatever it is – this conversation is improvised.

SR: But what is unique with you is that you manage to realize something of that in performance [laughs]. I've seen you do it in a workshop situation or gathering and I've seen you do it in a straightforward performance and I don't know if it's something you're necessarily consciously thinking about …

MN: No, something that has just happened really. Well, I remember the first time that it sort of happened, when I broke away from being more just focused on the voice – because John used to sometimes tease me and say: you're so theatrical he would say [laughs] – but I remember the first time it happened, it came when I was doing a gig with my ex-husband, Harry Vince, who was a trumpet player, and I can't remember who else was on that gig, maybe Chris

Francis, a sax player. Lol [Coxhill] was doing a solo gig – and I remember, whichever group we were in, I was struggling and I was struggling so hard, and I was too young to know to stop and I didn't know what to do and I found myself thinking, 'I'm lying, I'm lying', and before I knew what was happening I was saying it. I was saying in front of the whole audience, 'I'm lying'. And once I said I was lying suddenly these gestures, I suddenly found myself moving and dancing and of course the fact that I'd been a dancer, it suddenly made sense – it just happened and it was from then I suppose that I realized, well goodness I don't have to – why do I just have to sing – and music makes me move anyway, so why not extend that and then of course there's the theatre and all your life and everything and yes, that's where I suppose was the birth of that. And for a while it was very difficult because the early improvised scene was pretty purist and a lot did not take kindly to what I did. They thought it was really dragging improvisation through the mud [laughs]. But I suppose I couldn't help it – it just became more and more of who I was or who I am and just felt more and more convinced that that's what improvising for me was, it was just a totality of whatever, of the history, the now, the other musicians, the environment, what's going on in the world, politically, all those things and it varies all the time as well.

SR: I'm thinking of a performance I saw of you with Phil Minton.[1] You incorporate surroundings, be it the chair or members of the audience, and I see it as softening the performing boundaries, allowing for the possibilities in the environment of the performance.

MN: That's a lovely way of putting it. I like that, 'softening', I like that. And I suppose it's because I surrender, when I'm really functioning fully and completely as a performing improviser or an improvising performer, or a being, just being, I suppose it's that thing of just surrendering – really when I surrender anything can happen, basically, it's total trust – it's total trust. If I start panicking or getting self-conscious, then of course you default to your skills, you default to your experience and you still do a strong performance because sometimes when you're struggling that can create other things that are just as powerful in a different way, you're just completely intuitive and it's all happening. But my favourite, definitely, is when I trust and when I trust and just let things, you know whatever happens – if there's a baby, or if there's a bird, just be open to whatever's there is in that moment, in those unfolding moments, yes. So that is very interesting. That's a lovely thing to say 'soften' – I like that.

SR: [Laughs] I think I first met you in Oval House [arts centre, London].

MN: And Peter Oliver, who died of course. Just really sad because he was another mentor for me. Do you know how I started running workshops at the Oval?

SR: No idea, no.

MN: Peter Oliver said, would you run a workshop and Harry [Harry Vince, trumpeter] said yes, and then he said to me, 'You do it', [laughs] and it was like, aagh! I don't know how to run a workshop – this was probably in 69, 70 – probably late 69 I think and I'd obviously just worked with John and I thought alright then I'll try a couple of John's pieces. So I went into this room and there was literally a room full of men with saxophones. I don't think there was any other instruments apart from saxophones, and I thought I'll try the sustain piece and I was very, very frightened and nervous and didn't have a clue. So I just introduced the piece and I said take a breath and play any note and keep just sustaining that and I think it lasted I think about a second before there was mass hysteria, screeching and honking – it was phenomenal on a lot of levels – but I'd forgotten what happened and I bumped into my ex … and I said I don't remember what happened and he said what happened was it went on for about an hour and when it stopped I said; that was lovely but do you think we could try it again and this time we could hold those notes a bit longer [laughs]. That was literally my introduction to running workshops.

       Peter Oliver said, well, there are some actors that want to sing, would you do a voice workshop? I went, alright and I got a 'teach yourself singing' book, one of those black and yellow series teach yourself books. And I started off, 'aaa', 'eee', 'ooo', you know, and then I brought in some of John's pieces which of course worked b-ea-uti-full-y with all those voices and that's really how I started. I was exposed at the Oval House to fringe theatre … as you know all those amazing things that happened at the Oval.

SR: Yes, I was there a bit later and it was home of fringe theatre at that time. That period is significant for improvisation. It was a period which reflected openness and all these groups which no longer exist were around.

MN: It was just fantastic and I think so many things were birthed there because Peter just believed in people. Theatre groups started there – there was none of this you have to audition, he just believed in that, and it's that same thing I found in John and I'm just so glad I came across people like that. That believed that everyone was creative, that was the basic, bottom line, no negotiation, everyone's creative and we're just going to create conditions for people to be able to discover that. And that's really just so deep in me thanks to people like Peter Oliver and John Stevens. Really. And I feel so passionately about that. And of course some people are, some of you are going to be so obsessed with it that you're going to build skills to the point where you become virtuosic in different ways but there is such a thing that I really love which I call social virtuosity, it's a collective virtuosity which is … you know, not streamed. And again, John was a master of that. Mixed ability virtuosity, that has its own particular power. There is something phenomenal about a group of different experiences, making really strong performance in music. And I think the Oval House was very much in that spirit as well.

SR: In some respects that is the most challenging notion. Isn't it?

MN: Yes, yes.

SR: It is something that you have also spent decades working with, I'm thinking of the Gathering, the open door to that. This is a part of free improvisation that isn't articulated well – people tend to know about the famous people but many of them were involved in this kind of activity.

MN: John gave up a lot to become involved in Community Music, consequently a lot of Europeans don't know about John and just how crucial he was to the history of improvised music because he put his heart and soul into sharing that in community. I think it is not talked about because it is either, you've got your individual virtuosity and of course the whole point with John was to create a community interaction, you've got that or people see it as something you do, some sort of charitable thing, you go and do this thing for people who are not really musicians – they're not seeing that it's not really about that – that's patronizing really, it's actually saying no. John created excellence, he believed that everybody could achieve that kind of excellence. Now, not everyone might go on to make a vocation or a working life out of that. But it has its own power and I know that from going to see community events. I've gone to see fringe events, I can't even remember what they're called, but I remember going to one and thinking wow! This is one of the most phenomenal, exciting, powerful pieces of theatre I've seen and it wasn't professional actors – which is not to denigrate those of us who have made art our work-life – it's just different aspects of the same process really and each has its value. [Pause] And I do love mixed ability excellence, I think it's just so exciting. Because you are drawing on this thing which is a birth right, you know if we're all creative then we've all got something to say and the Gathering really brings that out for me too. There's a Gathering now in London as you know, that's been going twenty years and the one in Wales has been going about eight or nine years … I love that about the Gathering too, that it can go anywhere, people get up and move and dance, we talk in tongues, we babble … it's quite crazy at times, it's just beautiful. I love it. I think the London one is settled more, it's more music. Although Agnes Henny has been coming, she's a film-maker, and she brings some beautiful films and we've had poets come and just spontaneously start to spout poetry or write poems. Painters come as well, so it's lovely but for me the Gathering is about it being open to people who are not practising artists of any kind but who have an artist in them because as I say we're all artists in some way or another.

SR: Have you ever in the Gathering had someone come in and you've been like, Oh I wish they'd just shut-up? [Laughs].

MN: Oh aye. You know it's quite interesting I've found it's something that you said earlier, softening, and I've found that when it's making me anxious and when I'm preoccupied with it, it hasn't worked ... often people compound a problem. I remember this saxophone player who used to come, he's a crane driver ... and he'd come into the London one at about half past ten at night. And we had an L-shaped room and he'd creep into the back ... and suddenly there'd be this absolute blast! Absolutely deafening sound. And then of course what would happen is everyone would have a knee-jerk reaction, so the drummers if they were there they would start hammering away – and then there was no space. And I remember we were talking about this and I thought well how would it be if we didn't change what we were doing, when he started, what would happen and we tried that, and do you know something, the actual way he was playing was that he would do this blast and then he would leave this enormous space. So in actual fact he wasn't the problem, it was everybody else thinking, oh right, we'll all pile in now, even though they didn't want to. So it's that thing of being authentic, if you're truly authentic, I do believe that sooner or later it creates a space for everybody, so even somebody ... he needed, he needed to play like that but he was also incredibly sensitive because he would play like that and we'd all, we wouldn't change what we were doing if we didn't feel like that – there'd be these huge spaces, where there were lots of little gentle things happening and then he would steam in again. So that was a real lesson for me.

SR: That's very interesting, yes. Knowing your part in a way.

MN: Exactly. Being strong in your own centre, being really totally committed energetically to what you're doing. And then whatever anyone else is doing won't throw you off balance. And that's a lifetimes practice to me, I'll be practising that till the day I die ... just building up that tolerance of diversity, genuine tolerance of diversity, of our different foibles and the things that would normally annoy us, and how do we deal with it and that's what The Gathering is for me. It's really about practising, what John once said, to be a social being – practising to be stronger individually and collectively, basically. So the Gathering is very much in the spirit of John ...

There's an organization called permaculture, which I think is permanent agriculture, anyway it came out of Australia. It's all about learning from nature observing nature ... it's about minimum input and maximum output. You're learning about how nature functions and they have these different zones and Zone One is maybe your herb garden, it's close to the kitchen, Zone Two might be your vegetables and so on, bee keeping might be a certain ... and then right to Zone Six which you leave alone, you don't actually interfere with, you just let nature do its thing. And so I often feel the Gathering is probably, it's not exactly Zone Six because we are in there energetically influencing things but it's probably Zone Five. Just let it be self-regulating however chaotic that might

SR: And you've managed to sustain it over decades …

be and trust that out of that chaos will come the clearings, will come the new growth, will come the coherence, and it does, when you trust it, and if enough people trust it then of course that affects the whole thing. It's wonderful, I love the Gathering.

MN: It is sustainable because it is open. If you look at nature, nature is constantly mutating, there's always something new, it's diversity. We know from commercial agriculture how that kills the fields; they don't rotate the crops. They don't let the fields rest. The more diverse it is the more sustainable it is. I think that's what makes it sustainable and that's why the Gathering has been going in London twenty years. I was there last night and it was phenomenal. There was were all these youngsters – people have been saying to me there are no young improvisers, nobody young is coming and last night when I went there were all these students and it was young, young, young – all playing with the older ones and I thought this is just fantastic. And I think that's what makes it sustainable, its diversity …

With John I was just young and inspired and in awe and a little bit infatuated. So I was a young woman who was just crazy and I wanted to – just soak it up. I've often thought, it's because I put up no resistance, because I was a little bit infatuated with John. Whereas his peers were probably much more sceptical, much more challenging of him, you know, people like Evan and Derek. You know with me I just surrendered and something happened in that surrendering that – Trevor actually said that I influenced them too, because I was always seen as the younger one, but I think there was something in the way I surrendered, because I was a young woman and I was just wow! And in that surrendering I found something, I discovered something, and it was by accident almost.

What I noticed in the London Gathering too, you'd get a period where it would be the same people and it would get incredibly coherent, almost insular, almost to the point where it was stagnating. It was so perfect, it was so beautiful everybody knew each other so well. And then somebody would come who would just completely disrupt everything – but it kept it fresh … It was very, very, very beautiful: everybody was like mosaics and lace and, you know, just improvising at its most sublime … and then Lizzy came, and she was one of the road protesters, and she was out there in the tunnels and up the trees. And she had this battered psychedelic guitar and she was taking guitar lessons and so there'd be all this [sings the group part: skip, de, dat, ska, dot, dup] you know, all this beautiful – and then she'd be sitting there going ching, ching, ching, ching practising her chords and [laughter] and it drove everybody mad, they hated it, but it was wonderful on another level because then she'd play and she'd annoy people and she'd pick up things and she was a complete anarchic spirit and quite annoying in some ways, but the more Lizzy came and the more there was that embracing and not excluding of Lizzy, then when she did start to free up and and, you know, she did some amazing things. So again that was another lesson for me. And that's really, my dream Simon is, my vision is to one day get to the point where we're strong enough to contain the extremes of someone having a manic episode, somebody being completely catatonic, someone else maybe doing [laughs] meditation and somehow the energy and the love and the music are actually making it all safe for everybody. That's still … we're scratching the surface but as somebody once said at a workshop, it's a deep scratch. That's my dream … because to me it is about being. Finding ways to be with people that are different, and being able to handle it, whatever, and that also goes into mental health, which is very close to my heart … I love it when the Gathering goes into those areas and yet it goes in a way that doesn't lose musicality. Ah, it's phenomenal, phenomenal.

SR: That scenario when you met John, Trevor and Evan, and perhaps Derek and others. You were the only woman coming in amongst all of that. And I know that you have been deeply involved in the Women's Movement and that that is a whole thing as well. Did you see yourself as the only woman at that time? Or did you feel, well this is just something else that's going on?

MN: It was before feminism. The Women's Liberation Movement really again raised my consciousness, it was another milestone like Dennis Rose, like John Stevens and then the Women's Liberation Movement really just completely changed everything. No, I – in fact I was very vulnerable. Thanks to Dennis and John I got some sort of male protection but before that I was very unprotected and greatly taken advantage of in many ways which left me very, very vulnerable and very insecure about myself as a person and I was so desperate to belong and be accepted by … because before the Women's Movement many of us girls and young women, we just thought unless men approved of us we were just nothing. Our whole aim in life was to be accepted and approved of by men, so you can't believe the radical change that came about through me being exposed to the Women's Liberation Movement – it was just like wow! And for a long time, typical, by accident, I got plunged into a lesbian, separatist community – suddenly – and it's like, what's this! Oh, my god – so for a while I didn't have anything to do with men, hardly. So in a way, that's probably what I needed because I got to the point where I realized I didn't need men and then, now, I can have proper, equal, loving, mutually respectful relationships with men that are really kind of, really healthy. But thanks to people like Dennis Rose and John who didn't take advantage of me, and who genuinely mentored me – because I mean there were men there who used me like an unpaid prostitute in many ways, you know. Because it wasn't like the casting couch, where you give me a favour … no it was literally you just service me, so that's um, quite a, quite a wound really in a way, it's probably why, that's another reason why I worked, again not thinking about it consciously – why I, for me I was so driven to develop my voice as an equal instrument, with any male instrumentalist. That wasn't conscious, it really wasn't, but I know that I felt I had to prove that I deserved to exist, on that scene, and then somebody like John as I say, well Dennis who first started me singing, properly and mentored me in that way, and then John who mentored me in using my voice instrumentally – and also listening, listening – I mean I just haunted Ronnie Scott's, I begged, borrowed or stole to get in there and then soaked up all that fantastic music. And then suddenly there's the Women's Liberation Movement, and I'm starting to work with other women and it was so amazing – and now, as I say, it's integrated, I feel I've integrated just the joy of working with women, working in mixed groups, feeling comfortable with male musicians. But it's also getting older, sometimes as you get older as a woman you start to settle into a more natural authority and don't feel quite so vulnerable. Obviously I still have some vulnerabilities. I think you need to be vulnerable in order to surrender to the music.

SR: But there was also a time with the Women's Improvising Group.

MN: Oh FIG. I called it the Women's Improvising Group. We were asked to do this thing for Music for Socialism and I said look, all I see is female singers and male instrumentalists – I'll get a women's group together. And I called it the Women's Improvising Group and when the poster came back they've called it the Feminist Improvising Group. So I thought, well alright, you don't know what you've unleashed, so be it [laughter]. We'll be it and we did. We became really militant. And that was an amazing group actually. That was absolutely irreverent and anarchic.

SR: I never saw that group.

MN: It was phenomenal, it was great.

SR: Who was in the group?

MN: Well it started off with me, Lindsey Cooper, Cathy Williams who was a rock pianist – used to play with progressive rock groups and Georgie Born. And then we came across Irene Schweizer, so Irene joined and Corinne Liensol was in that first one too, Corrine was an amazing mixed race trumpet player. And then there was Annemarie Roelofs, who is a Dutch trombonist – she was fantastic. Angele Veltmeijer who was also a sax player and playing in a women's band called Jam Today. She'd never done any free improvisation and she just steamed in. I remember the first gig with Angele and we used to have this funny thing we'd go: ' A one, a two, a one, two, three, four' [sings wildly, laughter]. She just steamed in there and that was great. And later Sally Potter the film-maker, who was a performance artist who sang and played a bit of sax. And again it was mixed ability – that was the thing that marked FIG.

185

Because you had musicians of phenomenal technique like Lindsey and Irene and others who didn't have such a strong technique but were amazing performers and again that was really open and I loved the openness of that. What happened to FIG, which was very interesting, different male groups, there was [name removed], and they'd say well we like you two, Lindsey and Georgie, but we think they're too theatrical. And then there'd be the jazzers like [name removed] and people going – Oh, we like you and Irene, you know, and there was a bit of divide and rule went on, because I think we were quite threatening and other musicians loved us like Lol, Lol Coxhill, Eugene Chadborne, Maarten Altena – there were lots of male musicians who were big fans but there were other men who really, really were threatened, in fact [name removed]. We did the Berlin Total Music Meeting and he actually complained about us. He said why did they book us because we couldn't play our instruments. Well this is insane – you've got women like Irene and, you know, I could use my voice. And it was a huge hit as well. The audience loved us but we were accused of being novelty – you have no idea of the vitriol we got.

SR: What time was this?

MN: The first gig we did was 1977 – and then it went from there right through to the early 80s.

SR: That's an interesting time from the point of view of anarchism in music, because that was around a lot then wasn't it.

MN: That's right because there was, you know, Alterations and Steve Beresford, and there was a bit of an upheaval anyway, that's right. But there was a real … and I think the fact that all of a sudden here was this bunch of women that were breaking all the rules – because we brought in all the theatre and humour and politics and we were just not purist at all. But there was some very powerful music as well. It was some very strong music. I loved it, I loved FIG. But then there were some women who wanted to close it. And my heart went out of it a bit then. We became a little bit of a pastiche of ourselves.

SR: What do you mean close it?

MN: They wanted even to reduce it – there were some women they didn't want. I won't mention names because it's all water under the bridge now but, they wanted to have just five which meant that some of the musicians who were part of FIG would have just not been in it and I was just so against that, so it all … it just gradually went. And that's why I started Contradictions, which was an open women's workshop-performance group – which would be literally open. If you set up as a closed group fine. Like Lady Diabolique, we are a trio, that's Lady Diabolique, that's an identity, but if it starts off that the whole point, to be an open pool of women improvisers – open to women who hadn't improvised – to have all that diversity and sustainability again and so for me, to close an open group just felt wrong. I suppose I wanted to experience the intimacy with women that I was experiencing in my life, through the women's movement. And if they hadn't called us FIG I don't know that it would have been quite so militant. The fact that they called us that … our relationships as women obviously influenced the music and our shared experience in discovering and practising feminism then came into play … There'd have still been that energy of being women with certain shared experience, but being labelled Feminist Improvising Group [laughs] actually ironically enough, set us off in that direction.

SR: Did they record at all? Did they make any recordings?

MN: Cassettes somewhere and I don't even know where. There are several cassettes. But we brought a cassette out and there's some fantastic stuff on that. There was a Stockholm gig in which a whole audience joined in and it was really powerful stuff. And also Contradictions on cassette.

SR: Contradictions was a development.

MN: Yes, a development, taking it back to what I'd hoped FIG would sustainably be, which was an open group. But I did quite a lot of workshopping with that and we developed even more into multimedia and again, we did theatre, we had dancers, we did sketches we did written stuff, we did improvised stuff, it was lovely in a way and lots of different women came through that: Sylvia Hallet and all different women, women who were experienced, women who weren't. Wonderful, wonderful stuff we did and Annalisa Colombara who's a visual artist, who did the most amazing slides as well and wrote a story that we did. We did a lot – we did something at the Oval House actually. Again, nobody videoed it, what a shame. Because we did something on madness – I did a workshop in which we picked that theme and everybody improvised in a circle, everybody just went round and round, and then I transcribed it. And turned it into a working script, a springboard, and we did a piece on that which was great and then we did Annalisa's story, 'Moon Fish'. A beautiful story about an abandoned worm that a fisherman has left in the sea who has all these adventures, a beautiful story. And then a piece called 'Revolutionary Times', which was all different songs, political songs and it was an amazing piece but nobody videoed it. And that's the story of my life, all these phenomenal things I've been involved in and there's no record of them.

John Butcher

SR: What is the place of free improvisation in your practice?

JB: It's something that my feelings about have changed a lot over the course of thirty years and it may not be much help to you but a sort of conclusion I came to recently was, when I had to write a little piece about what they call free improvisation, was in a way how irrelevant the fact that free improvisation was involved was to me than it had ever been. Because when I thought about what really enthuses me it was actually the music of a few score musicians around the world, who happen to use improvisation in the course of their music making but it was those actual musicians who interested me.

SR: Who were those musicians?

JB: Well, we're going back to the early pioneers like Derek, Evan and John Stevens up to comparatively more recent players like Toshimaru Nakamura or Burkhard Stangl and I'm interested in them as musicians and the music they produce. If you look at that range of people that got involved with improvisation with a gap between them of something like twenty-five years. As the vast variety of aesthetics come into play, sound aesthetics being used, one theory is that improvisation is a part of all of it but for me it was becoming less and less relevant. It was a bit like saying, you know, I like pianists because they play the piano. I like these musicians because of the music they make, they use improvisation in different ways as their tool.

SR: Improvisation in education is under-acknowledged, not understood – as Derek Bailey described in his book.

JB: It depends a bit on how you use the free in that.

SR: I think he just uses improvisation. We can hang the *free* up to rest for a while, because it's the improvisatory practice that I think … so given that. What do you think? I view you as an improviser, I saw you the other night and the duo that you did there with the percussionist – it was an improvisatory engagement.

JB: Oh, without a doubt, I'm an improviser. Maybe we're seeing things in slightly different categories. We can discuss what improvisation means and different aspects of improvisation but if we're talking about, well it's a forty-year-old body of work now, we could say that what is meant by the practitioners by free improvisation is something that was very much a product of its time and that time has become extended. And it may be very much a time that has passed. You know people who come into things that involve free improvisation are very often making music in a very natural way, they're actually making music in a way which is more akin to a composed process or the outcome is very [inaudible word] … and they're aiming for a particular kind of music and they're filling in the details through improvisation but the extent to which they are doing free improvisation is radically different from, and much less than say it was throughout the 60s and 70s. And I think it's quite [inaudible word] to use the word 'free' because once something has been that elaborated, precedents are set and the possibilities of further freedom within that method become more and more narrow and I'm not sure how much of an aesthetic of people looking necessarily for freedom in their work these days. I'm of a generation, ten or fifteen fifteen years younger than the real pioneers of this. So I really do feel a part of that and can really register that feeling of in the early days breaking from what I and many people thought of as accepted ways of making music and that environment doesn't exist anymore. Anyone with any interest in anything outside of mainstream music has easy access to so many aspects of experimental music and improvised music, they're almost like genres now and idioms and they're working in a completely different world than I was working in …

SR: When I use that term 'free improvisation', I'm not sure where I got that term from.

JB: … People use different words you know …

SR: I can see why the term 'improvisation' is more useful and free improvisation can suggest a particular period and a particular association to processes and thinking – distinctly of a particular period. The terminology is problematic. I suppose for my purposes, looking at the phenomenon of creating music without a score.

JB: Right.

SR: And the phenomenon of creating music at the point of performance and using spontaneity and other things to do that, and that's what I'm trying to articulate. And I think I agree – there is now a canon of free improvised music. But there is another view that this music has always been around, it just was never documented, it was situated differently, which I find very interesting, especially when you think of Eurocentricity and ideas like that. Have you got a particular view of orthodoxy, style, or even dogma? It seems that there are quite naturally, within the London scene for example, these cohorts, these associations, you know, perfectly natural human developments occur and long standing relationships develop – and for audiences as well, maybe they like to think I'm on safe ground there. Maybe an obvious one would be between free jazz and lower case sensibilities, or that kind of thing?

JB: Well it's easy to recognize it, and I suppose the question is how much a hindrance it is and how much an advantage it is, again, if you listen to certain individuals. If you listen to the Schippenbach Trio with Paul Lovens and Evan Parker, it is clear that they have in a sense created their own canon and in a sense their own orthodoxy within which they work and, in a way, you're never going to be surprised in any broad sense by the music they make but I think their music has evolved on a very profound level and the way they operate within it is very profound. They're effectively three mutual composers going out and creating their music, which is a continually evolving body of music through the practice of improvisation. It's not free improvisation in the sense that if you were teaching a class to a group of people who'd never encountered the idea of working without musical scores and you're trying to introduce them to different ways and ideas of performing together. It's a process of incredible depth. To anyone who's familiar, even casually, with this kind of music it's not something that's going to surprise them greatly. Maybe its profundity may surprise them on occasion but its methodology and its broad-brushstrokes won't surprise them.

SR: There's a clarity about using that trio as an example, as one of the longest standing trios, it's interesting. That idea that you pinpointed about the continuing evolving thing, is that unique to improvisation I wonder?

JB: Well, I suppose if you look at how Mozart is performed, there is an evolving tradition of that as well. It's taken over if you like from a music that Mozart conceived to a tradition of how that music is performed, by what kinds of orchestras, there was a time when it evolved without thought almost into being performed by the orchestra created for the Romantic tradition, those kinds of instruments. Then people started moving back towards smaller orchestras, period instruments. So many evolving things in terms of what tempi are used, how you deal with string vibrato, these changed through the decades, so there's an ongoing, independent of Mozart, history in the evolution of performance practice. I mean it would be more interesting if Mozart was doing it. Which is why it's so interesting that it is Parker, Schlippenbach and Lovens because they're the true creators evolving their own music.

SR: Yes. People often cite Bach and Beethoven particularly as known for being improvisers over composers in their own day. This kind of idea supports the need to research why improvisation practice is left out – I'm thinking of school education.

JB: If you're doing this with a class of people who haven't encountered the possibility of operating like that, that's when you're going to get closest to the concept of what free improvisation is. With so little concept of what other people have done.

In the last say fifty years of popular music making, improvisation has been an important element. What that's been used for through rehearsal, studio work to develop a finished product which doesn't contain much improvisation. But the process of making it from The Beatles up to hip hop music, improvisation will be a part of arriving at the end result. Now that's a particular mindset which many people have. You use it to get somewhere which is comparatively immutable. I had this with dancers as well, you start off working with an improvisational practice and slowly as you develop they want to end up with a fixed product, through the improvisational scheme. Which I don't mind as a process but then I get completely bored when I'm having to regurgitate the product. I've got no interest in doing that ... So there's that tendency towards something only having value once you've been through all the options and you've fixed all the options and you've chosen the best option to produce the final piece. I like it when you haven't chosen the options yet and the ingredients are highly mutable at the performance stage. I think that's what I think improvising performers do, we do have vocabulary and ingredients but they are malleable enough if not to be ever changing then really fluid at the true moment of creation.

SR: Could you elaborate on this a little bit because this is very interesting point – why it is that you like, let's say, engaging with this process rather than settling on a product and how those things are differentiated for you, in your life [laughs].

JB: There are a number of sides to that, I mean I think one of them I – it's like a tautological situation in that the kind of music you're making couldn't exist unless it was being made comparatively spontaneously, in the moment, the intrinsic nature of the music, the end result of it engages with what it means to deal with spontaneity. And the other thing is I'm interested in being the performer as well as, if you like, the composer. And I do consider myself to be a composer it's just that most of my compositions are realized through comparatively spontaneous performance. And then, perhaps the most unique thing about this practice is that if it's group playing, it's a collaborative process involving the possibly slightly [inaudible word] but often contradictory creative input of other people. Things that you wouldn't have thought of yourself, things that you may not agree with, things that will force you to operate in a way that you weren't expecting. And I find that very intrinsic to the improvising process and what makes it when it works, almost the most interesting music you can get.

SR: I think that's one of the particular features of your music – having heard you in different settings. How do you prepare for that John? I commented to Mick Beck on the duo that you did. I said I really like the way John seems to be able to latch onto the other thing that's going on and then, I don't know what it is, but you seem to be able to turn and extend. Is that something you've practised or is it through reflection or you've analysed it. And you seem to be able to do this in different contexts. I heard you with Phil Minton as well. Not all saxophonists would team up to do a duo with a vocalist, you know.

JB: It is my particular interest. It is this thing of how to maintain your own personality, yet use it to make musical sense with the people, musical sense with the people you're working with and to accept their intentions to be as important as your own. You don't want to go to the performance with too fixed an agenda of what you're going to do.

191

SR: There is a theme here for education. For example, if there is a group of nine boys and one girl, these things become vividly clear – the need for adaptability ...

JB: If you like, that'd be the most ever present political aspect of the music, really harping back to the days of the polemicists such as John Stevens and Maggie Nicols. That kind of improvisation as a model of how people can interact in a broader sense.

SR: But, you've gone down that road a long way and uncovered some important stuff. Even players who are really well known and people love, you're not necessarily going to find them in the multiplicity of settings, particularly with an instrument such as the saxophone. Which can obviously be a lead voice, so, how have you worked on that?

JB: Well, the thing you want to avoid is being a chameleon.

SR: You want to avoid being a comedian?

JB: Chameleon [laughter].

SR: Oh, chameleon.

JB: You know, where you're just doing a Zelig thing.

SR: You want to avoid being a chameleon.

JB: Where you're just changing to fit into the circumstances. You have to bring something which is, as much as possible, uniquely you. And that's something you can't really consciously do. Either you manage that or you don't, I think. And I'm kind of an obsessive; I'm quite obsessive about music in many respects. I think improvising saved me. Because when I used to write music back in my student days, I was a control freak. This was with bands, I'd be writing the bass guitar parts, the guitar parts you know. I was just trying to control it all. And then I kind of dropped that because it was kind of, unhealthy. I obviously have the same personality and same kind of obsessiveness but I find it much healthier to operate in an environment where I'm continually trying to avoid what I would call failure but it's an inbuilt part of the process. I was asked something recently, and this was kind of a humorous comment but it actually captures something I believe which is: after an improvisation I often feel if I'd known I was going to that, I would have done it better. But I didn't know I was going to do that.

SR: [Laughs] That does sound like Woody Allen.

JB: It's not always a comfortable feeling, at the end. But it's so intrinsic to the process that you don't know what it is that you're going to do, by and large. Obviously you know, it's a saxophone, I've been playing it for thirty years, you know. Actually this particular week was interesting. By sheer chance I had six concerts in London: one with Ikue Morrie and Chris Cutler, who I haven't played with before; three nights with John Russel's Qua Qua Qua, largely musicians I haven't played with before; a solo concert opposite this doom, drone guitarist Steven O'Malley, American. Completely different audience, everybody's about twenty-five – I wasn't playing with anybody, that also changed how I play. I did an opening solo set for that. The knowledge that I was playing before that kind of audience, affects how I play.

SR: How did that affect how you played?

JB: It was Café Oto and it was packed, there were a hundred and something people there. The knowledge that there were maybe three people in the audience who may have heard of me or heard any of my music, obviously has an effect. If I play a gig with twenty people and I know that they've all heard concerts by me in the last few years, that creates a different psychological state than a room full of people who've never heard of you.

SR: Yes, did you find that quite nice?

JB: Yeah, I played about five short pieces, that was brought about by the fact that there was a slight pause in the first one and they started applauding before the end of the piece, which a more familiar audience would realize it was just a pause before continuing. That kind of set a mould for me. So the audience really affect – and this is the other thing about improvising, in public anyway, it's that where you play affects what music you play. I mean if you'd been blindfolded you would have known that was John Butcher playing, but within the detail it affects how you play.

SR: Did you find that the audience did the other thing that an unfamiliar audience might do and that is make noise?

JB: No, I kind of started reasonably loud to attract attention. And then take it down when you feel you've got them, with you. Until you can almost take it down to a pin drop then and people go with you in that kind of environment, like Café Oto. I've had a harder time – I think it's also because it's quite intimate, you're playing there on the floor, it's not on the stage, with the audience all around you. I've done gigs like opening for The Ex, the Dutch group, and that'd usually be on the stage with a big PA, a lot of people talking around the bar at the end of the room. I found with that you can kind of get half the audience, you can get the half at the front and you never get that half at the back. And even when you take it down it doesn't make any difference. I think it's to do with the physicality of the setup, being on stage with a PA and they're waiting for an energetic rock group, and a bloke comes out with a saxophone and plays a freely improvised saxophone solo …

There's a quality that's been developed by, well they're not that young now, but they're younger than me, musicians in Berlin and to some extent musicians in London and Japan, where there's very strong consensus about what music they want to play. It's very clear they've decided the music is going to sound like this and a lot of the music I think is very good, I enjoy it very much but, first of all, I do think it's a music that doesn't tell us very much about improvising and in a sense it doesn't involve a great deal of improvisation, there's a lot of layering of slowly evolving sounds. A lot of musicians operate in this way now and they're very precise and they're very careful and controlled. In the right hands it's very beautiful music but improvising is such a small part of it. So much of the decision-making has been made before hand, it's almost like realizing an indeterminate score except the score isn't on a piece of paper – you know, that says within this time frame play a long breath sound; within this time frame play as pure an A as you can with few harmonics, you know, and you're adjusting it like you might play an indeterminate score. It doesn't feel like it has the qualities of improvisation to me. And there are scores of musicians who call themselves improvisers who work like that.

I think it's a state of mind, [playing very quiet music] if you go into that world your ear also goes into that world, you're involved in the minutia of sound so suddenly to bring the dynamic up is [inaudible word]. There a sort of international version of Chris Burn's Ensemble and it was with the Berlin musicians and some of the London ones and one of these Berlin musicians had invited this guy [name removed]. Anyway, we were playing quite quietly and he was playing a very nice bass drum and at one point he wacked it so loudly the clarinet player nearly bit his mouthpiece off, everyone in the group jumped out of their skin and it ruined the piece of music, but it was a very dramatic event. And he's been doing a few comparatively radical things. He put together an evening of duos with people who hadn't played together before and the audience had to vote on the best duo. And the winner won a prize. It was kind of a comment on hierarchies in improvised music, what it means to say something is better than something else ... I wonder if there has always been an element in improvisation where you're looking for something new, you're looking for something radical. Most of us realize actually that's not such a necessary ingredient but young people coming in there's almost [inaudible word] radical to them. And I wonder if this is some sort of a response to that. The only place to go now is to very publicly critique the whole process.

Some years ago I was asked to give a sort of lecture demonstration to the Royal Academy of Music for their new Improvised Music module ... That was run by [name removed], he's not an improviser, of course, they usually aren't. And they were interested students and they knew a bit but what I found amusing was that to get their credit for the module they had to write a graphic score which was then assessed by the tutor, you know this was the improvisation module ... So that puts your finger on certain aspects of the problems of dealing with what we would understand as improvisation within an academic. Improvisation is so inaccessible to objective criteria of any sort that if you're having to assess things, this presents problems.

SR: On the face of it assessment is problematic but if you just unpack it a little bit, what's involved in improvisation, what's involved in free improvisation. Most education foregrounds the individual, so once you move slightly away from that and, say, let's foreground the group.

JB: … Well, it's interesting how you think about schools and that communal process in education how sports are held up like that, learning to work as a team. And it's always in competition against another team. We have criteria of how we win and how we lose, and you operate communally to beat someone else. Which of course is not what group improvisation is about.

… I learnt so much from going to gigs. You know I was free improvising before I knew there was scene. There was just something in the air. You know I was trying to copy the weird bits off Mothers of Invention records with my brother, or copying bits of Stockhausen, electronic music. What I realized I was kind of doing was free improvising. I'm talking about when you're sixteen, seventeen, eighteen, this sort of thing. And then through listening to jazz in London, I listened to people like Derek [Bailey] and realized there were people who dealt with these issues in a very profound way. And it all came through gigs. Recently I've started, for my own interest, trying to get hold of all the early iconic records like early AMM. Things I've never heard. Because a lot of people refer to them like that's what the history of improvised music is, just these tiny snap-shots. It's quite fascinating to hear these things that have become iconic records: *The Topography of the Lungs* and *AMM Live at The Crypt*, particularly these things from the late 60s to early 70s are quite fascinating.

SR: There's a commemorative thing for Paul Burwell at Matt's Gallery [London]. I'm just thinking of how the past can replay in the present. How the events can be replayed sometimes on a global scale. I've heard that John Tilbury has told a story of how there were two people in the audience for an AMM gig of theirs and one was Ornette Coleman …

JB: Fortunately most of the AMM are still with us but once people die the proportions of things can change in a peculiar way. The thing about Paul is that during his time in London with the LMC he was a very dynamic, inventive, original, intriguing figure. He didn't really believe very much in recording. There's very little recordings around. So he's largely unknown outside of our local scene.

SR: I guess the Bow Gamelan.

JB: They travelled, and I think Hugh Metcalf put out about one LP. They were a performance spectacle as well.

SR: Yes, people in the art world may not know about Paul Burwell the improviser but they will know about Bow Gamelan. That's a sort of different connection.

JB: Evan told me about a gig he put on with Paul Lytton, Derek Bailey solo and AMM in the early 70s and nobody came. It was a room above a pub in Acton and nobody came … John Stevens was in Ealing and I think he went to Ealing Art College as a lot of people did. It reminds me of how much in those days, for me it was a two-pronged thing. It was like jazz in its early days, you learnt by doing it. Trying to deal with people was how you learnt it. By learning it, it's how you came to that web of ideas and experience that leads you to some sort of voice in the way of operating.

SR: I think that's a critical point for education.

JB: The value of seeing people, Oxley and Evan, from my point of view was really to be inspired by the extraordinary music they were managing to make through the process …

SR: I think there's something important about seeing that music in those pub rooms in London …

JB: What I've always enjoyed about the small gigs is that the audience and performers are there mutually to spend that one hour, or whatever, with this unrepeatable experience. It won't happen again. And even if there's a recording of it, that's a different experience. And back then there weren't recordings of most of the gigs. So it's just like a moment of time that you've decided to share attention on something that can't be regained. Which is another reason why it is culturally devalued compared to the score, the saleable art product, the reproducible performance.

SR: I think that people who are new to the music, who might come, say the friend or the relative, can pick up on that quality quite quickly, even if they are completely unfamiliar with the music.

JB: Yes, yeah …

SR: That registers at some human level.

JB: That's a rare thing in our society, Western societies really, isn't it. Everything can be saved for another time. You know, you can save your television programmes, you can download at whatever time you like, whatever you like. To have a sensory experience which is only going to happen on that moment is very unusual.

Pauline Oliveros

SR: What is the place of improvisation in your practice?

PO: Well, it's a very important thread throughout and I've always improvised. When I was composing music with conventional notation, if I got stuck I could improvise. So my composition teacher Robert Erickson encouraged me to improvise and we were all encouraged by Robert Erickson to improvise. Lauren Rush and I were at school together in undergraduate years at San Francisco State and when we graduated we were all studying with Erickson privately. And Terry got a commission to write a piece for a film, a five minute film and he didn't have the time to write the music so Lauren and I went into the studio and we recorded five minute tracks for Terry, we improvised the music. That was my first improvisation in that way. And Terry took a track and used it for the film, and it was quite successful and I remember saying, hey this is fun, we should do this. So we got together maybe once a week or so and we improvised, and we discovered something very important which was that if we talked about the improvisation before we did it, it usually fell flat, but if we just sat down and improvised and then record it and then talked, then it was very interesting and we advanced our practice.

SR: What do you make of that?

PO: Well, rather than trying to get some kind of plan that you have to follow, like you have to follow a score instead of that you're communicating with one another directly. Spoken conversations don't have to happen before you play and the dialogue is in the sounds that you're making and the way you listen. So the working methods that I got out of it, and used ever since is: play first, listen to it then talk about it. Then you learn from that, because you are translating something that is embodiment, embodied sound making then translate it into spoken word after the fact which really the right way, the right order.

SR: I'm very interested in that because there's an almost an unsaid, shared understanding of that.

PO: Well, now it is, yes.

SR: We understand that we mustn't talk about it …

PO: You're going to kill it if you do.

SR: I played with a sax player this afternoon, and we hadn't talked at all, and it was very good. And I think this has potential in education. [Pause.]

PO: You have to trust the situation, you have to make it safe.

SR: I'm interested in the latency in the telematic free improvisation, the latency can be part of the communication. [We had been participating in group improvisations, connecting with other musicians via the internet, linking multiple global locations.]

PO:	It certainly is.
SR:	Using a score it can feel like something else.
PO:	It's interesting because when I talk about telematic transmissions and so forth, the first thing that anybody says is what about latency. 'What about the delay!' [laughter]. And I think I heard somebody talking about how many meters would equal so many milliseconds, but we're dealing with latency all the time. I mean if you're in a concert hall and you're one end and I'm the other, there's latency … And, I remember a very interesting experience, I have a piano piece that was written for one piano, eight hands. Very precise in terms of rhythmically. I had four world-class pianists rehearsing this piece, gathering together on one piano. You know, they got it and they were playing really well. The rehearsal room was downstairs from the concert hall that they were going to play in. And so it was very interesting because they had it, and it sounded really good downstairs in the rehearsal room. Then for the concert they didn't really have a proper sound check, and they started the piece and they fell apart pretty quick because there was about a half second latency, you know and it threw them off. All the time we're dealing with latency. We're dealing with latency between the ears. A lot of the time, sound is very slightly delayed in order that we can locate the sound.
SR:	OK, I can be the devil's advocate here and say that improvisation, the attraction is that it is very visceral, between people and that's why people are drawn towards acoustic instruments. And that's why it works really nicely in small clubs because you've got that closeness and all the rest of it. So how does that fit next to the notion of telematic.
PO:	Well, I think if you want very sophisticated technology, you can have whatever you want. You can have very intimate space and it can feel very close. We did a performance last night and Chris (Chafe) was in Toronto and we could hear each other very, very clearly and it was like we were in the same room, I mean it was intimate. So I'm saying, depending on the technology and set up. I mean there's a lot of problems to solve, the visual one is really important and it's nowhere near satisfactory at the moment, where you have a window to look in and see the people you are playing with. But then the sound might not be located properly, to do with the image you are receiving, so there's a lot of a difference to make.
SR:	Yes and certainly, when we did the telematic performance in five places simultaneously [laughs]. And certainly I was thinking of doing it with kids in other countries.
PO:	I've done it. It was a very interesting project. We had two schools: one in Troy, New York and one at Mills in California. And there was a shared drawing programme, where kids could draw on both sides on the internet, on a shared tablet. So that was really wild, it was fun, but there was also sound happening. We weren't focusing on music for that particular one but the shared drawing

space was pretty interesting. We had webcams going and we had sound. We were using just regular Internet. But the kids had been emailing one another. There were a lot of different levels of communication that went on with this project. So it was a very successful project. Fun, a lot of fun. I think shared space is a really interesting goal. If you can get really, really clear transmission, really good technology, to bring children together from different parts of the world.

SR: Thinking about the inter-disciplinary aspect of improvisation …

PO: I've done a lot of work with dance and a lot of work with theatre as well.

SR: Do you take from there, from other areas.

PO: Sure, I've absorbed whatever the dialogue is. And I've worked with a lot of dancers in a lot of different ways and I think of myself as an auditory-kinetic type. I really feel space and energy in space, movement as well as sound. I'm less visually oriented. Not that I don't visualize. You know there's seeing and hand eye co-ordination involved. You're sounding before you know what it is you're sounding, there is delay in fact, about half a second. It's possible to experience this, you've probably experienced this – you're improvising or reading or whatever and you realize that you're sounding it and you become aware of it slightly after it – and, oh, how did I do that? But the body knows what to do and this is a very important aspect to improvisation – allowing the body to lead …

Creative consciousness. It comes from somewhere but it is not necessarily the conscious mode that it comes from. The definition of that word is very – well you're awake and we have different modes of consciousness. The body consciousness is faster than the thinking consciousness. So, the body knows things before you can spell it out in words, is one way to say it. For example if you are in sudden danger, your body moves …

SR: … Body language and so on, there's all sorts of things happening before anybody has opened their mouth.

PO: That's right … In any sensory experience the body takes one tenth of a second. If you take part in highly specialized training, it can be reduced to one eightieth of a second.

SR: Is that to do with Lester Ingber and 'attention processes'.

PO: Yes, Lester Ingber was my teacher for some time.

SR: I want to do more work on the body.

PO: It's really essential, it's really important. It's what is. If you talk about being it's right in there and having awareness upfront, right there instead of meandering around and missing most of what's happening. I mean I bet you know quite a few musicians who do that.

SR: You mean who wander around.

PO: I mean they're just not with it. I'm mean they're with something but they're not with what's happening.

SR: [Laughs] Cornelius Cardew said something like, what people do tells you what they've got in mind.

PO: Yes indeed. So reaction time is important and I try to work with that ... to get some understanding of that. I have a class that I teach at RPI (Rensselaer Polytechnic Institute) in Troy. It is for two semesters. It is really a sitting meditation. But what I'm attempting to do is to expand awareness so that they begin to understand that there is an infinite expansion towards inclusiveness of waveforms they can perceive, that's very open.

SR: Can you explain?

PO: Well. As we sit here there's a lot of sound going on. It's about modes of attention, inclusive attention and exclusive attention and being able to negotiate both at once. Your focal attention is only momentary, it's only brief but then it can be sequential. But the sequence of focused attention, we're getting waveforms but we're also getting packets ... You have a kind of smooth analogue way of processing and you have digital packets. But exclusive attention when you are trying to narrowly focus on some detail, to understand speech for example, your attention is focused on the speech, in order to detect it, understand it, interpret it, all of those things. But sometimes we are focusing in that way and also it can be expanded to include whatever else is happening around. It's fuzzy, it's fuzzier than focus. You do that in music you know. You're aware of the ambience as well as being in a focused manner.

SR: You could play with someone and listen in a way that you're really focusing in on every detail of what they're doing and then you can listen in a very different way, perhaps to the overall effect of what they are doing. So people talk about different ways of playing but there are different ways of listening.

PO: The different ways of listening are more interesting [laughs]. If you're listening in a narrow way it may not fit with what else is happening. I think one of the interesting things is, you get a group of musicians together to play, and who's going to make the first sound?

SR: And there's always that moment.

PO: There it is. It's a beautiful moment because anything could happen. And nobody knows necessarily in an improvisation what is going to happen ... nobody will go whooooaaa, I hope.

SR: I know one or two that'll do that [laughter].

PO: I do too! [laughter] I think that that moment is really special. The moment the first sound is there then the waveform collapses – meaning that the potential has now got a direction. Whereas before it didn't have any direction. That's what makes it so special, you know.

SR: When people have been doing it for decades, sometimes there's that moment and you might know what they are likely to do. I just wonder with people who've been doing things for a certain time, who've become known for doing certain things …

PO: Of course.

SR: So how do they keep it special?

PO: I just do something. I mean how long can you hang on to that moment. I mean can you listen for an hour.

SR: You could make it a very long moment.

PO: Well why not? It is special anyway.

SR: I was thinking a lot about endings and it seemed that there were endings, quite a lot, which weren't really endings but token endings like going to a tonic by chance or something.

PO: Holding that ending moment is also special.

George Lewis

SR: I'm interested in the place of free improvisation in your practice – you freely improvise, what do you do?

GL: Well, first I try to pay attention [pause] to my environment, you're creating an environment – you're also interacting with one, so you have to pay attention. And before you ... the whole time you're there you're bringing all this baggage you've got to the space. I guess some people say you should get rid of it but you can't, so basically you should try to use it since it's there, or it'll use you (laughs) but that's to be as prosaic as possible about it, basically, you're involved in the exchange of information and maybe there are some goals that you have, momentary ones, or perhaps over-arching ones or, you know you might evolve some plans you have to reach certain momentary goals or satisfy, but when you're playing with other people of course you can't count on your plans coming to fruition so you have to try to figure out what other people's plans are and then see how you can work with those, and the way you figure that out is by basically listening to them. I mean over the years I've been pleased to believe that I've developed a certain kind of empathy that sort of allows me to get a sense from the sound, from the attention. And that's not so unusual, I mean people always imbue attention to sounds or gestures or movements it's part of a human or [laughs] animal birthright and even machines can do it. So I find myself involved in thinking about that as a part of what an improvisatory moment is about – what's going on more or less.

SR: When you say paying attention – you began by saying paying attention – can we talk more about that?

GL: Sure, sure.

SR: Do you have specific things that you do – I mean say if you are walking down the street to the gig and you may be paying attention to finding the place but is there something else ... even if you are alone in a room and you feel like improvising – do you prepare yourself in any way?

GL: I don't know, I spent the last twenty years stripping a lot of that out of my practice, the idea that there is some big difference in going on the stage and doing something and you know that thing you said about walking down the street. Increasingly I find the same structures are active all the time, and so I can learn just as much from that process of walking down the street as I can playing with some certified person, or even a not so certified person or group of people. And that's what comes from paying attention [pause, big laugh]. You know you are much more alive to possibilities for growth or change or interventions of different kinds; you're engaged in a continual kind of analysis of what's going on, what other people are doing, what the environment is doing. And it's not always possible to keep all that in your head. I mean, I've had a number of experiences where, certain things I just don't hear, um, and I'm always a little frightened of that, because, you know, I try to hear as much as I can, I try to keep as many senses moving as possible, at all times and, you know, certainly during a musical performance. But it doesn't always happen and I've had two incidents particularly that I remember in which some incredibly annoying or disturbing incident occurred in the audience which I didn't hear or even know about until they told me about it afterwords because that, I mean, if it had happened as part of the music, then that's another part of the agility in the definition there as to what's in and what's out of the music, I had an idea right there what was in and what was out, and so the person who made the disturbance didn't enter into the music [slight laugh] and um, maybe the person that should have …

SR: Could you have brought them in?

GL: Well sure, and that would have been OK, it's like that old Cage thing, you know, open the window, sure, it doesn't disturb the music. So you like to be aware of those things, because there is survival value in that kind of awareness [laughs].

    … People seem to use intuition as the space that goes beyond knowledge whereas I kind of feel intuition is based on what you know, and it is a version of what you know which you can call upon and intuition generally, for me, comes from a combination, comes from that awareness and information and interpretation. So, you know, I've got to the stage now where you can sort of tell what's going on and I wouldn't call it intuition – well maybe you would call it intuition but it's an intuition that's firmly grounded in information that I have taken great pains to amass and filter and achieve and analyses and work with and understand, and that's a funny thing. So you can call upon those resources when you need them. But the idea that they're separate from knowledge – I can't really use that in my own practice. I need to have a strong sense that I am somehow hearing what people want or what they're interested in. It's not so hard to imagine, you know, whether they're distracted or whether they are unsure of themselves. These kind of things are pretty much audible – they're audible not just to a trained musician but they're audible to anyone who has lived with another person for any period of time and can [laughs] hear when that person is having problems [laughs] so it's not anything that is unusual.

    … I remember reading about those musicians who say they blank their minds, you know the phenomenology of this I'm trying to point to a bit – you know and they're not thinking about anything when they play and all that. I think that's great, it's just not my experience, I find that there is a definite conscious strain going on, you know I'm trying to direct my attention to particular features in the given environment that I think I can use or work with or alter or revise and those features can change and in a way that's a kind of methodology, just something you never hear about with so called free improvisation, which is a word I think I learned it in London. Because when we were doing it in Chicago someone like Roscoe, you'd say: well, what's happening in this part of the music? Oh you're open there [laughs]. Nobody'd ever say you're free, they'd say: oh, you're open there, so it was open improvisation. So later I heard about it being free improvisation, but that's OK, who knows, there might be some ideological difference in the terminology embedded there.

… When you are trying to play with someone, whatever instrument or whatever they're doing, you're interacting with them, you're not even playing with them, it should come to you at a certain point, some sense of their intentions, it should come, and maybe people could be tuned into that and could allow, tuned in as a question of method. Or, another way to think about is that you have – I have certain methods, which are very simple actually. One of them is, I kind of presume that my presence as a sound maker isn't really needed, my presence to be party to the information exchange is needed, I need to be listening and paying attention, I don't ever let that go, but I might decide not to make a sound for long periods of time because it's a matter of trust, you know, if someone is doing something and it seems like it's working why should you come in. A lot of people come in because they're nervous, or they're upset, or they feel they should come in or they believe in call and response, things I don't really do anymore; you know call and response sounds boring. My thing has been call without response and I try to tell people this. If someone makes the call you don't have to respond because you're already listening, just let it go and see where it goes. Over the long run what you get is a great deal of variety in the texture and in the orchestration. Everyone isn't playing all the time and you can kind of let things go for long periods of time because what ends up happening is that at a certain point, whether it's through boredom or need for change the situation is going to change, it's inevitable, it's going to come into your lap, [laughs]. It's going to happen. It might not be for a while but it's going to happen and you can decide what kind of change you're looking for and at that moment for me methodologically that may be the right moment to, if you feel like making a sound then you can make it. And that probably is the moment when you can find something new that emerges in the performance. I find that to be a way of extending the life of the performance and extending the power of the gesture, potentially over long periods of time, maybe a very long time. But it does require you to sit back and relax and enjoy other people and what they are doing and to trust that they are going to do the right thing and that you don't really have to do anything, they're fine and even if they're not maybe you should just let them work it out. Do you ever watch the Bulls basketball team?

SR: No.

GL: But you know about that right, and the coach?

SR: No [laughs].

GL: Oh, you don't – anyway this guy Phil Jackson, he's the coach, and he's the coach of the Lakers, and he had this book right, and the book is all about improvisation in basketball and it's based on this theoretical book written by his assistant coach in the 50s, all about improvisation in basketball and he kind of combined that with systems. He would say this funny thing like, the team would be losing and usually the thing is you got somebody saying: 'The team is loosing take out person X and put in person Y'. But his thing was: 'Well the team is losing we'll let them work it out', [laughs] and so they're out there working it out. That's why it's so entertaining to watch, even though I'm not a big basketball fan, you can see them working it out improvisationally, how to do things, it was an expression of trust in their ability to work it out for themselves and I learnt a lot from that for improvised music ...

If it dies, it dies, I mean you crash but you don't necessarily burn, you know [laughs] so you can have the possibility for enhancing larger values than just the aesthetic of the situation.

SR: It reminds me of being in improvisations where I'm sitting there and I'm not happy, I'm thinking of particularly large groups – things can go on and very often a response to that is, you hear people trying to impose something else ...

GL: We covered all that when I went to Glasgow [Glasgow Improvisers Orchestra]. This is where it started, this thing I'm telling you about, it started right there in Glasgow with those guys. And I was very happy, I was very gratified because they released a recording of it. And what it was, it was a recording of the rehearsals leading up to it, we were supposed to play this piece – like it was something out of Stanislavski, or we were going to do an improvisation on Othello – well fine give us the play – give us the text – well not right now [laughs] – we're going to give you the characters first, we're going to give you the situation first and you're going to improvise on it. You know this right? It's in *An Actor Prepares*. [Stanislavski's book describing an approach for actors].

SR: Oh, yes.

GL: There's a whole section called improvisation with Othello. So I read this years ago and it made a great impression on me because here was a situation where, finally I could use it. Instead of playing the piece we would play the preparation for the piece. My thing for the last few years had been improvisation in large groups because that's where the frontier of attention and communication really resides in the field and personally I find there's a dearth of methodology there, effective methodologies for doing that, and it's been a problem for a very long time.

SR: With the large group?

GL: Yeah, it's been a problem for a very long time and you know Derek (Bailey) used to complain about it, back in the old days, 'Company' days. He'd have his things, small groups, and then somebody would say: 'Let's all play together,' and Derek would say: 'That never works' [laughs]. And that's amazing, you've got all these guys, there we were in like the 80s and you guys were getting started in the early 60s, and it still doesn't work – well why doesn't it work? [Laughs.]

SR: … 'Conduction' (guiding improvisers) shifts the onus of responsibility and it becomes very much – in many ways I think people go to that as a way of resolving this problem.

GL: Well, what problem are you resolving?

SR: Well, you can decide on the textures, of the density of an enormous group of people, you can pick out individuals …

GL: Yes, but that's a static problem – there are bigger fish to fry in improvisation than aesthetics and we found that out in Glasgow with the GIO. I felt that some people were pretty frustrated with what had been going on, people would come in and they would impose their piece and you had to play it or a conduction and people didn't feel they had a chance to say what they wanted to say there. And some people felt that they couldn't say certain kinds of utterances because it didn't fit in with a certain kind of stylistic sort of, you know, presumption. I felt there was a lot of hostility and I kind of felt it, like I was the next jerk who was bringing his piece in – I didn't want to do that. So I said let's bag the piece and let's try to play. So the first time we tried to play it wasn't that good and so we started to work out ways we could try to play better. And what it meant was that everyone had room to be a part of the proceedings and to do what they felt, because the thing about improvisers is they're smart, they have ideas. And so what you can do as an individual is you can find a way to put yourself in a position of creating a space for someone else to do what they want to do, you know [laughing] you can do that, you can really do that. So that is a methodology, that's not a moral precept, so there are ways of doing that. So that's something that we decided, that that is going to be part of our method. It's the equivalent of in basketball, you don't hog the ball, you pass it around to someone else who can make the play. So that was one thing and the other thing was that there weren't any rules about what you could play, you could play whatever you would want. And the other thing was that critique was suspended indefinitely. That was very much an AACM thing, nobody ever said 'Oh your concert was this or that,' – you gave your concert, people came to it, that was it. Generally they said they liked it. A lot of the problem with certain kinds of Western notions of keeping your critical faculty active is that, actually it's not a critical faculty, it's trying to rip people to shreds in order to show you are being objective. Whereas I've always found it's better to tell people it's good, you know it might be good, they might live up to it – I don't lose anything, no one's waiting for me to give the word from on high about what other people are doing or the strength of their work – it doesn't matter what I think, it's what they think that's important. The next step here was to realize that it was about personal transformation – you would have to come to the improvisation as a changed individual and that you transformed yourself as the kind of human being who can operate in a large space, and a lot of that was quite prosaic and obviously if everyone's playing all the time the textures are not going to be that diverse – so that means, realistically, in a large group, you're going to spend most of your time listening …

So they were listening and they were getting pleasure from listening, the thing was to take pleasure from listening to your fellow people on the stage, listen to the outcome of the thing and think about what kinds of pleasures this was producing, what people were learning from the experience, what people were finding out about the other people, finding out about things you hadn't really considered. To let in thoughts that had nothing to do with the music necessarily at that moment, let them in. This is the way I've always worked but I think what we started to find was, that's why I was so gratified to see that they had released these improvisations, because we had been rehearsing this for a number of days and then on Friday afternoon it worked, everybody liked it, and they put that out on a record, and I think they named it 'Friday Afternoon' or something [laughing]. But suddenly people felt as if they owned this, they could take ownership of this. That it was theirs, they had made it, but it was very quiet a lot of the time but it had a lot of energies, sometimes it would be very energetic, sometimes it would be very quiet, sometimes maybe one or two people were playing and maybe that person would play for a while and nobody felt the need to chime in or add a little bit or adornment and all those things you know, people didn't do that and so as a result you could hear that, it opened up the space, you could hear people play. Everybody likes the idea that they were being listened to and some people felt they were being listened to for the first time since they'd been in the group. That people were listening to them in a new way …

You were talking about conduction. They've had all kinds of conduction and what Butch did was great, he gave it a name, he gave it a vocabulary, he gave it a practice, he did all these things – whereas people used to get up and wave their arms and do stuff and you'd have to interpret and do all these gestures, now Butch gave it a form. It's not responsibility that's lacking because – people who are being conducted by Butch or someone or one of those Sound Painters, they do have a responsibility and they're executing it, they're discharging their responsibilities. I don't have a problem with conduction but I don't want to conduct anybody. I want to sit in my space and I want to be able to view and intuit and empathize with the flow of intelligences through the network of the players. That's what I want and that's what my research object is in improvisation right now, local intelligence. Look, you can read about it, the Javanese Gamelan people are talking about it, you get these flows that are happening, the drummer is doing one thing and the flow goes to the little biddy guy, the tiny xylophone there and other people start to pick up on it and finally the whole leviathan starts to move with that rhythm. Suddenly this thing starts to move slowly and accelerating you know, what you're hearing is the flow of intelligence and thinking. You can hear a similar thing in these improvised music things, you're always hearing the intelligence and the intension regardless of what they're doing, you're always hearing it, but I sort of wanted to hear a lot of different variations for that. I felt that the various conducting schemes interrupted that or made that more difficult to hear and maybe to a certain extent people felt that it maybe solved problems but they weren't the problems I was interested in, they weren't my problems. So you felt good and you got a good outcome for your piece and everyone liked it, so what, you know. I mean did you learn anything about the nature of, the things that you can learn from improvised music, the nature of consciousness or the nature of communication, things that really matter, things that you can really learn from improvisation that you can learn all the time. And I thought that's why they were on stage but I guess what they really, what some of them were really on stage for, was to create a nice commodity, that they could package in some way and that they could get a repeatable outcome from. That's a different problem, that's not my issue – not now, maybe it was a long time ago.

… Those musicians themselves [GIO] who are extraordinary – extraordinary not for the usual reasons, or in addition to the ordinary reasons; they've been together for a long time, they are a community, they come out of the community, they're very generous with each other, their music was the place where you're supposed to have these generosities. Oh, and I forgot to mention an important part of the process – we had some extensive discussions we actually did more discussing than playing. So we'd play and then we'd talk about it and critique what we were doing. I don't know if you've read, I have a little article it's called 'Teaching Improvised Music', it's in the Arcana collection?

SR: Yes.

GL: It talks about all that kind of stuff we were doing – it's the same stuff. If you look at it it's exactly the same stuff. We're playing, we're critiquing. At first people would say things like: I can't just stop what I'm doing and start talking, and I'd say: Well why not? You're already talking [laughs] – of course you can. It's just that they had a self-conception of this is my playing and this is my other life. This is my heightened consciousness and this is about my conscious life and so to mix those up and break up that romantic conception of the improviser made it easier.

SR: So, discussion is part of the method.

GL: Well it's part of the – we're self-teaching, we're learning from each other. We're self-teaching. We do an autodidact process, with the outcome of which we don't even know [laughs]. So we're teaching ourselves to do something that we don't really know what it is. We're just looking for an outcome and we'll know it when we see it, and that's a part of improvisation too – opportunist as Stephen Greenblatt would say.

SR: Can I ask you about spontaneity in improvisation and familiarity?

GL: Oh boy.

SR: And how you experience spontaneity and familiarity in your musical practice?

GL: What's that mean, familiarity? You mean just being familiar with something?

SR: Well, someone develops a vocabulary and they introduce that into a situation – but this music is also about spontaneity …

GL: I don't know I kind of felt that spontaneity is overblown, most people aren't that spontaneous, they're doing mostly the same thing, there are all kinds of little rituals that people do, you know that they do every day, just to get through their everyday lives, and they use the same version of those repetitious rituals when they play music. Music is just one domain of the improvisative experience, you know, and as you start to find out how vast that experience is, how many levels it has, you don't want to privilege music over all the others, which ends up making a limitation on it.

Composers also belaboured that over years, between composition and improvisation. There's often the claim with composers that we, and I include myself in that, are able to create things that don't rely on repetition because we have a chance to write it out, well if that were true you wouldn't be able to tell Wagner from Bach, but people can, I mean we look for those structures, Bach looked for them too. People are not that able to transcend, they can change but they always bring their previous stuff with them. So there's always such familiarity. There's this interesting book that you may like, it just came out it's by this British neuroscientist, it's called *The Actor's Brain* by Sean Spence (2009). He's got a whole section on improvisers attempting to be spontaneous and attempting to create new stuff [laughs] and how hard it is and how neurologically it's an impossible task [laughs] you know. But he doesn't take a position of what you get from the attempt to overcome these apparently neurologically imposed limits on spontaneity and newness. He quotes Steve Lacy and Charlie Parker and all these people. Because back in the day he was doing brain scans on people while they were listening to Theolonius Monk this guy you know [laughs]. So the thing is I'm with him, once you admit that there aren't that many novel situations, then you're prepared to see the novelty in new combinations … once you get there you revel in the combinations which are potentially infinite. He quotes Thomas Owens' (1979, dissertation) book on Charlie Parker extensively, which I thought was the most ridiculous thing I'd ever read [laughs] I mean Owens had this incredible … he wrote down a hundred motifs that Charlie Parker would repeat and recombine, some of them were only two notes long – I mean that's not a motif, that's just two notes [laughs] … and subjected it to Schenkerian analysis [a system for analysing tonal music]. The upshot was that there was nothing new there. But somehow, how did the impression arise that Charlie Parker was so spontaneous, or even John Coltrane? You hear the same things over and over, but what accounts for the power of it, it's not in the spontaneity that's for sure, there's something else there.

SR: What is it?

GL: Well, I don't know, but let's take out all the things that obviously don't work [both laugh] and start there, you know one of those Sherlock Holmes things, once you've eliminated all the obvious things then however improbably, this is the truth, so … [laughs] So what was the other one, was there something else?

SR: Familiarity.

GL: I guess they are the two sides of that coin. If you don't stick with the familiar you've got the spontaneous, and everyone's trying to avoid the familiar and stick with the spontaneous. The problem is most of the time what spontaneity produces is the familiar. The other thing is we don't want people to be too spontaneous you know. I mean spontaneity is pretty easily achieved and sometimes it's not really wanted. Like I could spontaneously have a heart attack or something. People talk about it as this unquestioned value, when it seems on reflection it is difficult to come by, in fact it's almost prosaic.

SR: In a way it's like trying to understand the nature of creativity.

GL: Well that's what we're trying to do, aren't we? I mean that's the real thing. I mean you didn't really want to know about free improvisation, I mean that's just a part of it all really and that's just this socio-musical location free improvisation. I mean there's this other larger issue there.

SR: There is a larger issue there and I just wonder about that term, the term itself is problematic, free improvisation, as you said before you also described it as: we're open on this section of music, with Roscoe Mitchell, and I've read Anthony Braxton using the term 'open form' improvisation. I don't even know where it came from, it's associated with Derek Bailey but he used *improvisation* for his book title.

GL: I don't know, maybe that would be a good thing to trace – where the discourse begins with free improvisation, I don't really know. But as it stands now it's a historical term and culturally charged term and as such that's OK, that's what it is. It's a marker for something that has definite roots – trans-cultural and trans-national but certainly it's been connected with particular communities of practice. I don't find it problematic at all because I don't think in relation to described music, or even a style, it's not descriptive of a style, it's descriptive of a set of histories and to a lesser extent ideologies, so that's what I think and that's what works for me.

SR: Right.

GL: So when you're bringing free improvisation to these people, you're also bringing a kind of canon. Free improvisation used to be anti-canon but not anymore. People really want to be associated with the canon of it, you know … Did you read Jason Stayeck's little paper [reads]: 'Free improvisation is less a type of music with a definable sound-scape than it is a set of strategies, deployed by musicians to engender a very inclusive space for music making. These strategies privilege the dialogic, the heterogeneous and the incommensurable … Free improvisation is also a set of beliefs or ideologies about what music is or what it could be. It is grounded in a politics as highly participatory … Extreme in its espousal of personal agency, unique in its combination of difference, favours the egalitarian but does so without renouncing the inter-subjective noise which is an inevitable residue of any interaction action highly communicable and personal. Has intense awareness that music both mediates and is mediated by the world'. I like this first bit about: 'a set of beliefs and ideologies but also a set of strategies' whereas I call it a socio-musical location, which is a different thing. So I kind of prefer that because it sort of allows me to sort of put limits on it [laughs] otherwise I'm stuck with this thing that sort of gets way out of hand, and I can't put limits on it and then it becomes impossible.

SR: Do you have a view of style, orthodoxy or dogma within free improvisation? I suppose in a way this is relating to everything that we've said. You can get a great improviser but they have their thing and it's coming from a distinct world. How is that fitting into the whole picture? For example a jazz player may have their way and it's about taking a solo. But sometimes it's about the collisions as well.

GL: Well a lot of people have thought this way. I'm not as much into it as I used to be though. I kind of like a unity of purpose these days. We're back to talking about stylistic differences which maybe is interesting as an art project, but we should be drawing larger lessons from improvisation at this point and I guess what is happening is, maybe the object is to try to engender, as Jason says, a space where we can do that, where we can consider these issues which transcend, that transcend music in some way. And certainly transcend the idea that the outcome of every encounter has to be this wonderful thing that we can all go home and feel good about or put on a record and all that. So in that sense, what we draw from the lessons in life seem to me to be the most exciting to me. I don't know about the rest, so you may learn a lot from someone who has a particular viewpoint, that they articulate, that they play. But then that person is maybe trying to learn too – again it hinges on the personal transformation thing, how open are you? How vulnerable can you make yourself, how open to change, how malleable, mutable as I think Evan [Evan Parker] used to say … maybe that kind of value system is what you could use. Because there are a lot of ways to go about things you know. Maybe part of the lessons with these kids who are permanently excluded is that you have to figure out a way not to be permanently excluded [laughs], which means you have to figure out some strategies to get what you want and at the same time find out when the battle is winnable and when it is not.

SR: Very often the one thing that was very difficult, people were very often unwilling to acknowledge the other person. So the drama and music created metaphors, analogies and pragmatic things at the same time.

GL: Hey, *Metaphors We Live By* (1980). How pragmatic can you get, [laughs] George Lakoff and Mark Jonson.

Mick Beck

SR:	I'm interested in the place of free improvisation in your practice. How did you begin to improvise?
MB:	Hmm, yes, I'm happy to start there and if it gets too prosaic, you can [laughs] give me a nudge.
SR:	How did you get into music?
MB:	I think – we had a piano in the house. When I was a child. And I used to spend ages, improvising, experimenting.
SR:	What age were you?
MB:	As soon as I could remember, three onwards anyway. And I do remember I used to sing as well. Probably to everybody's chagrin and eh, typical kiddies stuff. I've no idea what the melodic lines were like, but they were ideas about puppy dogs [laughs] and all sorts of things. And then on the piano I do remember loving the generation of chords, and leaning on the black notes and just making a lot of racket. And so my folks said would I like piano lessons when I was six or seven and I said yes, please, and as soon as I started them, it killed it stone dead.
SR:	Can you remember what the teacher was like?
MB:	Um, he was called Mr Doggit and he was a bit dogged. And there was no imagination there. It was him playing very simple things on the piano.
SR:	Was he a good teacher for an unsighted child?
MB:	I don't think there was a problem there in itself. I think he was a fairly formal classical teacher.
SR:	I'm thinking of the dots.
MB:	Yes, I learnt Braille music subsequently. I learnt Braille music and went on to various other teachers at school. And the Braille music system is very clumsy.
SR:	How on earth does that work in relation to using your fingers to play?
MB:	You can only do it using one hand at a time, in terms of sight-reading, so called. But it is a comprehensive system, in that it does show you which notes you're supposed play and with which fingers, all those sorts of things. But I laboured on with that system for a number of years always feeling frustrated and a bit bored with it. Coming across a few pieces as I went through the elementary grades that I did like and enjoying being able to play them but more often than not, not doing much practice and becoming de-motivated. And in parallel to that I'd started playing the ukulele when my hands were not big enough to play the guitar in skiffle groups, and that was more fun. And then I decided that, I'd made some recordings of myself playing the piano and thought that sounds just like I'm playing a typewriter. And I gave it up. At the same time I fell in with a group of people at school who were interested in things moving towards jazz, some of it was jazz.

SR:	What age were you then?
MB:	So this would be thirteen, fourteen that sort of age. And I got hooked on some of the jazz. The biggest impact was when I started listening to bebop. The standard greats from that time: Coltrane and Parker and Cannonball Adderley and Eric Dolphy.
SR:	And you were playing?
MB:	I was playing nothing at this time because I'd given up the piano. I still played the guitar a bit but more in a blues way. I didn't really develop my guitar technique because I was interested in Flamenco guitar when I settled on the guitar and I had, for a kid, probably not a bad Flamenco, Flamenco licks. But then school bands loose their players on a regular basis, you know people leave school, and they needed a saxophonist. So somebody said well why don't you take up the saxophone. And under the influence of the aforementioned players and people like Yusef Latif and a few others, I picked up the saxophone. And I had a few lessons and decided because I'd had the experience of the piano, I thought well, I'll just go it alone. So that was what I did with the saxophone. Which meant I think in terms of learning to play jazz, I was a bit slow on picking up things like the chord structures. I got some of them from the guitar but I never really got engaged in that too much. And although I went through the rest of school and my university days playing jazz I was tending to do it more from a melodic ear context rather than chordally. And I also found when I left university that I was playing less and less because I was being diverted by getting a career off the ground and girlfriends and this, that and the other. So I sort of gave up playing in me twenties and then returned to it when I was nearing thirty.
SR:	So you were working for the civil service?
MB:	Yes, yes, which was fairly demanding, the longish hours and it was fairly intense stuff so there was a bit of an energy issue. But I took nine months sabbatical leave at the time Marion and I got married which was back in 1978 and spent that time jacking up my musical skills, my knowledge of chord structures and this, that and the other. And when I came into that phase and started playing jazz again, I found that whereas I'd been quite assimilated by playing jazz earlier, that there was something boring about it. The more I learnt about the chords and playing the changes, the more boring it got. So I then got my mind opened up to the free scene that was around in the late 70s.
SR:	In Sheffield?
MB:	No, in London.
SR:	You were living in London then.
MB:	Yes.
SR:	So that's quite a good time in London.

MB:	Yes, in fact my interest in the free scene had gone back further than that in London. It was really from 1970 onwards, where I started listening to people like Bob Downs and Barry Guy and then some of the stuff with Derek [Derek Bailey] and then coming across Evan's [Evan Parker] playing, and Harry Becket and various people. So I, as it were, exposed myself to some interesting players and it was then that I started to play more actively again that I realized that I wanted to be in their ballpark rather than the playing of the changes ballpark.
SR:	So when did you become involved in free improvisation as a player?
MB:	As a player it would have been '79, '80. First tour I did was with Will Evans and Paul Rodgers in 1980. When I was working my way back into music I came across people like Steve Berry, the bass player from Loose Tubes. He was a good player who, in jazz terms wanted to push the boundaries and the Django Bates crew and that sort of thing. Before them there was Mike Westbrook and Mike Gibbs and all those people had a big influence on me.
	So returning to your underlying question, I realized there was something, that wasn't playing a detailed, defined structure, which could be released in terms of energy, intensity output, which could be accessed by playing freer and I was after that.
SR:	Can we talk a bit more about what you mean by that? How you identify that, or how you identify it in yourself.
MB:	I think it's quite visceral really, it's things like, I'll mix metaphors, or language anyway, there's tingle factors. You hear people doing things and you think that sends a shiver down the spine. And it might be because of a bit of technical hi-jinx. Or more likely to do with sequences of notes and implied chords and stuff, which would really excite me and then the other bit of metaphor or idealism is what it felt like to be in a group where a sense of musical oneness which can go beyond music where a oneness was being created. So the feeling of being on a creative high and losing one's self in that creative process rather than intellectualizing or making it into an abstract where I'm saying to myself, 'Oh this is going on now, I think I ought to do this'. So it's stepping aside from that logico-deductive space into more emotional fields I suppose.
SR:	So there are emotional possibilities, within …
MB:	I think I thought the emotional possibilities from free improvisation were greater than those that could be achieved from closed structures and in some ways I still do believe that – in terms of access, what I can access. And I am not saying people who play from such closely defined structures don't generate such a feeling. But the freer way into it is my access point, if you like, or my line of entry.
SR:	What do you do when you improvise freely?
MB:	For me there's quite a distinction between what I'm doing if I'm soloing, compared with what I do in a group because if I'm in a group then it's 80 percent

to do with listening and responding. Obviously not in a straightforward call and response but more widely, acknowledging that OK: X is doing this, I'm having this reaction, I think I'll do Y. Because, and there is a because, I think it would in some sense add something. I use the word 'add' I suppose, distinct from the word 'complement'. There's the dimension of doing something which is complementary and there's the dimension of doing something that is completely different, in opposition. So I suppose at an ideas level there's an over-arching notion for me which is that if I'm involved in a piece of music which is improvised, then my aim is to make it into an interesting piece of music. And that does override.

SR: I'm just thinking about this and also the previous thing we were talking about which is this interesting relationship between the cerebral and the emotional.

MB: Yes.

SR: If indeed those two things should be separated at all. You described how it's eighty percent listening and then you make a decision about how you choose to respond. Could you describe how you might experience a feeling [laughs] or an emotion in relation to that? Are you led by emotion? I suppose I'm interested in how we locate ourselves within the visceral aspect of free improvisation that we like?

MB: Because I'm a wind instrument player it's something that is going to be quite naturally centred in the diaphragm area. So there's going to be a feeling coming from that centre of my body, there's a sort of grrrrrr, that really gets me, and that's really what I want to do. In response, and the response will be quite an emotional one, it may be anger or excitement or pathos but it's going to be quite markedly on the emotional spectrum, and it's going to have physical repercussions. In the sense that I am feeling sad, happy, excited.

SR: I'm thinking of that YouTube clip[2] we were talking about before [Mick Beck, Tom Jenkinson (Squarepusher), Paul Hession].

MB: Yes.

SR: Where you're clearly 'in the zone', so whether or not it's right to talk about in terms of: I hear this and then there's this decision there. Of course there are decisions because that's all we can make but it seems that there is something else going on there as well. Things are happening fast. Things are happening faster than we can...

MB: Think. Yes. I certainly experience that. It's the speed. And the speed is part of the excitement. To be able to do things almost ahead of yourself, that's really fucking exciting. I love that. It's partly an ability to let go and it's partly, you know there's a technical element to it. Certainly in my case, that's partly why I practice, in order to do things fluently. So yes, I think it's those two things: fluency and control without it feeling like control.

SR: Right.

MB: And here we're going to go into another dimension, we're talking about emotion but the parallel for me was in the meditation arenas, the yoga domains, that sort of stuff. Which of course people also equate with the spiritual dimension and for me spirituality – I've actually got quite a down to earth view of spirituality which is for me that it is not that far away from determination. It's a bit different, but it's choices, it's making choices and sort of standing by them. And all that links into what we were just talking about in terms of the capability to do what is just at the back of your mind, partly because I've been working on the effects I think I might like to generate and can pull them out when the time is right – a bit of waffle there …

SR: No not at all, the opposite in fact because although we were talking about emotion, I am very interested in the totality of improvisation, and the way in which people perceive it. How much we know of what we do is obviously limited. What do you think about while you're playing?

MB: Being in the moment. Being in the moment, very much. It's the sense when it's going well, the sense of being supported and supporting. So the oneness of the group – that's the zenith. I wouldn't say quite that I don't have to think about anything else, that's not quite true. When things are really buzzing and the group feels like one, there's a sort of imperative desire to keep that oneness going – so what little things do I need to keep the momentum there. And there's something about maintaining momentum that requires change so there's a need for change, or development. The process doesn't stand still.

SR: If you feel this isn't …

MB: Cooking.

SR: What do you do, or think.

MB: Then I do think analytically. But I think quite widely. What can I do to generate some interest here? So there might be an element of what do we need, if we're all flapping about, like in that opening piece that we experienced last night, you know the full ensemble. There's sometimes a need for people to have something to latch onto, in order to generate a focus, because there's not enough focus in the group to generate a sense of direction, or momentum. Those words direction and momentum are metaphors because they are physical and probably what we're talking about is not really described as physical but anyway, they're not bad metaphors I think.

SR: So what would you do? [Laughs] I think that's quite interesting.

MB: Well it depends on which background you come from. My response is, I've done quite a bit of practice to become a fairly good technical player in certain respects. One thing I might well do is draw on some of that technical knowledge, in order to suggest some new material for the group to kick off from, or pick up on. I can imagine, not in opposition to that, but there is another approach which is that I'm going to let my mind go as blank as I can and let random sounds emerge and see if they suggest anything. And the problem with that is that what will tend to emerge is the clichés, that you've been rehearsing with yourself for any number of years [laughs] but I think some improvisers are more skilled at completely letting go and coming in with a completely different line.

SR: Yes, that relates to how you balance spontaneity and that which you already know.

MB: It's a never-ending question or quest, that issue of balance. There's never ending loops, aren't there. You're in this situation where you think not much is happening, and you think I could do that, but on the other hand that's one of my licks, or a few of my licks and people have heard them before and think, oh, he's doing that again, and therefore I won't do that I'll do something else and so you are casting around for things other people might not expect you to do and so you're trying to second or third guess yourself, so I won't do this because it will relate to this and they'll know that set of licks and they'll recognize that. But on the other hand I can do those licks really well [laughter]. And in this case what this bunch of wankers actually need is something quite zizzy – so I could sock it to them, you know, and say fuck you, I don't really care whether you've heard these before, on this occasion it might be what you need [laughter]. So I think those circular processes certainly go on for me. Again, we talked about speed and they go on very fast. And if you do reach the situation where you're nearer to the oneness position then those loops, those circular processes go more into the background and you somehow, just can make noise which is communicative in some way. I was put in mind a bit of the group I had with Simon Fell and Paul Hession. We'd been doing a gig in Leeds and it really had taken off, so it was one of those situations where there was a oneness in the group and somebody came up to me afterwards and said: 'You don't really need an instrument do you, it just sort of seeps out of your pores,' [laughs] and there was something in that – that the oneness with the group came out in a oneness with the instrument and when I think, I was using my voice and my body in a way that just communicated, whatever I did, and that was the moment.

SR: That's very interesting. You transcended your role as a ...

MB: ... player of the saxophone ...

SR: Do you have any ideas about style, or orthodoxy or dogma in improvisation?

MB: Well, I recognize for myself I know that all the work I did on jazz is going to have a big impact on what I do, so if you like I'm acknowledging that the free jazz mode is the one that's the most natural to me. But I don't think that means that I expect other people to come from the same place or operate in the same parameters as me.

... I think there is something about music because it requires the development of sophisticated motor skills, in one way or another, whether it's manipulating a laptop or an acoustic instrument and the way you develop motor skills is largely through practice. So to me I couldn't care less whether somebody has learnt a particular theory but I think they're far more likely to generate some interesting music if they've done a lot of practice. I know some of the practice methods I use because they're right for me, and if I'm asked to give people lessons then I will hold them up as possible ideas but if they choose not to do those then that is absolutely fine. But the key thing is whether they are motivated to practice at all, I mean spend time.

SR: You were talking about your other work as a counsellor and I'm interested whether you make any connections to your thinking in improvisation in relation to that kind of activity, at any level whatsoever?

MB: There is a quite distinct overlap of allowing yourself to be in the moment and going with an instinctual level of response ... I think that's the bit about being in the moment. There might be some things going on and you think: oh, I don't know what the fuck this means and what that is but don't try and struggle to understand it too much, just go with the flow and say and do things which are just instinctual and it might reveal something to you immediately but it might take a couple of sessions for you to think, ah, when this was going on it was probably a reflection of this that or the other ... there is a parallel in what I was talking about drawing on technical expertise, technical knowledge in that as a counsellor you obviously learn certain ways of intervening, which may unlock some of those knots, or may undo some of those knots. But I mean, your reflections about how something may feel later on, may lead you to different interpretation of what is or was happening, which can be very informative to both the counsellor and the client.

Tristan Honsinger

SR: What's the place of free improvisation in your practice?

TH: It's … it's … like the theory of gravity, the gravity … that we are here … so, improvisation is up or down – in direction. And when you're going up you tend to realize you're going up and you're listening to what is around you and you decide to go down and in that split moment, deciding to go down or up is basically the principle of improvisation. And when you decide, it can be a surprise in changing direction. This is an example of improvisation – the moment surprises you, but at the point of deciding to go down or up can be very important in the whole spectrum of the thing – it's kind of like catching something that is in movement – for me this is what improvisation is, the moment of change can be totally important to what comes.

SR: You used the analogy of up and down and sometimes in music people use the terms up and down but you also used the term 'gravity' and I'm thinking that you're using the …

TH: When you go up you can defy gravity – that's the wonderful thing in music is that – the up maybe is a sublimation of down – but we all know that in the end you come down, but flying is a sort of musical, I suppose that's why music is so special, is that we can fly when we're supposed to be down.

SR: When we're talking about music the language always comes up short and yet there are accepted metaphors we use like a 'heavy' group or 'fluid' music. So I like the up and down although I am also slightly confused because if I am to write down 'up and down' a lot of people will understand that in terms of pitch. But we're not only talking about pitch.

TH: We're not only talking about pitch.

SR: So, as well as pitch what are we talking about?

TH: We're talking about … well, I'll bring water into the discussion, because water is undividable, you can't divide water, water is one of the elements that you can't divide, alright air as well, these very important things that benefit us but are totally, these words, what is the word, water is of a consistency but it doesn't care about our practice of dividing. And I think something happens in music where the connection becomes one, then we're in the way of water and this would also be another way of saying it's anti-gravitational in a certain way. When we become one, we are flying together and I think, yes I think music has this, we have made this language I think for some of these reasons – reasons to become one and to float I would say. If you look at Pygmy music or some African, a lot of African music, its practice is not for anyone. It's like I remember going to Derek's [Derek Bailey] house and having a play and there's no people it's just what we do. And I think for me these can be the most revealing sessions in improvised music – playing in the kitchen with another person, or two other people, where there's no audience. And I think that for example, Pygmies, it's been recorded but there were no people watching, except for the one who was recording and they're all floating together, it's one thing. It's so beyond analysis, this state.

SR: Derek Bailey said in an interview: 'I'm interested in playing, rather than performing', and that seems to fit in with what you're saying …

TH: Well, Derek he never looked – this thing of looking, for him, annoyed him, so he would always play like this [mimes looking at held guitar].

SR: It annoyed him?

TH: Yes.

SR: To look at the audience?

TH: Well, to look – just to look, he was always like this.

SR: Was he shy when he performed.

TH: No, because he could also just stop playing and say something to the audience, which is a different thing … I'm totally different from Derek in the sense that I do open my mouth and do very odd things. He's immobile, he was. I'm very mobile in the sense of that's who I am, what I am. Whereas Derek was very stoic and immobile, when he played, that's what I learnt, something about the importance of … because.

SR: Of what?

TH: Of movement, just movement. Someone who is moving is moving anyway. I move around but basically being mobile or immobile is up and down … Well I have to say, the first time I played with Derek was in Masse in Paris – and he brought it out on a record. It was maybe half an hour or something like that. People were laughing, and I don't remember what I was doing but I'm sure it wasn't Derek they were laughing at – but it was just what I was doing in my movement that cracked them up, so it is this contrast between the immobile and the mobile that - because Derek was very dry in his humour, I'm not so dry, that I move around I would call it wet, more than dry, the wet and the dry …

When I discovered improvisation I also saw a retrospect of Buster Keaton. I was living in Montreal at the time. I went to see all of his films. I saw many short films – and I'm absolutely sure that he influenced me completely in the fact that I'm in front of people. It's kind of like a fake thing, it's pretentious and fake.

SR: What is, the situation?

TH: Yes, the situation is very unnatural, people are here and you are here. It's not like …

SR: And there are expectations.

TH: Exactly. So, from the beginning I was influenced by the theatre. And also reading Becket for the first time.

SR: Have you played with Phil Minton?

TH: Yes, there is a group with Phil Minton and Luc Ex [bass guitar] and Serene, a Senegalise percussionist – very fine, a very great player … I like working with Phil because he obviously – the thing of the English scene is they never run after … except for Evan, Evan likes to imitate but a lot of English improvisers don't, I mean they won't react obviously and so you have that tension that you don't get normally from, let's say, German improvisers, as such, or the Dutch.

… Free improvisation came out of maybe the tail of free jazz, and now free jazz is slowly disappearing and so free improvisation is the thing. The Germans call it free jazz – they don't call it free improvisation. 'Oh, you play free jazz'. 'Yes.' But, basically I think England is the first, is the beginning of free improvisation, I would say, in Europe. And now it shows its colours in a way because people aren't really that interested in playing for fifty minutes full out like Brotzmann, well Brotzmann still does it – he's free jazz now, basically.

SR: There's also some interest in free jazz – the immediacy and connections to noise music for a younger generation, the visceral thing and the less 'plink-plonk'.

TH: Well, for instance, I've been playing here (Berlin) for the last couple of months and we actually stop together and we experience the silence and the audience is like – it's a very good audience, I would say, the German audience, because they will give you more than what most people will give you. I mean the respect, so there comes out sometimes maybe eight seconds of silence, which is incredible, so this is where it's going. And this is really so beautiful, this thing – who's going to start, you know.

SR: You started in New England?

TH: I grew up in Massachusetts – I went to a conservatory which is like university level – you go after high school. I went to New England Conservatory back in '67, '68. It was a disaster because the cellist who was there at the interview who said you can come – I said I'd like to study with you, he said fine. But then he went on sabbatical, he went to England … I went there and played with an older cello player who taught from the Symphony, the Boston Symphony. So I decided, I went to Peabody and studied with quite a well-known cellist, didn't like him and therefore I left – I went to Montreal in 1969. It was basically, I'd had enough of classical music. But I didn't know I was going to become an improviser – it was the days of youth and confusion and what have you.

SR: Was that even a term then. Did people say: I'm an improviser?

TH: No, it was free jazz. I started because I was in love with this very, very lovely woman, she still is lovely and a friend of hers decided, OK I want to do some theatre. He didn't have a clue what he wanted. So I went with my girlfriend's sister who played the Baroque flute. So we get to this space and I said well what do you want us to do. And he said I don't know, just do something. I said OK, so we start and it was wow. I said I guess I'm going to leave this classical business behind. From one moment to another I decided, yes this is my life. So just a little understanding made me decide, yes this is what I do, so.

SR: In performance?

TH: No, just in a rehearsal. He didn't do anything – but I had discovered my life. Which is quite amazing.

There was a group called the Jazz Libre du Quebec and they were a backup band for a famous chanson singer. They played arrangements of songs and then they met Noah Howard and playing with him –they decided OK we do that – we play free jazz. And this was the only thing that was happening – this was the late 60s in Montreal – absolutely nothing, and I was playing in the street … playing in the street I met people who let me hear the early FMP records, the early Incus, the early ICP, so I said I think I am going to go to Europe. I felt much more attached to their way than the free jazz way. Because it was either going to New York or it was going to Europe and I decided yes, I go to Europe.

SR: Was there a scene in New York then to do anything other than free jazz?

TH: No, no. I mean John Zorn, I met them after I'd … maybe in 78 – already they had started. This was John Zorn, Toshinori Kondo, Eugene Chadbourne – prior to that there was nothing. So it was … I was closer to free jazz at that time. But I heard this music and thought, yes. It was 'The Topography of the Lungs' [Evan Parker, Derek Bailey, Han Bennink. 1970. Incus Records]. I don't know I think it's maybe the first Incus Record. It really impressed me – so I said, yes, I go. Basically I met Han the first time. I flew to Amsterdam because I had a Dutch friend who said Tristan, come on it's all happening in Europe. We met in Montreal and we had a group together and he said yes, we can do it. So I went there.

SR: Was it all happening there?

TH: Oh, yes it was all happening. Of course it took me a year before I got into the thing.

SR: Did they let you in?

TH: No, they didn't let me in (pause). No, no, no, so it was really difficult. I remember playing at the Bimhaus when it opened, and I played with Han. I came into the dressing room. I said: Hi, I'm Tristan and I want to play, and I took out my cello and Han was like: 'Yes, listen to him', this is in the dressing room and Han is playing like soprano or something. This is the early 70s and Han is like – he has this huge Chinese cymbal and I sat just in front of this Chinese cymbal and I didn't hear a note that I played the whole evening and I still remember I had the ring of this cymbal in my head for at least four hours after the concert. So this is my introduction to Europe. And then I didn't have any money so I went out in the street in Amsterdam and they arrested me, they took my cello away.

SR: Because you were playing?

TH: Yes, and so, with a friend we got a lawyer and we got the instruments back. And I said fuck Amsterdam, I'm going to Paris. So I went to Paris the next day …

SR: You hitched?

TH: Yes, and then I started playing in the streets.

SR: You didn't have anywhere to stay?

TH: I had one connection, and finally I had a *pensione*, you know a room, so I managed to survive every day, playing in the street. And then I went back to Amsterdam and I remember I came back the first night and I went to the Bimhaus and Irene Schweitzer was playing with Louis Moholo and Louis didn't want to play … so they'd heard of me and they said would you like to play tonight. So I ran back to my place, got my cello and I played the gig with Rudiger Carl, Irene Schweitzer and I forget maybe there was – and I replaced Louis, and a friend of his said hey Louis there's a Czechoslovakian cello player, he was South African as well, he's really good and I meet Louis at the bar, he's drinking, and I smile at him and say 'Hi,' and he says: 'What are you smiling for?' And that was my introduction to the South African way … And so it started then, actually when I came back all the doors were open. It took me six months staying in France because I toured and went all over the place in France and then I came back and all the doors were open, yes, but it was a very great time for me because it was like a school, I also thought I'm not ready, for these people, so playing every day in the streets it was a great school – I mean for six months every day – playing … and then Han [Bennink, ICP] said: 'Misha, [Mengelberg, ICP] listen to this guy', and so Misha listened and then he invited me to his house and it started to happen. And then I met Kowald and I get invited into the Globe Unity; and I met Derek (Bailey) in the streets in Paris. I was playing. I didn't know. He walked past, and somehow he found someone who knew me and they gave him my phone number, and he called me and said would you like to come and play with me tonight, I said sure, because I'd heard him play, yes, of course, of course. He said I'm playing with the Steve Lacey Sextet – I'm the guest and if you like to come down we play in the break. So we played for about ten minutes and that was the beginning of England. So it was like Switzerland, Germany, Holland, England.

SR: So that's mid 1970s?

TH: Yes '75.

SR: When you improvise, what do you do?

TH: [Very long pause] I … it's basically like stepping from everyday life and all of a sudden you're standing on the table and there's absolutely no difference except that you're in a parallel world with the real world. So you kind of take a step, or dive or whatever into this other world I would say but it's almost a mirror of what everyday life is.

SR: Is that the same experience as when you were alone with Derek, or on your own or say when you are in Wendel [music venue] and people are talking …

TH: It's all really the same, of course it's a … but I don't see it as an abstraction, I see it as a … um … a … farce, as something to do with everyday life.

SR: How do you view familiarity and spontaneity in improvisation – do you view that as important? You have material you know …

TH: Yes, of course.

SR: And yet there are other aspects to the performance, or the experience, and the experience changes for the audience so there's something else going on there as well other than the material that you know.

TH: The whole thing is, when you start thinking about it the complexity of, of, let's say a concert, all the things that are influencing you, the audience, the place, whatever I think has a great deal to do with the outcome of, and I suppose the only, the only thing is to be prepared for this complexity. I would say that it's, and of course spontaneity is, part of this complexity, I would say. So, I think it comes down to experience and really being part of this complexity offers a possibility that, that this complexity transforms into some kind of simplicity. So if you have the confidence to realize the complexity, then you can become simple, I would say. Because it's kind of like, seeing, that, you are just a crumb [picks up a cigarette butt from the ashtray] you're just like that in the complexity, but if you understand that you are like that in the complexity, then you can offer simplicity. And I would say, spontaneity is maybe another way to express the same thing, but I would have to say that spontaneity is overrated.

Alan Tomlinson

SR: What is the place of free improvisation in your practice?

AT: The improvisation that I do, it's as free as I can get it. It's not free, it's within your own constraints, your own licks, your own motifs that you've heard a thousand times, that you've played. And then you think: oh dear me, I'm not playing that again am I? So it's not free, it's not that free at all. Well, I don't think …

SR: How do you experience familiarity and spontaneity in your musical practice?

AT: Do you mean when I practise or on a gig?

SR: In your work as a musician.

AT: Well you see I've not got a composer's mind, I don't infinitely invent and I don't think a lot of improvisers do. They've got their own little devices that they do and they more or less stick to them. That's why you can hear someone playing and you can say: oh, that's Charlie. So, I don't think so-called free improvisation is that free. I don't give it a lot of thought. I try my best to play well; I try my best to put on a good performance. I've seen such boring and lifeless improvisation over the years, I try to avoid that like the plague really. People who will witter away for twenty minutes and don't get anywhere, there's no drama in it, no life in it, there's no coming in it, there's no going in it. I'm sure you've seen it yourself. I avoid that. I can't stand it: lifeless music, limp music – music with no charm.

SR: So how does that relate to technique?

AT: No, no. I think you need a big technique. As good a technique as you can possibly achieve. And then it makes up for one's lack of invention. I've got a good technique; I've practised over the years – I've always striven to achieve a good technique, and sound. And I've taken lessons over the years, from different orchestral players when I was younger, the proper players who can really play the trombone. So I've learnt properly; I went to music college as well and I play other kinds of music. I sit next to people sometimes who can really fucking play, and I try to play as well as I can.

SR: Who do you mean by those who can really play?

AT: Good people who have been to music college, they are trained properly, they sit up straight, they don't spit notes out with their tongue, they use their diaphragm properly, they make notes that project. Well-trained people, it's good to sit next to them and you can play exactly in tune with them, when I do other kinds of music that is. So I try to acquire as good a technique as I can and I try to bring that to bear upon improvising. When I can't think of anything to play I can rely on technique. I think I've got strong chops, physically I've got strong chops and I can play a solo for half an hour without falling flat on the floor, I think. Well over the years …

SR: Those people who've got the technique, who really can play who you're sitting next to, and then they say what are you doing tomorrow Alan? And you say I'm going to do this free improvisation. What's the response, and can any of those improvise?

AT: No, no they can't. They don't do that at all. Like the jazzers, they don't improvise. Well, they don't play that sort of music, it's not in their realm of thought even.

SR: The jazzers?

AT: The straight players. I don't do a lot of straight playing. A little bit.

SR: But for them the goal is …

AT: It's very limited – it's technique based. And the jazzers that I play with, they don't play improvised music generally, even though a lot of them are good players, very good players. They can't improvise because – they sound like jazzers when they do improvise. As you know, you've probably heard them. Years ago there was a lot of them about, there's still a lot of them about. The first note they play is 'ba-dup' and you think: Oh, fucking hell, here we go, the old scooby-doobies, [clicks fingers] the old jazz merchants. And they're good players a lot of them but they've spent so long learning jazz that they can't get it out of their system, they can't play free music very well. It sounds like they're in the wrong genre almost: jazz licks with no rhythm section and it doesn't work.

SR: Do you think they don't hear it or they just dislike it?

AT: They've not acquired a technique whereby they could play this sort of music, properly, I don't think.

SR: Do you agree with Cecil Taylor when he says people won't be honest, when they say they don't like my music it's really that they don't understand it?

AT: I don't know about understand it, I don't understand it myself, sometimes. Generally I like it but I don't always like it. I mean I hear myself on things that I've played and I think it's rubbish, often. It doesn't sound very good on playback, it might be alright on the gig but generally that's why I haven't made many records.

SR: So you did all the training – when did you become involved in the free improvisation, what's the story?

AT: When I was at music college I was listening to Alan Civil, one of the Mozart horn concertos. Alan Civil was a very famous principal horn in the BBC Symphony, a fabulous player. And in the cadenza he broke into chords and I was having a shave at the time and I nearly cut my throat.

SR: He broke into chords, he played multi-phonics.

AT: Yeah, because it's not that new that stuff, you know. Weber wrote it in the 1820s for his French horn concerto. So, it's not new all that carry on. So I got my trombone and I tried to do it myself and a little bit later on I heard Globokar on the radio playing *Sequenza V* by Berio. So I got that out and bought it and started to learn those techniques.

227

SR: When was this, roughly?

AT: 1970 maybe, a bit before that. I was still at music college in Leeds. And then I discovered improvised music and that took my fancy. See I was in the Jazz and Light Music College and I wasn't a jazz player, I couldn't play jazz. But I got in because they needed people to fill the numbers out, and I got on the Pre-diploma Course, I don't know what it's called now. In other words a year of study before I went onto the three-year course proper. Because I was going to take O levels and A levels to get myself into another music college but I got into there instead because they needed the numbers. And then I bought a record of John Stevens and Paul Rutherford and Trevor Watts.

SR: That was a step in the direction away from Berio …

AT: Yes, but it was still that kind of music, if you know what I mean, that side of the fence so to speak.

SR: I've heard some people say free improvisation; there's nothing new about it; people have always done this, but it's not been documented. That it's something that's always been done, around the world. I think Braxton said that.

AT: They probably freely improvised but within the constraints of their own culture. If they dropped me into the middle of Africa two hundred years ago with my trombone, they'd think who's this? I could improvise with them but … people improvise within their own constraints. I'm sure; I'm sure they do.

SR: Do you see free improvisation, or improvisation as a tool for the professional musician or something beyond that?

AT: It is becoming so now – some of the music colleges have improvising and some of the modern compositions have improvised sections within them. Though I think most of them improvise in a very constrained way, not like so-called practising improvisers like myself and others would play. Though it is accepted as a sort of a norm in music college. Like jazz, jazz is accepted as a norm in most of the music colleges, they all learn jazz now, to a certain extent. And I think they do learn to play freely in music colleges, but it's all very technique based. I mean I did a little bit at the Royal College of Music once at the junior department, for a friend of mine and most of the pianists were trying to play as many notes as they could without listening. Their concept of what it was was quite askew; they'd not had experience of doing it. Though they could actually play. Some people were very reticent to improvise.

SR: So you encountered resistance?

AT: In a way yeah, yeah, but that's only through upbringing and training.

SR: So, in a way it's a bit like a cultural thing, if we dropped you with your trombone two hundred years ago … really it's to do with …

AT: Their culture … Yeah, I would say.

SR: When you're freely improvising what do you do?

AT: Do you mean my thought processes?

SR: Yes, whatever, your thought processes or …

AT: I'm trying to create something that's of interest to the people sat in front of me, basically, and myself. If I see a bunch of, a load of bored faces, I've failed, you know. I normally bring a theatrical element to my playing, something a bit visual. I mean I don't overdo it but I mean I don't stand there like a statue and play and twenty minutes later step from the spot when I've finished; I don't play like that. I try to use the space. There are certain devices you can use. You know when your invention is floundering there are devices you can rely on, that I can rely on, a few I suppose. Getting back to what I said at the beginning, none of it is that free. I've just come back to the beginning now haven't I. An element of drama as I said before, an element of coming and going. Not some flaccid, limp dick music like a flat fucking pond. You know I've seen so much of it. I would hate to play like that. If I thought I played like that I'd give it up; I'd just play other music. People are listening to it as well. Bear that in mind as well. It's not self-centred music. Like any performance, when people have paid to listen to it, they should be engaged in it in a way, in the whole process, I mean I do play to an audience to a certain extent, certainly when I'm playing solo. When I'm playing with other people, that's different again you're constrained by the way they play. I do try to engage people to some extent in my playing.

Sven-Ake Johansson

SR:	I want to ask you about the place of free improvisation in your practice and you were telling me about the boxes [SAJ's studio space has a lot of cardboard boxes in it] and the 20th anniversary of Echtzeitmusik [real-time music].
SAJ:	Yes it is an organization here [Berlin]; it's called Echtzeitmusik and I'm supposed to have an evening. For performing of course you need some money, you need a director for it and to rehearse it in like a week and good players who can read music and play with a bow [to bow the boxes]. They will do this piece in a forty-five minute performance. Very big boxes in a standing section, smaller boxes section sitting. So you have a spectrum of this white noise music which comes out of the cardboard.
SR:	Is it the first time you've performed this?
SAJ:	Yes, this will be the premiere.
SR:	I saw you did a piece with twelve tractors.
SAJ:	Yes. This is a piece I did fifteen times in different parts of Europe. I never did it in England but I would like to. The old tractors are best because they have only two cylinders. The can make a kind of polyphonic rhythm, very slow.
SR:	I'm interested in what the notion of free improvisation means to you.
SAJ:	It's not so free – you study a style all your life and when you do that you cannot do – just free. And you have to be ordered to do that. And you make your own choice. Between training and what you find out, you mix it with other players or you play alone. So, it's not notated but it's memorized. I think it's a kind of … you cannot just do anything.
SR:	So the free part of that suggests to you anything.
SAJ:	Anything can be added to it or … ? No.
SR:	Let me put this another way. What is the place of improvisation in your practice?
SAJ:	My practice?
SR:	Your music – your work with sound. Your early record with Peter Brotzmann and Peter Kowald, I don't think is written music. I wondered if you have ideas on that?
SAJ:	This is a very long time ago. And it is very different today. At this time I would say, this was a kind of artistic step beyond a kind of jazz music, which existed at the time, which was just a little part of improvisation, because it's mathematic music, because it was the old song form all the time. And this was a kind of step out in the cold water; you don't have to use your instrument, the sound of your instrument. It was not music in that case; it was to find out what the instrument can do. What you can do with the instrument, more or less, a step out to – to find out what the instrument could bring. And it was at that time very special – young artists, it was energetic music – fast and loud – yes, because that's how it was at that time. Being fast and being loud

and express, not yourself, but kind of express and use the instrument and see what the instrument could do. So it was not an idea about music, so much. It was playing together and then everyone had a little solo, and it kind of divided the time between the three persons. And this is also a decision you make.

SR: So there were decisions before you …

SAJ: No, during playing.

SR: So that way of sub-dividing the trio. That was a spontaneous thing.

SAJ: Yes.

SR: That's interesting, that you say it wasn't a kind of music …

SAJ: It was a kind of art sound. It became later a kind of music when you started to put in musical structures, elements which comes from music at any time. At first it was a kind of very loud expression, beyond the borders of what existed before and what we were training and listening to, as a musician we listened to mathematic music, jazz music mainly. This is my view of it now.

SR: Did you study music yourself?

SAJ: I was not academic trained. Not in the classical academic way. Since a very young boy in the orchestra, the dance orchestra.

SR: In percussion?

SAJ: Yes. It was mainly by ear. I was not a person who could play the percussion by reading music.

SR: You mentioned an 'art sound'. I don't think Brotzmann or Kowald came from music training background. I think it was art school and languages.

SAJ: Yes. I came from the orchestra, dance orchestra mainly. Kowald was a languages man. He studied Greek and he worked as a translator in the court. And Brotzmann was graphics, art.

SR: There were some Fluxus ideas?

SAJ: Yes, that was more performance, it was not music. But he was impressed by some of the people who were with the Fluxus.

SR: So your practice now you see as significantly different. Does the way you develop music now bear any relation to that?

SAJ: Yes, of course. But the sound is different. It could not stay, otherwise I repeat myself [laughs] – because I try to come out of something, try to find new experiences and challenge to find other materials, and this is still going on … finding new challenges … curious about your own way and the communication with the other players. But the backgrounds are the same. The sound and the form has to change because I'm curious about how we can communicate. The most interesting things, which are not full of clichés.

SR: There're people who spend their entire life within the limitations of a single instrument, whether it's a saxophone or piano, but you don't see that as your way. You prefer to go away … for example, from the drum kit.

SAJ: Yes. I still practice on this though. The drum kit, as we know, belongs to the dance orchestra. It belongs actually to history. Where there weren't enough people in the orchestra so one person has to do the job of two or three people. So they found this mechanical stuff. And then it went in the jazz scene as a kind of classic. I play that too, I play jazz, in the meanwhile, a lot of concerts, classical jazz form. That's what I started out at, mathematic music, and I do that quite a lot, in different formations here in Berlin ... as well as the modern music ... I do this kind of classic form.

SR: I'm very interested in these different points of view. Some people stay within one framework/instrument for their lifetime and others move to other ways of making sound, to other instruments or music practices.

SAJ: Musicians or composers have different views. Some do a very special gesture for a very long time, or they use classical forms of music to do a kind of collage. I found out very early in my percussion, solo work, to explore the sound, not the ringing cymbals and the drums, but make shorter sounds, and make different sounds, and new communication with other players. It was easier to bring in other material than the classical. Sometimes you try to imitate some other things that you have heard or be on a certain level with another instrument. So you have to find material which communicates with it.

SR: I saw you in a gallery/series called COMA in a trio with Mats Gustafasson [saxophones], and Werner Dafeldecker [double bass]. And you had cloth on the drums and you moved the cloth on and off the drums.

SAJ: Yes, sounding and not sounding. Also, you can make the shape of the room. You can let it ring or you can stop it.

SR: So, is it only about limiting the sound?

SAJ: Yes, or stopping it from ringing out. Sometimes the room is ringing and it is like closing the door ... With the piano it's the same thing but you don't see it. In this case it is performative, you see it but with other instruments you don't. You are making the music visceral, you see how it is constructed and how it is done, maybe for some people that's interesting. Some people say it is a performance but it is just handling ... ways to get the sound as I like it.

        [SAJ then takes me to a glass display cabinet along the length of one long wall of the studio, in which his works are displayed: publications, photographs, recordings, artefacts of performances.]

SAJ: Let's take a look here ... [looking at an early record cover]. This is to do with making the music of that time – a *drive,* so the music goes forward, at that time. As we spoke about earlier, you used your instrument not to make melodic forms but rather to find out what the instrument could give in sounds, that is so in these early works. This is a later idea about fifty minutes of ventilation sound. And this from '72, with a Dutch group, we played with early free electronics, instrumental music in the Roundhouse in London at a festival. It was mixed media.

SR: That was an interesting time at the Roundhouse in 1972. I think AMM played around then.

SAJ: They played also. [Indicating the different artefacts.] This is the last solo work: bowed cymbal and snare drum. And this is with Christine Sehnaoui from Paris. So it's just bowed drums and cymbals, it's not this kind of patterned music. This is also something that has to do with cardboard sounds. These drawings are from unreleased material from Swiss Radio in 1967 – and there are twelve originals. The early trio that we spoke about. And this is a book made from the original sleeves …

SR: When you sit at your chosen percussion, what do you do?

SAJ: As a soloist or when I play with some people in a performance, I just start. I have different sound combinations I worked out in the last ten or fifteen years and I try to organize, this informs other instruments and their intentions to play. And it comes out a little bit different every time, depending on the players and with the same players it is also different, we make the structures, we make the same because this is something that interests us all. We can't do everything, we are specific, in the structure of sounds, so we try to work in this kind of way.

SR: In your opinion how would somebody develop those skills? You have been doing this for a long time. Some people say they can't improvise.

SAJ: They are used to academic music. There are many reasons why people don't want to improvise. Maybe they are afraid to play music in public without having a score. Or they want to play music with a score only. There are many reasons. Maybe they don't want to be direct, making their own decisions in music; they are used to being given the decisions in music. They don't want to blame themselves for things that can go wrong or whatever. Mainly they are not used to it. They are used to playing pieces from a piece of paper or by heart, from notation. They don't see themselves as composer and instrumentalist at the same time, that's too much. That's the main thing at the end, you are the composer and the instrumentalist at the same time, which is our job.

SR: From the dance orchestra to the Peter Brotzmann Trio was a big step. 'Mathematical music' to 'art sound'.

SAJ: Yes, it was a big step, it was in cold water. You don't understand all music, you sometimes have to do something very different. The sound of the instrument, find out what the sound can be, not think about old structures – jump to the new experiences. Where you do communication by listening to the sound. But this was not the first experience – with this trio, this is the first recording, my first experience was in a quartet in Sweden, which was mixed media, time music and open sequences and so on, that was earlier work with open forms and sounds instead of normal instruments. That started in '62.

SR: You mentioned mixed media. There seems to be a strong relationship to art, contemporary art. Is that something you've been aware of? A lot of the work you have shown me is integral …

SAJ: I work as a visual artist in my scores and papers, it goes in the direction of scores and drawings, is integrated in the visual art scene. I am in the Biennali here [Berlin]. I also have a concert on the 21st but mainly I am invited as a visual artist. In the biggest house in Oranienplatz, but I also have a concert on the same day at the Kunste [Akadamie der Kunste], a solo presentation. So I am also an artist – special musician. And also qualities from the visual art scene come into my work as a musician. So it's not from the academic school.

SR: I've read that you use theatricality in relation to your work. Would you agree with this?

SAJ: No. People see me moving from one thing to another but it's just music stuff, playing this and the other. A piano player has to stick to his instrument but my instrument is here, there and everywhere, more or less so I have to move a bit, and they say it is theatre but it is, I have nothing against it but … I do visual acts but for me it is also music. I have a rubber cymbal and people hear a big cymbal in their heads, sometimes and they see the cymbal. Not hearing, but they see the sound. I play with this seeing and hearing and turn it sometimes backwards round.

SR: You play with the visual side of musical performance.

SAJ: Yes. Expectations, or the visualization of musical sound, in some parts.

SR: Do you see improvisation as a tool for professional musicians or as something more than that?

SAJ: I would say it was always a part of the music. But the last century it was more or less forbidden. Every composer always had a chance to improvise over their themes, or whatever, parts were improvised. And the big symphonic orchestras were not trained to do that at all. They didn't want that … the music school is also called the conservatoire [laughs] to keep that. And all these orchestras they have to keep that. In all the schools you have to train and do this business, and keep this classical music and fill these orchestras. They are not interested to do something new, or improvise, or find out new things. They are there to be paid to play that stuff … they are trained to repeat the classic.

SR: Do you see your music as a challenge to this?

SAJ: No, it's so far away.

SR: The term 'free improvisation' is connected to the period when the music came through: the 1960s/early 1970s. That music was raising questions about accepted norms.

SAJ: And there was no record company who was ever going to use this. So musicians started out small record companies to make their own records. Music played on stages was only made by big companies. So that if you wanted to present your music, you had to do your own recordings.

SR: FMP [Free Music Production].

SAJ: Yes, they started early, Brotzmann was earlier. I made my early work one year later than him. Companies like ESP records.

SR: And Incus with Derek Bailey. I have one last question. How do you position familiarity and spontaneity? It seems we want familiarity and we want spontaneity in improvising but how do these two things work together?

SAJ: Sometimes when you remind yourself of a thing which might work in this kind of music, and really thrills you, then you have to do something different, whatever, in order not to repeat yourself. For the listener it may be quite good sounding music. But if a new communication, a new experience doesn't happen, then you have no reason actually to go on the stage.

SR: So it's not sufficient just to go through your thing.

SAJ: No you have to show the spectators and yourself that you are trying to find out some new communication and combinations of sounds and to not repeat yourself … it is better than just to do a very sure thing that you know can work. You have to find out in the concert of course and be very close with the others to do that. And there is no recipe for how you can do that. To do unexpected things for yourself, that you never did before, it brings new experience of sound.

Bob Ostertag

SR:	What is the place of free improvisation in your practice?
BO:	I'm trying to think of when I first ran across the notion of free improvisation. I suppose my first notion of improvisation was when I was a kid I played guitar in rock bands when I was 14 years old through to 17 years old. So I guess my first encounter with the notion of improvisation was the guitar solo [laughs] you had the sort of rock song form and you played the song and there were two verses and two choruses and a bridge and then there was the guitar solo [both laugh] … I don't think the word 'improvisation' was really in my vocabulary at that point. There were *guitar solos*. Or maybe there was a piano solo or something like that. I don't think we ever used the word 'improvisation' to refer to the guitar solos. And then there were the jam-bands, you know Cream and Jimi Hendrix. I don't think we called it improvisation, I think we called it a jam. Because my last year in high school we formed a band that did what we'd later call free improvisation, or what I'd later encounter as free improvisation. We'd get together and turn out all the lights and just play whatever came to mind. But we called it jamming, I don't think we had the word 'improvisation', I don't think I really encountered the word 'improvisation' until I went to college. So when I first found *Bitches Brew* (Miles Davis, 1970) and a couple of Cecil Taylor records and the early Weather Report records, I think those were my first records that made it to my little isolated, quasi-suburban world. I think I thought: oh these guys really know how to jam … So you'd play in a rock band in which there'd be a guitar solo and then you'd take that concept to the next level which was jamming where everybody played a solo at the same time (laughs). Then when I was back in my hometown I found a record of the Music Improvisation Company. I think that's the first time I encountered the word 'improvisation'.
SR:	Jamie Muir and …
BO:	Derek Bailey, Evan Parker, I think there.
SR:	Hugh Davis and Christine Peters.
BO:	What became Company.
SR:	So how old were you then?
BO:	Must have been seventeen. I don't know how I got my hands on that. It was about the time I got my first Cecil Taylor record. I can't remember what Cecil Taylor record it was – but I remember thinking what the hell is this! And I remember I couldn't figure it out at all. I definitely couldn't figure out if I liked it, but I was definitely drawn to it and it was like, wow, there is something there that is totally beyond me, I've got to figure that out. And I probably felt the same way about the Music Improvisation Company. You know Hendrix I totally understood; Cream I totally understood – so when I found the electric

Miles Davis I thought that's like Jimi Hendrix except he's playing the trumpet but when it came to The Improvisation Company and Cecil Taylor it was, well, what! I couldn't think of it as a logical extension of anything in my musical universe. It was something completely from a different planet.

… I couldn't really read music very well. I knew where the notes were on the stave, but I couldn't sight read or anything like that, so we would learn songs off the records but since we were kids we usually couldn't play them right. So we'd adapt whatever the parts were on the record to whatever our skill level was, leaving out lots of notes and turning arpeggiated phrases into strummed chords and things like that. That's kind of improvisation, for sure, and we definitely understood that what we were doing was different from what we would have been doing in a music class, we would have been learning to read classical music from scores. And I don't think we could have put it in those terms but we definitely understood that there was a right and wrong way, that when you were confronted with a score, the range of possible right things you could do was vastly reduced from if you were learning a song off a record. If you were learning a song off a record as long as you sort of, more or less got the gestalt of the song [laughs] it was right. If you got the verses in the right place and the chorus in the right place and the singer sang the notes that were in the melody, then that was right … So, we'd learn Jimi Hendrix songs off the record, I certainly did not play the guitar parts anything like Jimi Hendrix – our 16-year-old drummer certainly did not play the drum parts the way Mitch Mitchell played them. But we felt like we were playing the song – right we've got that song, let's get another one [laughs]. And we understood that that was a very different activity from getting piano lessons, learning pieces from the piano repertoire and if we'd been doing that, what our teacher viewed as, OK, you've got that song was very different from what we were doing. And then we understood that in all these rock songs there was a point where there was supposed to be a guitar solo [laughs]. And some guys would very diligently learn the guitar solo off the record and do the guitar solo note for note that was on the record and then some of us would just kind of fuck around [laughs] and that was the guitar solo. But then you would hear the live rock bands and you'd think, oh, he didn't do the guitar solo in the same way as it was on the single and so it was clear there was a realm of freedom that was the guitar solo that was less constrained and that's why when we started doing what we talk about now as free improvisation it would be like what if we all solo at the same time … [laughter]. Once a set there'd be a drum solo and if you really wanted to stretch it at some point you gave the bass player a bass solo. I don't think there was ever a rhythm guitar solo.

… Hendrix is an interesting figure. And you know his approach was so improvisatory at the core. The improvisatory core at the centre of his music was a result of a total lack of stability in his life. He grew up extremely, extremely poor. You have to remind yourself that poverty like that exists in a country like the United States. Going to the back door of Burger King at closing time to beg for food, that kind of poverty and a highly unstable home life. And his whole life he sort of assumed that instability was the norm. His whole world of contracts was completely chaotic, what mattered to him was what he got at the moment. So he would sign these pieces of paper and he really didn't care, it's like, is there a cash advance? And do I get it now? And the way he formed his band was, he got a gig at a club and went to the guitar store, Manny's or Sam Ash's [New York] and he recruited people from the guitar store to play with him that night. The members of his band were sales people from the store he recruited that day, they were just the ones who happened to be there, he didn't really look around. There's a story about him playing this big gig in London. Eric Clapton and the Rolling Stones came and Sgt. Pepper's had been released that day and he turned up a bit late and walked into the dressing room with a copy of Sgt. Pepper's and he said OK I want to open playing Sgt. Pepper's so this is how it goes [laughs]. And I don't think they had a record player, just learn the bass part and that's the first thing they did on stage – and you know McCartney was there. It's just the ballsiest thing. It was his MO, it was just the way that he worked, it was never about replicating anything. It was like in the moment and his music conveys that. So it was Hendrix and Cream doing these long jams, and the Grateful Dead. The one that really captured my imagination was Hendrix. My cultural background was so white that we didn't really have any exposure to the jazz tradition. Didn't know anything about it really. I grew up in redneck country, ranches and cowboys, in Colorado and New Mexico. So, I didn't know anything about John Coltrane, Ornette Coleman or Charlie Parker.

But then I was taking guitar lessons and living in northern Colorado. The nearest town that had any music scene was Boulder, which had a university and lots of drugs and my music teacher said there's this group called Weather Report and you should go and hear them. This was early, early Weather Report, just after they released *Body Electric* (1972). And I had never heard them and I just went to the show because my teacher told me to go and I had my head taken off that time – I was totally unprepared for what that was. So it was before Weather Report got into that groove thing, it was much more free. So that was the first time I'd ever seen a performance of anything like that. And then I went for a trip with my parents to New York City … We were such hicks, we were country bumpkins. And one night I got to choose what we did and somehow I found in the paper this Cecil Taylor gig in some club [laughs] and I took my parents to see Cecil Taylor [laughs] … Oh my dad hated it so much. He said: We should send him to the piano Olympics [laughter] – it's not music.

And in a way I could see what my father was saying because there was such a physical assault on the piano, what Cecil was doing at the time. It was a tiny little club. It was the Cecil Taylor Unit. I was just watching this guy at the piano. So that changed everything, seeing him.

I never got to see Jimi Hendrix play – I almost saw him in fifth grade when we made a deal that I would go to an opera with my father if he went to a rock concert with me. Denver was the nearest big city and this must have been '68. Woodstock had just happened, so there were all these Woodstock wanna-be festivals springing up. So Denver had this three-day rock festival and I got to pick which night, and Hendrix was playing but there wasn't anybody else on the bill that night that I was interested in. So I didn't pick that night which turned out to be a good thing because there was a riot and Hendrix didn't even play, so I wouldn't have got to see him anyway. And the bill I got to see was [laughs] so absurd: it started with Big Mama Thornton, The Flock, Three Dog Night, followed by the original Frank Zappa and the Mother of Invention followed by Iron Butterfly [laughter] …

SR: Good grief! 'In-a-Gadda-Da-Vida'.

BO: Exactly, it has a drum solo [laughter] … so I got to see The Mothers of Invention sandwiched between Three Dog Night and Iron Butterfly. And I think the Mothers of Invention had just released 'We're Only in it For the Money'.

SR: So that was one of the best times to see them.

BO: Absolutely. Probably the best time – because I was only in fifth grade I was so overwhelmed I don't even know if I heard any of them [laughs].

SR: I was thinking of the groups you've got, the more recent groups. And from all that early experience, how do you relate that to what it is you do now? Or do you not relate that, do you see what you do now as quite different? And I know that you do so many different things as well. It's not like you've got a fixed practice, like a violinist.

BO: You know I haven't been playing much in recent years – I haven't been performing much. And I've been thinking about stopping entirely, which is probably on the horizon for me, to stop performing entirely for some period of time [pause].

SR: With the group with Justin Bond, I didn't know it was Otomo Yoshihide that was the third member of the group. Was he using turntables? Justin Bond was using voice. What were you doing?

BO: I had a keyboard sampler. I had that sampler I played for ten years. That was probably the riskiest improvisation I'd ever done.

SR: Why? Isn't free improvisation always risky? Except maybe Justin Bond's (drag artist) reference, was that the thing?

BO: Justin was such a wild card [pause] and we had no idea what was going to happen, fundamentally what was going to happen. Like was Justin going to start singing show tunes. There was the possibility that the concert might suck, that Justin might start doing something that Otomo and I would have no idea how to respond to. And I'm not somebody who has a strong theatricality – like, you could put Justin and Han Bennink together on stage and there wouldn't be that kind of risk because Han could go toe to toe with anything that Justin could do. In the last PantyChrist concert we did Otomo Yoshihide sort of quit the band [laughs]. He was never really that comfortable with Justin; Justin was too queer for Otomo.

SR: The setting is interesting. I think if you're performing in a setting in which people are used to free improvisation it's one thing and if you're performing in a setting in which they're not it could be a completely different event.

BO: The way that group came together was, I'd always wanted to play with Justin and Otomo was coming to town. Otomo rang me up and said he was coming to San Francisco, could I organize a concert for him? So I thought this would be the chance to play with Justin. So I organized a concert and there were two sets and the first set was Otomo and I and Mike Patton [voice]. And the second set was Otomo and I and Justin. And of course the place was packed out with Faith No More fans, they're a stadium, platinum selling, heavy metal band … I don't find that band interesting but they have a huge following. So all of these Faith No More fans came to see their hero. The first set was hard enough for them because they had no idea it was going to be this noise thing and that Mike wasn't going to sing any words and they had no idea that Mike wasn't going to be in the second set. So, [laughs] when Mike didn't appear and this guy in a women's bathing suit appeared in his place and started getting a tan with her tanning lotion, I think people were absolutely dumbfounded, people were like, what the fuck. I half expected that chairs were going to start flying [laughs] … So then we had a very small European tour where we did three dates in Switzerland, one in Germany and one in Gent. And those were all to free jazz audiences who were as unprepared for Justin as the Mike Patton fans had been. The way we started the concerts were sort of composed, because the Pope had just put out a record. Pope John Paul, I don't know if you know that? The Pope made a record it was on Sony, it was him reading Psalms and giving homilies over sort of ambient, world-beat grooves.

SR: Was it really?

BO: Yes, it was. I immediately thought OK, so we need to sample the Pope. I mean we're PantyChrist. I wanted to put out another CD entitled: 'PantyChrist: The Pope remix' [laughs]. The way the concert started was that Otomo and I went on stage first and made this big noise, blaaaa, and it gradually sort of settled down into a drone, it became quieter and quieter and the lights would go down until the stage was dark and there was just this drone and then we'd have this white down spot come on, with nobody in and then you'd hear the Pope's voice say, it was from the record: 'The man who does bad things avoids the light, for fear that his bad deeds will be exposed. But the man who does good things walks into the light'. And Justin walks into the light where he just sort of has a grouchy schoolteacher outfit on, looking very angry with a cocktail. Walks up to the mike and says, 'Welcome to Mummy's Club Ariola' [laughs]. And that's how the concert began and from there on it was improvised, no idea what was going to happen. And every now and then Justin would run out of things to do, he would be at a loss. You know there's that moment on the record where he starts screaming: 'Shut up, get me a tranquiliser, I can't stand this music. I didn't get my fingernails painted petal pink to come here and listen to this shit' [laughs]. So, yeah it was risky. So that was it for PantyChrist performances. They were not an easy group to book believe me. There was one other time when we played in Portugal – at that point Otomo wouldn't do it anymore. Justin was just too queer and I don't think Otomo felt comfortable around that sexuality. And also Otomo couldn't understand the words, his English wasn't that good back then. And Justin and I thought that was funny that one of the musicians couldn't understand anything that Justin was saying, we thought that was part of the concept … So he wouldn't do it anymore. So, we got Jon Rose. And Jon Rose is like Han Bennink, he has such a theatrical confidence. It's fantastic, fantastic. He does all kinds of electronic modifications with his violin. In fact I would say that Jon is the most successful integration of acoustic and electronic of anybody I've ever known … Jon had this MIDI set-up where he'd generate MIDI data with his bow. He could actually play that in a very deep sense in a way that few people I've seen have accomplished. But he's also inherently a charismatic and theatrical presence on stage. That was brilliant to watch him and Justin and of course they didn't know each other and they'd go on stage together. It was such fun to keep my eye on Justin during those performances as it began to dawn on him that the third guy on stage was a straight guy who could be just as creative and in your face as Justin could be - and this sort of light going on. I really enjoyed that. Justin's become quite famous now. He's a movie star, a celebrity – Justin has sold out Carnegie Hall twice. Justin has taken drag where drag has never gone. He's a celebrity. *Time Out* published this list, the ten iconic people of New York City, one of them was Justin Bond. He's become totally at another level and travels with a personal assistant, tailored suits …

When I left my home town and went to school, went to Oberlin Conservatory, they had a music improvisation class, and that was the first time I encountered the notion that there was a thing called improvisation that you could study, in a systematic way, and the class was utterly dreary and boring and it immediately became the class that it was hard to drag yourself to. And then Anthony Braxton came and taught a workshop and it was a revelation and I thought

OK, this is what I want to do – my first encounter with improvisation in any rigorous or systematic way was this horrible class where the guy who taught it never improvised at all.

SR: Was that the meeting with Braxton that led to playing with him?

BO: Yup.

SR: How do you experience spontaneity and familiarity in your practice?

BO: If you do this for any length of time you develop a palette or a grab-bag of tricks, you can rely on. So then that becomes the practice, trying to transcend your own cliché. When I think of improvisers that really come to mind, who are really inspiring improvisers in that sense, the first one would be Monk, who every time he sat down somehow conveyed the sense that he was taking a really fresh look at the piano – look here's an E over here – how can I use that, and when you compare his various recordings he never plays the same tune the same way twice. And he always conveys the sense that he is discovering, generally discovering new things, every time he sits down to play, which I think Hendrix did too. Just going on a TV show and just stopping the song because really he was in another place. Let's just do this, I don't care if it screws up the performance, just do that. Those two performers really I think convey that sense of discovery. And you know who else, at his best, Bill Frissel – there's a lot of Bill Frissel's music that is not my cup of tea. A slice of his work speaks to me speaks quite deeply, and I've seen him play on more than one occasion in a way that just conveyed that he was taking a fresh look at the guitar, he was finding things, he was not re-sequencing his greatest hits of guitar licks – he was actually finding something and searching and discovering right there. And I think there's very few people who can do that over a lifetime …

SR: I'm thinking of you and technology – changing technology, in one way, addresses familiarity. With players like Derek Bailey and Phil Minton I think it becomes more of a life's practice – like a yogi who gets up every day and does yoga because that's their life's practice. Have you never been drawn towards this kind of practice?

BO: Well actually I do yoga everyday – an hour and a half, two hours when I have time – at least an hour.

SR: And in your music practice?

BO: Well I think, that kind of life practice has to be corporeal, that life practice has not to do with technology. Like you can do that if you're Phil Minton and you have this voice and you are going to encounter your body every day. You check in with your body … There's painters, they get up every day and they paint, that's what they do. There's novelists who get up every day and write, it is a life's practice. And I think what is more interesting to them is the practice rather than the result. The result is what it is but it is this practice of having this discipline that becomes the language through which you organize your life, that's what matters. And I've never had that relationship with music, I'm more concerned with the result. I want to produce music that I think is interesting, I want to keep growing and not repeat myself. I tried very much to create a body of recorded work that has no redundancies, that goes from A to B to C to D. Well now I'm more out of the scene, but when I was more in the scene I was always being asked by people, come on let's make a record, let's get together and go into a recording studio and make a record and I always said no, I don't want to do that. And people like that have hundreds of records. I don't know how many records Evan Parker plays on – hundreds, Fred Frith – hundreds, John Zorn … I want to have twenty records from a coherent body of work. If you don't hear one of them then you've missed an important piece of what I've put together. I don't want to have a thousand records of which if you've listened to ten then you get the idea of what I was doing. I remember Zorn would always walk around with his saxophone and if he'd meet someone who was a musician, he'd be like, OK, let's play, let's play, and he'd play with everyone. I've never been like that, it always takes me a while to find the person I want to play with. I don't want to play with everybody. And it's probably to do with the fact that I'm not as versatile a musician as John is. But people I really feel resonate with me are few and far between, they don't grow on trees … The people I run into over the years that I really feel I resonate with playing improvisational music, there's not that many.

SR: You had a rich beginning.

BO: Yeah.

SR: And that's unusual I think. But you were straight into playing with Anthony Braxton …

BO: Yeah, big band with George Lewis, Kenny Wheeler, Marilyn Crispell … yeah it's a good start [laughter].

Notes

1 Readers can find a video of the performance featuring Nicols and Minton mentioned in this chapter online: https://www. youtube.com/watch?v=C48F8iMvhCk). Accessed 26 January 2017.

2 Readers can find the clip featuring Mick Beck, Tom Jenkinson and Paul Hession through the following address: https://www.youtube.com/watch?v=Z_5PX1crLHo. Accessed 26 January 2017.

References

Ainscow, M., & Booth T. (2003). *The index for inclusion: Developing learning & participation in schools.* Bristol: Centre for Studies in Inclusive Education.

Agrell, J. (2007). *Improvisation games for classical musicians.* Chicago, IL: Gia Publications.

Allen, S. (2002). Teaching large ensemble music improvisation. *Radical pedagogy.* Retrieved from http://radicalpedagogy.icaap.org/content/issue4_1/01_Allen.html.

Amedeo, G. (2009). *The descriptive phenomenological method in psychology.* Pittsburgh, PA: Duquesne University Press.

Amon Düül. (1969). *Psychedelic underground* [Vinyl record]. Germany: Metronome.

Amon Düül. (1993). *Collapsing/Singvögel Rückwärts & Co.* [CD]. France: Spalax Music.

Apple, M. W. (1998). Selling our children: Channel One and the politics of education. In R. W. Mc Chesney, E. M. Wood, and & J. B. Foster (Eds.), *Capitalism and the information age* (pp. 135–49). New York: Monthly Review Press.

Arendt, H. (1977). *Between past and future: Eight exercises in political thought.* London, UK: Penguin.

Arroll, M., & Senior, V. (2009). Symptom typology and sub-grouping in chronic fatigue syndrome. *Bulletin of the International Association of CFS/ME, 17*(2), 39–52.

Artaud, A. (1958). *The theatre and its double.* New York, NY: Grove Weidenfeld.

Atlee, J. (2007). *Isolarion.* London, UK: Transworld.

Atlee, J. (2015). *Station to station: Searching for stories on The Great Western Line.* London, UK: Guardian Books.

Attali, J. (1985). *Noise: The political economy of music.* Minneapolis: University of Minnesota Press.

Austin, J. L. (1962). *How to do things with words.* London, UK: Oxford University Press.

Bachelard, G. (1958). *The poetics of space.* Boston, MA: Beacon Press.

Bailey, D. (1992). *Improvisation: Its nature and practice in music.* London, UK: The British Library.

Bailey, D. (1992). *On the edge.* London, UK: Channel 4.

Barker, M. (2003). Satanic subcultures? A discourse analysis of the self-perceptions of young goths and pagans. In T. Waddell (Ed.), *Cultural expressions of evil and wickedness: Wrath, sex, and crime* (pp. 37–57). Amsterdam, the Netherlands: Rodopi.

Barnhill, E. (2006). *The daily improvisation.* Retrieved from http://ericbarnhill.wordpress.com/facts-about-improvisation/.

Barrett, L. F., & Lindquist, K. (2008). The embodiment of emotion. In G. Semin, & E. Smith (Eds.), *Embodied grounding: Social, cognitive affective, and neuroscience approaches* (pp. 237–262). New York, NY: Cambridge University Press.

Barthes, R. (1972). *Mythologies.* New York, NY: Hill and Wang.

Bateson, G. (1979). *Mind and nature: A necessary unity (Advances in systems theory, complexity, and the human sciences).* New York, NY: Hampton Press.

Beard, D., & Gloag, K. (2005). *Musicology: The key concepts.* London, UK: Routledge.

Beckett, S. (2010). *Waiting for Godot.* London, UK: Faber and Faber.

Beins, B. (2015). *The Sealed Knot: 'Common objects' reviews.* Retrieved from http://www.burkhardbeins.de/releases/unwanted_object_reviews.html.

Beins, B., Kesten, C., Nauck, G., & Neumann, A. (Eds.). (2011). *Echtzeitmusik Berlin: selbstbestimmung einer szene/self-defining a scene.* Berlin, Germany: Wolke Verlag.

Belousov, B. P. (1985). A periodic reaction and its mechanism. In R. J. Field, & M. Burger (Eds.), *Oscillations and travelling waves in chemical systems.* New York, NY: Wiley.

Benjamin, W. (1936). *The work of art in the age of mechanical reproduction.* London, UK: Penguin.

Benson, B. E. (2003). *The improvisation of musical dialogue. A phenomenology of music.* Cambridge, UK: Cambridge University Press.

Berkowitz, A. L. (2010). *The improvising mind: Cognition and creativity in the musical moment.* New York, NY: Oxford University Press.

Berliner, P. (1994). *Thinking in Jazz: The infinite art of improvisation.* Chicago, IL: University of Chicago Press.

Bernstein, D. W. (Ed.). (2008). *The San Francisco Tape Music Centre.* Berkeley, CA: University of California Press.

Biggs, M. & Karlsson, H. (2010). *The Routledge companion to research in the arts.* London, UK: Routledge.

Bishop, C. (2006). The social turn: Collaboration and its discontents. *Artforum,* 179–185.

Bishop, C. (2012). *Artificial hells: Participatory art and the politics of spectatorship.* London, UK: Verso.

Blacking, J. (1973). *How musical is man?.* Seattle, D.C.: University of Washington Press.

Blazanovic, M. (2012). *Echtzeitmusik. The social and discursive contents of a music scene* (Unpublished doctoral dissertation). Humbolt University, Berlin, Germany.

Bonwell, C., & Elison, J. (1991). *Active learning: Creating excitement in the classroom AEHE-ERIC higher education report No. 1.* San Francisco, CA: Jossey-Bass.

Borgo, D. (2005). *Sync or swarm: Improvising music in a complex age.* New York, NY: Continuum.

Borgo, D. (2007). Free jazz in the classroom: An ecological approach to music education. *Jazz Perspectives, 1*(1), 61–88.

Born, G. (1995). *Rationalizing culture: IRCAM, Boulez, and the institutionalization of the musical avant-garde.* Berkeley, CA: University of California Press.

Bourdieu, P. (1977). *An invitation to reflexive sociology.* Chicago, IL: University of Chicago Press.

Bourdieu, P. (1986). The forms of capital. In J. Richardson (Ed.), *Handbook of theory and research for the sociology of education* (pp. 241–258). New York, NY: Greenwood.

Bourdieu, P. (1993). *Sociology in question.* London, UK: Sage.

Boudrieu, M. C., & Robey, D. (2005). Enacting integrated information technology: a human agency perspective. *Organization Science, 16*(1), 3–18.

Bourriaud, N. (2002). *Relational aesthetics.* Dijon, France: Les presses du réel.

Bourriaud, N. (2010). *Radicant.* New York, NY: Lukas and Sternberg.

Bramley, C. (2015). *Too important to be left to the musicians: Un-musical activism and improvised fiction* (Unpublished doctoral dissertation), Newcastle University, UK.

Braun, V., & Clarke, V. (2006). Using thematic analysis in psychology. *Qualitative research in psychology, 3*(2), 77–101.

Braxton, A. (1970). *For alto* [Vinyl record]. USA: Delmark Records.

Braxton, A. (1985). *Triaxium writings* [Vinyl record]. USA: Frog Peak Music.

Brentano, F. (1995). *Descriptive psychology.* London, UK: Routledge.

Brentano, F. (1998). *Philosophical investigations of time, space and the continuum.* New York, NY: Croom Helm.

Brocki, J. J. M., & Wearden, A. J. (2006). A critical evaluation of the use of interpretative phenomenological analysis (IPA) in health psychology. *Psychology and Health, 21,* 87–108.

Brook, P. (1968). *The empty space.* London, UK: Simon and Schuster.

Brooke, R. (1991). *Jung and phenomenology.* London, UK: Routledge.

Brötzmann, P. (1968). *Machine gun* [Vinyl record]. Germany: Bro.

Brötzmann, P. (2013). *Ljubljana jazz festival: Interview with Peter Brötzmann.* Retrieved from https://www.youtube.com/watch?v=xtuxx403LJw.

Brotzmann, P., & Rouy, G. (2014). *We thought we could change the world: Conversations with Gérard Rouy.* Berlin, Germany: Wolke Verlag.

Brotzmann, P., Bennink, H., & Van Hove, F. (1975). *Balls.* Berlin, Germany: FMP.

Brown, J. S., Collins, A., & Duguid, S. (1989). Situated cognition and the culture of learning. *Educational Researcher, 18*(1), 32–42.

Bruner, J. S. (1961). The act of discovery. *Harvard Educational Review, 31*(1), 21–32.

Buarque de Hollanda, B. B. (2011). *In praise of improvisation in Brazillian soccer: Modernism, popular music, and a Brasilidade of sports.* http://www.criticalimprov.com/article/view/1229.

Burr, V. (1998). Realism, relativism, social constructionism and discourse. In I. Parker (Ed.), *Social constructionism, discourse and realism* (pp. 13–26). London, UK: Sage.

Butler, J. (1993). *Bodies that matter: On the discursive limits of sex.* London, UK: Routledge.

Cage, J. (1961). *Silence.* London, UK: Marion Boyars.

Cage, J. (1969). *A year from Monday.* Middletown, CT: Wesleyan University Press.

Cardew, C. (1967). *Treatise.* New York, NY: Gallery Upstairs Press.

Cardew, C. (1971). Towards an ethic of improvisation Cornelius Cardew. *Treatise handbook.* London, UK: Edition Peters.

Carles, P., & Comolli, J-L. (2015). *Free jazz/Black power.* Jackson, MI: University of Mississippi.

Chan, C. (2008). An interview with Fred Frith: The teaching of contemporary improvisation. *Critical Studies in Improvisation/Études critiques en improvisation, 3*(2).

Charmaz, K. (2000). Grounded theory methodology: Objectivist and constructivist qualitative methods. In N. K. Denzin, & Y. Lincon (Eds.), *Handbook of qualitative research* (2nd ed.) (pp. 509–535). Thousand Oaks, CA: Sage.

Charmaz, K. (2006). *Constructing grounded theory: A practical guide through qualitative analysis.* London, UK: Sage.

Ciborra, C. (1996). Improvisation and information technology in organizations. *ICIS 1996 Proceedings.* Paper 26. http://aisel.aisnet.org/icis1996/26.

Collingwood, R. G. (1938). *The principles of art* . London, UK: Oxford University Press.

Coltrane, J. (1963). *Alabama* [Vinyl record]. CA, USA: Impulse!

Coltrane, J. (1966). *Ascension* [Vinyl record]. CA, USA: Impulse!

Conquergood, D. (2002). Performance studies: Interventions and radical research. *The Drama Review, 46*, 145–153.

Coffield, F., Moseley, D., Hall, E., & Ecclestone, K. (2004). Should we be using learning styles? What research has to say to practice. *Learning.* UK: Skills and Research Centre. Retrieved from http://www.itslifejimbutnotasweknowit.org.uk/files/LSRC_LearningStyles.pdf.

Costa, J. T. (2014). *Wallace, Darwin, and the origin of species.* Cambridge, MA: Harvard University Press.

Craft, A., Jeffrey, B., & Leibling, L. (2001). *Creativity in education.* London, UK: Continuum.

Crawley, J. (2005). *In at the deep end: A survival guide for teachers in post compulsory education.* London, UK: David Fulton.

Critchley, S. (2009, June 8). Being and time, part 1: Why Heidegger matters. *The Guardian.* Retrieved from http://www.theguardian.com.

Cropley, A. J. (2001). *Creativity in education and learning: A guide for teachers and educators.* Oxford, UK: Psychology Press.

Crossan, M., Cunha, M. P., Vera, D., & Cunha, J. (2005). Time and organizational improvisation. *Academy of Management Review, 30*(1), 129–145.

Crossley, N. (2009). *Reflexions in the flesh: Embodiment in late modernity.* Buckingham, UK: Open University Press.

Csikszentmihalyi, M. (1991). *Flow.* New York, NY: Harper Collins.

Damasio, A. (1994). *Descartes' error.* New York, NY: Penguin Books.

Damasio, A. (2000). *The feeling of what happens: Body and emotion in the making of consciousness.* San Diego, USA: Harcourt.

Darwin, C. (1976). *The origin of the species.* New York, CA: Gramercy Books.

Davies, H. S. (2002). *Sounds heard.* Chelmsford, UK: FMR.

Davis, M. (1970). *Bitches brew (Tanglewood live).* Retrieved from https://www.youtube.com.

Davis, M. (1970). *Bitches brew* [Vinyl record]. USA: Columbia Records.

Dean, R. (2006). Book review - Playing ad lib: Improvisatory music in Australia 1836–1970. *Critical Studies in Improvisation/Études critiques en improvisation, 1*(3). http://www.improvcommunity.ca/about/research.

Debord, G. (1995). *Society of the spectacle.* New York, NY: Zone Books.

De Certeau, M. (1984). *The practice of everyday life.* Berkeley, CA: University of California Press.

Dennis, B. (1969). *Shoreditch: Experimental music school.* Retrieved from https://www.youtube.com/watch?v=hsigOnPJTtA.

Dennis, B. (1970). Experimental music in schools: Towards a new world of sound. *Handbook for teachers.* Oxford, UK: Oxford University Press.

Derrida, J. (1992). *Acts of literature*. London, UK: Routledge.

Derrida, J., & Malabou, C. (2004). *Counterpath*. USA: Stanford University Press.

Dewey, J. (1997). *Experience and education*. New York, NY: Touchstone.

Donaldson, M. (1978). *Children's minds*. London, UK: Fontana.

Dreyfus, H. (1991). *Being-in-the-World: A commentary on Heidegger's being and time*. Cambridge, MA: MIT.

Dreyfus, H., & Dreyfus, S. (1992). What artificial experts can and cannot do. *AI & Society, 6*(1), 18–26.

Dreyfus, H., & Hall, H. (1992). *Heidegger: A critical reader*. Oxford, UK: Blackwell.

Dreyfus, H. (1979). *What computers can't do*. New York, NY: Harper and Row.

Durant, A. (1989). *Improvisation in the political economy of music*. Retrieved from http://eprints. mdx.ac.uk/8193/.

Ediger, J. (1993). Imaginative listening and the reverberations of the world, presented at 'Turning of the world' conference, Banff Centre for the Arts, Banff, Canada.

Ferrand, E. T. (1961). *Improvisation in nine centuries of western music*. Germany: Arno Volk Verlag.

Fischer-Lichte, E. (2008). *The transformative power of performance: a new aesthetics*. Abingdon, UK. Routledge.

Fischlin, D., Heble, A., & Lipsitz, G. (2013). *The fierce urgency of now: Improvisation, rights, and the ethics of cocreation*. Durham, NC: Duke University Press.

Fiumura, G. C. (1990). *The other side of language*. New York, NY: Routledge.

Ford, C. C. (1995). Free collective improvisation in higher education. *British Journal of Music Education, 12*, 103–112.

Flowers, P., Duncan, B., & Knussen, C. (2003). Reappraising HIV testing; an exploration of the psychosocial costs and benefits associated with learning one's HIV status in a purposive sample of Scottish gay men. *British Journal of Health Psychology, 8*, 179–194.

Foucault, M. (1970). *The order of things: An archaeology of the human sciences*. New York, NY: Random House.

Foucault, M. (1972). *Archaeolology of knowledge*. Oxford, UK: Routledge.

Foucault, M. (1980). In C. Gordon (Ed.), *Power/knowledge: Selected interviews and other writings 1972-1977*. New York, NY: Pantheon.

Foucault, M. (1991). *Discipline and punish: The birth of the prison*. London, UK: Penguin.

Freire, P. (1996). *Pedagogy of the oppressed*. London, UK: Penguin.

Freud, A. (1975). *Introduction to the technique of child analysis*. Manchester, NH: Ayer Company Publishers.

Freud, S. (2005). *The unconscious*. London, UK: Penguin.

Friedman, K. (1998). *Fluxus reader*. Chichester, UK: Academy Editions.

Gardner, H. (2006). *Multiple intelligences: The theory in practice*. New York, NY: Basic Books.

Gadamer, H-G. (1990). *Truth and method*. New York, NY: Crossroad.

Gadamer, H-G. (1994). *Literature and philosophy in dialogue*. Albany, NY: SUNY.

Gibson, J. J. (1979). *The ecological approach to visual perception*. Boston, MA: Houghton Mifflin.

Giddens, A. (1987). *Social theory and modern sociology*. Redwood City, CA: Stanford University Press.

Gillick, L. (2006). *Proxemics: Selected writings, 1988-2006*. Zurich, Switzerland: JRP Ringier.

Giroux, H. (1997). *Pedagogy and the politics of hope: Theory, culture, and schooling*. Boulder, CO: Westview/Harper Collins.

Giroux, H. A. (1983). *Theory and resistance in education*. New York, NY: Bergin and Garvey.

Giuffre, J., Swallow, S., & Bley, P. (1962). *Free fall*. USA: Columbia Records.

Glaser, B. G., & Strauss A. L. (1967). *Discovery of grounded theory. Strategies for qualitative research*. New York, NY: Aldine de Gruyter.

Glaser, B. G., & Strauss, A. L. (2005). *Awareness of dying*. New Brunswick, NJ: Aldine Transaction.

Goehr, L. (2004). *The imaginary museum of musical works: An essay in the philosophy of music*. Oxford, UK: Oxford University Press.

Goffman, E. (1990). *The presentation of self in everyday life*. London, UK: Penguin.

Goldberg, R. L. (1998). *Performance: Live art since 1960*. New York, NY: Abrams Books.

Goorney, H. (1981). *The theatre workshop story*. London, UK: Methuen.

Gray, J. (2002). *Straw dogs*. London, UK: Granta.

Gray, J. (2011). *The Immortalisation Commission*. Retrieved from https://www.youtube.com/watch?v=hcnCmx7F6a8 7.7.15.

Green, L. (2002). L. *How popular musicians learn. A way ahead for music education*: Aldershot, UK: Ashgate.

Gould, G. (1996). Forgery and imitation in the creative process. *Glenn Gould Magazine, 2*(1).

Greeno, J. G. (1994). Gibson's affordances. *Psychological Review, 101*(2), 336–342.

Grotowski, J. (1968). *Towards a poor theatre*. New York, NY: Simon and Schuster.

Guignon, C. B. (1983). *Heidegger and the problem of knowledge*. Indianapolis, IN: Hacket.

Habermas, J. (1975). *Legitimation crisis*. Boston, MA: Beacon.

Hammersley, M. P., & Atkinson, P. (1983). *Ethnography: Principles in practice*. New York, NY: Routledge.

Harriet, J. (1961). *Free form* [Vinyl record]. UK: Jazzland.

Heble, A. J. (2003). *Landing on the wrong note: Jazz, dissonance, and critical practice*. New York, NY: Routledge.

Heble, A. J., & Wallace, R. (Eds.). (2013). *People get ready*. Durham, NC: Duke University Press.

Heidegger, M. (1962). *Being and time*. New York, NY: Harper.

Heidegger, M. (1968). *What is called thinking?* New York, NY: Harper.

Hickey, M. (2009). Can improvisation be 'taught'?: A call for free improvisation in our schools. *International Journal of Music Education, 27*, 285–299.

Holiday, B. (1939). *Strange fruit* [Shellac recording]. USA: Commodore Records.

Holmes, M. (2001). Emotional reflexivity in contemporary friendships: Understanding it using Elias and Facebook etiquette. *Flinders University Sociological Research Online, 16*(1), 11. Retrieved from http://www.socresonline.org.uk/16/1/11.html.

Husserl, E. (1982). *Ideas pertaining to a pure phenomenology and to a phenomenological philosophy*. London, UK: Kluwer Academic Publishers.

Husserl, E. (2001). *Logical investigations*. London, UK: Routledge.

Hutchins, E. (1995). *Cognition in the wild*. Cambridge, MA: Bradford Books.

Hytonen, E. (2010). *Flow experiences as means of identity and motivation formation in professional jazz scene*. Paper presented at the Royal Northern College of Music Conference.

Iñárritu, A. G. (2014, October 15). *Birdman movie interview - Alejandro González Iñárritu*. Retrieved from https://www.youtube.com.

Ingber, L. (1982). *Karate kinematics and dynamics*. Boston, MA: Unique.

Jackson, P., & Delehanty, H. (2014). *Eleven rings: The soul of success*. New York, NY: Penguin.

Jackson, R., & Waterman, E. (2010). *The improvisation toolkit resource list*. Retrieved from http://www.improvcommunity.ca/research/improvisation-toolkit-resource-list.

Jaques-Dalcroze, E. (2015). *The Jaques-Dalcroze method of eurythmics*. Kyiv, Ukraine: Leopold Classic Library.

Jaworski, A. (Ed.). (1997). *Silence: Interdisciplinary perspectives*. Berlin, Germany: Mouton de Gruyter.

Johnston, K. (1987). *Impro: Improvisation and the theatre*. Oxford, UK: Routledge.

Jones, L. [Amiri Baraka] (1963). *Blues people: Negro music in white America*. New York, NY: Payback Press.

Kaprow, A. (2003). *Essays on the blurring of art and life*. Los Angeles, CA: University of California Press.

Keaton, B. (1926). *The general*. USA: United Artists.

Kenny, B. J., & Gellrich, M. (2002). Improvisation. In R. P. G. E. McPherson (Ed.), *The science & psychology of music performance: Creative strategies for teaching and learning* (pp. 117–134). Oxford, UK: Oxford University Press.

Kester, G. (2004). *Conversation pieces: Community and communication in modern art*. Oakland, CA: University of California Press.

Klein, M., Heinmann, P., & Money-Kyrle, R. E. (Eds.). (1955). *New directions in psychoanalysis: The significance of infant conflict in the pattern of adult behaviour*. London, UK: Karnac.

Korsyn, K. (2003). *Decentering music: A critique of contemporary musical research*. New York, NY: Oxford University Press.

Kugler, M. (2000). *Die Methode Jaques-Dalcroze und das Orff-Schulwerk, Elementare. Musikbung*. Frankfurt, Germany: Lang.

Lakoff, G., & Johnson, M. (1980). *Metaphors we live by*. Chicago, IL: University of Chicago Press.

Lakoff, G., & Johnson, M. (1999). *Philosophy in the flesh: The embodied mind and its challenge to Western thought*. New York, NY: Basic Books.

Landgraf, E. (2011). *Improvisation as art: Conceptual challenges, historical perspectives*. London, UK: Continuum books.

Lange, B. R. (2011). Teaching the ethics of free improvisation. *Critical Studies in Improvisation/ Études critiques en improvisation, 7*(2).

Lao Tzu & Lau, D. C. (1964). *Tao Te Ching*. London, UK: Penguin.

Laver, M., Heble, A., & Piper, T. (2013). *Ethics and the improvising business*. Retrieved from http://www.criticalimprov.com/article/view/2946.

Lavie, M., & Willig, C. (2005). 'I don't feel like melting butter': An interpretative phenomenological analysis of the experience of 'inorgasmia'. *Psychology & Health, 20*(1), 115–128.

Lehman, S. H. (2012). *Liminality as a framework for composition: Rhythmic thresholds, spectral harmonies and afrological improvisation* (Unpublished doctoral dissertation). Columbia University, New York, NY. Retrieved from http://www.scribd.com/doc/184695341/Stephen-h-Lehman-Dissertation#scribd.

Lenvinas, E. (1987). *Collected philosophical papers*. Dordrecht, the Netherlands: Martinus Nijhoff.

Leone, L. (2010). A critical review of improvisation in organizations: open issues and future research directions. Paper presented at the Summer Conference. Imperial College London Business School, June 16–18 2010. London, UK: Druid.

Leontev, A. N. (1978). *Activity, consciousness, and personality*. Upper Saddle River, NJ: Prentice-Hall.

Levin, R. (1992). *On the edge*. Retrieved from https://www.youtube.com/watch?v=SVexDvUi1DA.

Levis, K. (1980). *Jackie McLean on Mars*. Retrieved from https://vimeo.com/12192828.

Levitin, D. J. (2007). *This is your brain on music: The science of a human obsession*. New York, NY: Plume.

Levy, S. (2010). *Hackers: Heroes of the computer revolution*. Sebastopol, CA: O'Reilly Media.

Lewis, G. E. (1996). Improvised music after 1950: Afrological and eurological perspectives. *Black Music Research Journal, 16*(1).

Lewis, G. E. (2000). Teaching improvised music: An ethnographic memoir. In J. Zorn (Ed.), *Arcana: Musicians on music* (p. 78–107). New York, NY: Granary Books/Hips Road.

Lewis, G. E. (2008). *A power stronger than itself: The AACM and American Experimental Music*. Chicago, IL: University of Chicago Press.

Lewis, G. E. (2008). Improvisation and pedagogy: Background and focus of inquiry. *Critical Studies in Improvisation/Études critiques en improvisation, 3*(2). http://www.improvcommunity.ca/about/research.

Lipsitz, G. (1998). *Possessive investment in whiteness: How white people profit from identity politics*. Philadelphia, PA: Temple University Press.

Litweiler, J. (1984). *The freedom principle: Jazz after 1958*. Boston, MA: De Capo Press.

Litweiler, J. (1992). *Ornette Coleman: A harmolodic life*. New York, NY: Morrow.

Livingstone, C., & Borko, H. (1989). Expert-Novice differences in teaching: A cognitive analysis and implications for teacher education. *Journal of Teacher Education, 40*(4), 36–42.

Lock, G. (1988). *Forces in motion*. New York, NY: Da Capo Press.

Lock, G. (1999). *Blutopia: Visions of the future and revisions of the past in the work of Sun Ra, Duke Ellington, and Anthony Braxton*. London, UK: Duke.

Lock, G. (2008). 'What I Call a Sound': Anthony Braxton's synaesthetic ideal and notations for improvisers. *Critical Studies in Improvisation/Études critiques en improvisation, 4*(1). http://www.improvcommunity.ca/about/research.

London Improvisers Orchestra (2009). *Improvisations for George Rusque*. London, UK: PSI.

Luhmann, N. (1979). *Trust and power.* Hoboken, NJ: John Wiley & Sons.

Luhmann, N. (2000). Familiarity, confidence, trust: Problems and alternatives. In D. Gambetta (Ed.), *Trust: Making and breaking cooperative relations* (pp. 94–107). University of Oxford. Retrieved from http://www.sociology.ox.ac.uk/papers/luhmann94-107.pdf.

Luhmann, N. (2005). *Risk: a sociological theory.* Piscataway, NJ: Transaction.

Luther, K. (2007). *Distributed creativity.* Retrieved from http://shamurai.com/sites/creativity/papers/8.luther.pdf.

Lyotard, J-F. (1984). *The postmodern condition: A report on knowledge.* Minneapolis, MN: Minnesota Press.

Lyotard, J-F. (1991). *Phenomenology.* Albany, NY: State University of New York Press.

MacDonald R. A. R., Byrne, C., & Carlton, L. (2006). Creativity and flow in musical composition: An empirical investigation. *The psychology of music, 34*(3), 292–307.

MacDonald, A. R., Hargreaves, D. H., & Miell, D. E. (2002). *Musical identities.* Oxford, UK: Oxford University Press.

MacDonald, R. A. R., & Wilson, G. B. (2005). The musical identities of professional jazz musicians: A focus group investigation. *The Psychology of Music, 33*(4), 395–419.

MacDonald, R. A. R., &. Wilson G. B. (2006). Constructions of jazz: How jazz musicians present their collaborative musical practice. *Musicae Scientiae, 10*(1), 59–85.

MacDonald, R. A. R., Wilson, G., & Miell, D. E. (2012). Improvisation as a creative process within contemporary music. In D. J. Hargreaves, D. E. Miell, & R. A. R. MacDonald (Eds.), *Musical imaginations: Multidisciplinary perspectives on creativity, performance and perception* (pp. 242–268). Oxford, UK: Oxford University Press.

Macey, D. (2001). *Dictionary of critical theory.* London, UK: Penguin Books.

MacIntyre, M. (1968). *New Regime: AACM newsletter.*

Magee, W. L., & Davidson, J. W. (2002). The effect of music therapy on mood states in neurological patients: A pilot study. *Journal of Music Therapy, 39*(1), 20–29.

Mandelbrot, B. B. (1975). Stochastic models for the Earth's relief, the shape and the fractal dimension of the coastlines, and the number-area rule for islands. *Proceedings of the national academy of sciences of the United States of America.* Retrieved from http://www.pnas.org/content/72/10/3825.short.

Mantie, R. (2008). Schooling the future: Perceptions of selected experts on jazz education. *Critical Studies in Improvisation/Études critiques en improvisation, 3*(2).

Maturana, H. R., & Varela, F. J. (1987). *The tree of knowledge: The biological roots of human understanding.* Boston, MA: Shambhala.

Mauthner, N., & Doucet, A. (2003). *Reflexive accounts of reflexivity in qualitative analysis.* Sociology, *37*(3), 413–431.

Mazzola, G., Cherlin, P. B., Rissi, M., & Kennedy, N. (2009). *Flow, gesture and space in free jazz: Towards a theory of collaboration.* Heidelberg, Germany: Springer.

McQueen, S. (2014). *Steve McQueen: My hidden shame.* Retrieved from http://www.theguardian.com.

Mead, G. H. (1932). *The philosophy of the present.* New York, NY: Prometheus Books.

Merleau-Ponty, M. (1962). *Phenomenology of perception.* London, UK: Routledge.

Midgelow, V. L. (2012). *Nomadism and ethics in/as improvised movement practices.* Retrieved from http://www.criticalimprov.com/article/view/2001/2705.

Miller, J. (2014). *How jazz drummer Antonio Sanchez improvised the Birdman score.* Retrieved from http://www.vanityfair.com.

Misztal, B. (1996). *Trust in modern societies: The search for the bases of social order.* Oxford, UK: Blackwell.

Monson, I. (1996). *Saying something: Jazz improvisation and interaction.* London, UK: University of Chicago Press.

Moran, D. (2000). *Introduction to phenomenology.* London, UK: Routledge.

Morris, L. D. *Conduction.* Retrieved from http://www.conduction.us/main.html

Mulderrig, J. (2012). The hegemony of inclusion: A corpus based critical discourse analysis of deixis in education policy. *Discourse and Society, Sage Journals Discourse Society, 23*(6), 701–728.

Murray, S. R. (1967). *Ear cleaning.* Toronto, Canada: Clark and Cruickshank.

Murray, S. R. (1977). *The tuning of the world.* New York, NY: Knopf.

Murray, S. R. (1992). *A sound education: 100 exercises in listening and soundmaking.* Indian River, Canada: Arcana Editions.

Nettl B., & Russel M. (Eds.). (1998). *In the course of performance: studies in the world of musical improvisation.* London, UK: University of Chicago Press.

Nicols, T. (2012). *An ethics of improvisation: Aesthetic possibilities for a political future.* Maryland, Lexington: Lexington Books.

Noujaim, J. (2013). *The square.* Egypt: Mosireen.

Office for Standards in Education (2003). *Daniel House pupil referral unit inspection report.* Manchester, UK: Ofsted.

Oliveros, P. (2004). Tripping on wires: The wireless body: Who is improvising? *Critical Studies in Improvisation/Études critiques en improvisation, 1*(1). http://www.improvcommunity.ca/about/research.

Oliveros, P. (2005). *Deep listening: A composer's sound practice.* New York, NY: iUniverse.

Parker, E. (2009). *Evan Parker on biofeedback.* Retrieved from http://www.youtube.com/watch?v=r_ZjoW8rcJs.

Pallant, C. (2006). Contact improvisation: An introduction to a vitalizing dance form. Jefferson, NC: McFarland & Co.

Palmer, R. E. (Ed.) (2007). *The Gadamer Reader: A bouquet of the later writings.* Evanston, IL: Northwestern University Press.

Paynter, J. (1972). *Hear and now. An introduction to music in primary schools.* Retrieved from https://www.youtube.com/watch?v=cLcelEsbvJI.

Paynter, J. (1992). *Sound and structure (Resources of Music Handbooks).* Cambridge, UK: Cambridge University Press.

Peters, G. (2009). *The philosophy of improvisation.* Chicago, IL: The University of Chicago Press.

Picard, M. (1963). *Man and language.* Chicago, IL: Regnery.

Poitras, L. (2014). *Citizenfour.* New York, NY: Praxis Films.

Prasad. R. (2011). English riots were 'a sort of revenge' against the police. *The Guardian.* Retrieved from http://www.theguardian.com/uk/2011/dec/05/riots-revenge-against-police.

Pressing, J. (1998). Psychological constraints on improvisation. In B. Nettl, & M. Russel (Eds.), *In the course of performance: Studies in the world of musical improvisation*. London, UK: University of Chicago Press.

Prevost, E. (1997). *No sound is innocent*. Harlow, UK: Coppula.

Purcell, A. (2007). Free radical [Ornette Coleman interview]. *The Guardian*. Retrieved from http://www.theguardian.com.

Ranciere, J. (2011). *The emancipated spectator*. London, UK: Verso.

Raphael, A. (2008). *Mike Leigh on Mike Leigh* (Directors on Directors). London, UK: Faber and Faber.

Reason, M. D. L. (2002). *The myth of absence: Representation, reception and the music of experimental women improvisers* (Unpublished doctoral dissertation). University of California, San Diego, CA.

Robinson, K. (2001). *Out of our minds: Learning to be creative*. Oxford, UK: Capstone.

Robinson, K (2010). *Ken Robinson says schools kill creativity*. Retrieved from http://www.ted.com/talks/ken_robinson_says_schools_kill_creativity.html.

Robinson, K. (2011). *Learning without frontiers: March 2011*. Retrieved April 25, 2011 from http://blip.tv/learning-without-frontiers/sir-ken-robinson-march-2011-learning-without-frontiers-4928095.

Rogers, C. (1983). *Freedom to learn for the 80s*. Columbus, OH: Merrill.

Rogers, C. (1988). *On becoming a person: A therapist's view of psychotherapy*. London, UK: Constable.

Rose, S. D. (2003). *The uses of digital video recording for teaching and learning music and drama in a pupil referral unit*. Best Practice Research Scholarship, Department of Education and Science, UK.

Rose, S. D. (2008). 'Articulating perspectives of free improvisation for education' (Unpublished master's thesis). Middlesex University, UK.

Rose, S. D. (2013). *Improvisation, music and learning: An Interpretive phenomenological analysis* (Unpublished doctoral thesis). Glasgow Caledonian University, UK.

Rose, S. D., & MacDonald, R. A. R. (2012). Improvisation as real-time composition. In D. Collins (Ed.), *The act of musical composition* (pp. 187–214). Farnham, UK: Ashgate.

Ross, D. (2011). *Activating bodies of knowledge: Improvisation, cognition, and sports education*. Retrieved from http://www.criticalimprov.com/article/view/1314/2234.

Rothman, J. (1997). *Resolving identity-based conflict: In nations, organizations, and communities*. San Francisco, CA: Jossey-Bass.

Rowe, K. (2001). An Interview by Dan Warburton. *Paris Transatlantic Magazine*. Retrieved from http://www.paristransatlantic.com/magazine/interviews/rowe.html.

Ryle, G. (1979). Improvisation. In K. Kolenda (Ed.), *On thinking* (pp. 121–130). Oxford: Basil Blackwell.

Samson, M. (2007). Improvisation & identity: A qualitative study. *Improvisation, community and social practice*. Retrieved from http://www.improvcommunity.ca/research/improvisation-identity-qualitative-study.

SARC. *Translating improvisation*. Retrieved from http://translatingimprovisation.com/

Sawyer, R. K. (2003). *Group creativity: Music, theatre collaboration*. New York, NY: Routledge.

Sawyer, R. K. (2004). *Creative teaching: Collaborative discussion as disciplined improvisation.* Retrieved from http://online.uncg.edu/courses/mue704/readings/unit9/Sawyer2004.pdf.

Sawyer, R. K. (2007). *Group genius: The creative power of collaboration.* New York, NY: Basic Books.

Sawyer, R.K. (2008). Improvisation and teaching. *Critical Studies in Improvisation/Études critiques en improvisation, 3*(2). Retrieved from http://www.improvcommunity.ca/about/research.

Sawyer, R. K. (Ed.). (2011). *Structure and improvisation in creative teaching.* New York, NY: Cambridge University Press.

Schleiermacher, F. D. E. (1978). *Hermeneutics: The handwritten manuscripts.* Oxford: OUP Publication.

Schlicht, U. (2008). "I feel my true colors began to show": Designing and teaching a course on improvisation. *Critical Studies in Improvisation/Études critiques en improvisation, 3*(2). Retrieved from http://www.improvcommunity.ca/about/research.

Schön, D. (1983). *The reflective practitioner.* London, UK: Temple Smith.

Schroeder, F. (2012). Network[ed] Listening – towards a de-centering of beings. *Contemporary Music Review, 32*(2-3), 215–229.

Scott, R. (2014). *Free improvisation and nothing: From the tactics of escape to a bastard science. ACT – Zeitschrift für Musik & Performance, 5,* 1–23.

Self, G. (1970). *New sounds in class: A contemporary approach to music.* London, UK: Universal.

Self, W. (2007). *Psychogeography.* London, UK: Bloomsbury.

Sinclair, I. (2003). *London orbital.* London, UK: Penguin.

Small, C. (1977). *Music, society, education.* London, UK: John Calder.

Small, C. (1998). *Muscking.* Middleton, WI: Wesleyan University Press.

Smith, J. A. (2007). Hermeneutics, human sciences and health: Linking theory and practice. *International Journal Of Qualitative Studies On Health And Well-Being, 2,* 3–11.

Smith, J. A., & Osborn, M. (2007). Pain as an assault on the self: an interpretative phenomenological analysis. *Psychology & Health, 22,* 517–534.

Smith, J. A., Flowers, P., & Larkin, M. (2009). *Interpretative phenomenological analysis: Theory method and research.* London, UK: Sage. Retrieved from http://www.ipa.bbk.ac.uk/references.

Smith, J. D. (2004). Playing like a girl: The queer laughter of the feminist improvising group. In Fischlin, D., & Heble, A. *The other side of nowhere: Jazz, improvisation, and communities in dialogue.* Middletown, CT: Wesleyan University Press.

Sonic Arts Research Centre. Retrieved from http://www.sarc.qub.ac.uk/.

Stallabrass, J. (2004). *Art incorporated: The story of contemporary art.* Oxford, UK: Oxford University Press.

Stanislavski, C. (1936). *An actor prepares.* New York, NY: Routledge.

Stanyeck, J. (2004). *Diasporic improvisation and the articulation of intercultural music* (Unpublished doctoral dissertation). University of California, San Diego, CA.

Stanyek, J. (2004). Transmissions of an interculture: Pan-African jazz and intercultural improvisation. In D. Fischlin, & A. Heble (Eds.), *The other side of nowhere: Jazz, improvisation, and communities in dialogue* (pp. 87–130). Middletown, CT: Wesleyan University Press.

Stein, E. (1989). *On the problem of empathy.* Washington, D.C.: ICS Publications.

Stevens, J. (1985). *Search and reflect.* London, UK: Rockschool.

Straus, A., & Corbin, J. (1997). *Grounded theory in practice*. London, UK: Sage.

Stuart, H. (2005). Disciplinary hegemony meets interdisciplinary ascendancy: Can interdisciplinary/ integrative studies survive, and if so how? *Issues in Integrative Studies, 23*, 1–37.

Sudnow, D. (1993). *Ways of the hand*. Cambridge, MA: MIT Press.

Swanwick, K. (1979). *A basis for music education*. London, UK: Routledge.

Todd, C., & Scordelis, A. (2009). *Causing a scene: Extraordinary pranks in ordinary places with improv everywhere*. New York, NY: Harper Collins.

Thompson, A. R., Kent, G., & Smith, J. A. (2002). Living with vitiligo: Dealing with difference. *British Journal of Health Psychology, 7*, 213–225.

Thompson, W. (2017). *Soundpainting*. Retrieved from http://www.wtosp.org/.

Thomson, S. (2007). The pedagogical imperative of musical improvisation *Critical Studies in Improvisation/Études critiques en improvisation, 3*(2). http://www.improvcommunity.ca/about/research.

Threadgill, H. (2011). Interviewed by Fischlin, D. 'A door to other doors': Improvisation and creation sound. *Critical Studies in Improvisation/Études critiques en improvisation, 7*(2).

Tilbury, J. (2008). *Cornelius Cardew: A life unfinished*. Harlow, UK: Copula.

Tucker, S. (2008). When did jazz go straight? A queer question for jazz studies. *Critical Studies in Improvisation/Études critiques en improvisation, 4*(2). Retrieved from http://www.improvcommunity.ca/about/research.

Turetzky, B. (2010). *What creativity means*. Retrieved from http://www.youtube.com/watch?v=zdez-nHEkWw.

Turing, A. M. (1952). The chemical basis of morphogenesis. Philosophical transactions of the Royal Society of London. *Series B, Biological Sciences, 237*(641), 37–72. http://links.jstor.org/sici?sici=0080 622%2819520814%29237%3A641%3C37%3ATCBOM%3E2.0.CO%3B2-I.

Turner, R. (2010). Steve Paxton's 'interior techinques': Contact improvisation and political power. *The Drama Review Fall, 54*(3), 123–135.

United States of America War Office (1969). *Improvised munitions handbook*. Retrieved from http://gunfreezone.net/wp-content/uploads/2016/03/improvised-munitions-handbook.pdf.

Van Manen, M. (1990). *Researching lived experience: human science for an action sensitive pedagogy*. Albany, NY: Suny Press.

Vaz, A. F. (2011). *Soccer, improvisation, clichés: Brazillianness in dispute*. Retrieved from http://www.criticalimprov.com/article/view/1428/2039.

Velleman, J. D. (2009). *How we get along*. New York, NY: Cambridge University Press.

Vygotsky, L. S. (1987). In R. W. Rieber, & A. S. Carton (Eds.), *The collected works of L.S. Vygotsky*. New York, NY: Plenum Press.

Watson, B. (2004). *Derek Bailey and the story of free improvisation*. London, UK. Verso.

Williams, C. (2011). Echtzeitmusik berlin: Selbstbestimmung einer szene / self-defining a scene [Book review]. B. Beins, C. Kesten, G. Nauck, and A. Neumann (Eds.), *Critical Studies in Improvisation/Études critiques en improvisation, 7*(2).

World Health Organisation. (1986). *Stress at the workplace*. Retrieved from http://www.who.int/occupational_health/topics/stressatwp/en/.